Nearly Universal Acclaim for *The Accidental Teacher* by Eric Mandel

"*The Accidental Teacher* is a fascinating account of a challenging year in what is for most of us above a certain age an alien world – the contemporary American high school. It's a perceptive, witty and often touching tale of success and failure, discord and harmony, frustration and satisfaction. More than a commentary on education today, it offers insight into how one man, at least, was able to deal with it all."

—Marc Okrand, creator of the Klingon language used in *Star Trek*, author *The Klingon Dictionary*, and renown linguist specializing in Mutson, the language spoken by the original inhabitants of Hollister, California—the setting for *The Accidental Teacher*.

"*The Accidental Teacher* is a compelling read—once I began reading I couldn't put it down until the end. A bittersweet, funny Quixotic-like narrative of the author's struggle to reconcile the reality of his classroom with the bureaucratic nightmare he found himself in.

—**Tim Hunter, Acclaimed Director** *Twin Peaks, Madmen, Deadwood* **and** *Homicide*

"I am tired, ready to go to sleep, but this is just too good, too engaging. A combination of Jonathan Kozol and Frank McCourt. It all seems too true. Heartbreaking and uplifting, and above all genuine. After just a few months of teaching Eric Mandel clearly respects and understands his students, especially the more eccentric, troubled, and somewhat neglected ones who can cause a teacher a lot of grief and whose value is not readily apparent either to themselves or others."

—**Andrew Lachman, Educator and Journalist, Master of Arts: Yale, Stanford, Columbia and Antioch**

"I am way too busy to read your stupid, self-centered narcissistic journal, Dad."

—**Lily Mandel, Slacker**

The
Accidental
Teacher

ERIC MANDEL

The
Accidental
Teacher

Outskirts Press, Inc.
Denver, Colorado

Outskirts Press, Inc.
http://www.outskirtspress.com

ISBN: 978-1-4327-4486-1

Outskirts Press and the "OP" logo are trademarks belonging to Outskirts Press, Inc.

PRINTED IN THE UNITED STATES OF AMERICA

If only...

Bullfighting in Spain with Hemingway, quarterbacking the *Detroit Lions*, a stint as goalie for the *Boston Bruins*, pitching to the Hall of Fame laden 1960 National League All-Star starting lineup, and going three rounds with boxing legends Archie Moore and Sugar Ray Robinson; these are just a few of the exploits of writer and bon vivant George Plimpton. Plimpton not only survived each of these challenges to go on and pen dozens of poignant stories describing his exploits, but he also made a mountain of money in the process. More surprisingly, Vanilla Ice made a bundle of bling pretending to be a rapper, and *Milli Vanilli* won a Grammy for best vocal without singing a single word.

So then how hard could it be for me, or just about anyone else for that matter, to cash in on this literary and cultural tradition of pretense and fraud; to stand in front of a captive group of teenagers, spout platitudes while pretending to be a high school English teacher for ten months—while being paid handsomely for my performance—and then to write a book about it???

I can hear all the bleeding hearts now:

What a pompous ass!

What about the poor kids?

So what!

If I can't pull it off and I turn out to be a miserable teacher, what harm is done? Yeah okay, some kids don't learn as much as they might have, but no one dies; besides the kids might even prefer my charade to the inside-the-box routines of some teachers they have had in the past. I mean this is nothing like the havoc inflicted by the most nefarious charlatan of our times whose scams have resulted in carnage and untold misery. That simple Connecticut Yankee native frat boy's ignoble performances include: toy soldier, Texas snake-oil salesman, major league team owner, cowboy governor, and of course the greatest and most stunning fake feat of all time: this recovering alcoholic and former cokehead's appointment to the office of the Presidency of the United States in spite of the fact his opponent outpolled him by more than a half-million votes.

Now that's a fucking flim-flam man!

Okay, now that I have hopefully piqued your interest with this steaming pile of hubris, let the real story begin.

Table of Contents

Preface

When you come to a fork in the road, take it.
                                    —Yogi Berra

Last year I made a decision that turned my life upside
down. And prior to the upheaval, my life was already tee-
tering on disaster.

In my younger and more vulnerable years the impetu-
ous decision that brought me to these pages might have
made sense, but not today. Why would a rational, skeptical,
recently-retired fifty-eight year-old suffering from stress-
related hypertension, recovering from back surgery and
without a teaching credential, suddenly decide to become
a high school English teacher, despite the fact he had not
set foot in an English classroom in over forty years?

The simple answer may have something to do with
his dormant desire to perform his tired old shtick in front
of a fresh audience, possibly reinforced by a false sense
of confidence afforded by pain meds prescribed for his
chronic back pain. As plausible as this may sound, there

was more to the fateful decision than simply drugs and some mild psychological disorder.

Over the years, as the stress and dissatisfaction of my job as facilities director for a local school district intensified, I had come to regret my earlier career-curtailing choice (a decision primarily based on the ideology of the *Sixties* and the anti-motivational side effects of a certain popular recreational aid) to promise myself, upon receiving my relatively worthless bachelor's degree in American history, to never return to school.

But the truth is I have long harbored a desire to teach. Over the decades, whenever I found myself lamenting my self-inflicted career cul-de-sac, I imagined myself teaching American history or politics in a college setting—and no, I didn't picture myself in a leather-elbow-patched tweed coat smoking a pretentious fucking pipe. So when out of the blue the opportunity arose, I was not going to let it slip away. I'm bright and have always prided myself on an ability to connect with teenagers. So despite a mountain of doubts and a stockpile of shortcomings, I was pretty confident that with some quality assistance I could pull it off.

The job was teaching English, and though I am well read and can write effectively in an emergency, I have never given even a scintilla of thought to teaching grammar or writing. "I can't define it, but I know it when I see it." Supreme Court Justice Potter Stewart once wrote in regard to pornography. That's exactly how I feel about decent writing. Don't get me wrong. I am excited about teaching English and have nothing but respect and appreciation for English teachers. I just never thought I would ever be one. While I'm a voracious reader, a glutton for literature and a crossword puzzle junkie, my complete lack of college-level English courses could represent a serious handicap.

The arcane rules of spelling and grammar remain a mystery to me. My gut-level bias against authority and my innate skepticism prevent me from accepting conventions at face value. My natural inclination and curiosity is to question dubious rules. In my view of the world rules exist to preserve order and maintain consistency. Many make perfect sense and are incontrovertible; for instance stopping at red lights does save lives. Others make no sense and are riddled with exceptions. Why *i before e except after c, or when sounded like a in neighbor and weigh*? Talk about weird!!! (Oops, I just discovered the updated addendum to this mnemonic device: *and except seize and seizure and also leisure, weird, height, and either, forfeit, and neither.* There is no *their* there. No wonder I get lost in the quagmire we call English; it's a miracle anyone can understand this crap.)

So perhaps a semi-literate former school bus driver ain't the best choice to be teaching English to our nation's youth. We shall soon find out.

And to complicate matters even further, the job was a Resource Specialist/Teacher position—meaning I would be required in my role as teacher to revise the normal English curriculum, teach students of normal intelligence suffering learning disabilities stemming mostly from processing disorders (dyslexia, etc) and/or attention deficit disorders, and at the same time, in my role as a resource specialist I would be required to manage a caseload of twenty-five individual students.

I've had experience with resource students through former jobs, and have spent time with some of my son's friends who were in resource classes in high school. I have always fancied myself, regardless of protestations to the contrary, a sensitive guy with a gentle sardonic wit and disarming sense of humor. So contrary to logic, and in spite of many well-meaning warnings from my friends, many of whom were teachers, assuring me that I had no idea what I was in for, I naively convinced myself that I would be able to amuse 'em, charm 'em, disarm 'em, and engage 'em—and at the same time be entertained by their shenanigans.

~o∽

Looking back, it is hard for me to figure out exactly what I was thinking when I launched myself, totally unprepared and unequipped, into uncharted waters. As my golden years approached I had become more and more the homebody, possibly even bordering on agoraphobic. I had become increasingly anxious and resistant to change. In my younger and more vulnerable days I traveled the world with hardly a care, experiencing everything from the exotic to the mundane; from downing liters of beer with former Nazis in the beer gardens of Munich, to getting hammered on some rancid traditional rice concoction with former headhunters deep in the interior jungles of Borneo. In more recent times however, I have done my best to avoid any situation containing even a modicum of uncertainty—traffic, big-box stores, crowds or even normal, run-of-the-mill lines in theaters or banks.

Over the years I have worked ceaselessly, albeit effortlessly, to live up to my credo: *Avoid fortune and fame at all costs. It could be lurking around every corner.* In the years prior to my career change I basically went to work, came home, napped, frisbeed the dogs, ate, watched some TV (consisting of a combination of sports, *ESPN*, *The Daily Show*, *Dirty Jobs*, *Anthony Bourdain* and *Antiques Road Show*), went to bed, and then got up the next day and did it, with minor variations, all over again. Excitement consisted of either an hour-long bike ride to the beach, or on rare occasions, an early night out with the wife, a half-dozen raw oysters and a pint of beer. I had grown, or perhaps regressed, to desire, even demand, that things be simple, and the simpler the better. Recently I have come to realize that the older I get the more I expect of others and the less I expect of myself.

I was in a decade-long rut and it was obvious I needed a change. My family and friends had been trying to shake me out of my doldrums for a while. Their advice ranged from quitting my job to finding a hobby. I needed to either change myself or change things in my life. One night in an attempt to avert the pressure I was feeling I told my wife that I was going to make a change, a real change. And when she asked how or what I planned on changing I answered, "I'm going to grow a beard."

∽

By now you must be wondering how does one actually obtain a genuine bona fide teaching job in a public high school with no qualifications whatsoever? For me it was the combination of fate, a desperate school district in dire need of warm bodies, and as with most life-changing events, serendipity. So with no planning and little effort, I ended up with a full-fledged job teaching English in a California public high school.

My fast track to teaching began one day in late July 2007, a few weeks after I had taken early-retirement from a job I had grown to hate. Unbeknownst to me, my wife Mary, a woman of unrivaled curiosity mixed with a strong dose of gumption, noticed during her daily perusal of the want ads (she wasn't looking for a job, just curious to see what was out there if she were), an ad **stating** something along the lines: *Attention college graduates, high school English Teachers wanted. No credential or experience necessary. English majors preferred. Salary $46-$74,000. Call Carol Havisham at 831-772-5532.*

The following day I stumble upon a voice mail message from someone named Ms. Havisham calling Mary about a teaching job. Befuddled and confused I ask my wife what the hell is going on. In her guileless manner Mary points out to me the ad she had highlighted in fluorescent yellow, and explains, "I wasn't calling for myself. I was just curious and I was thinking that maybe Lily or Simon (our twenty-something kids) might be interested."

I respond with what I thought was the obvious—neither Lily nor Simon was an English major—and more importantly—neither one had ever shown the slightest interest in becoming a teacher. Then it hit me—*Hey what about me? I didn't major in English, but I always wanted to teach and I got nothing to lose.*

On a whim, and before I can talk myself out of my cockamamie scheme, I pick up the phone and call Carol Havisham. After several awkward minutes attempting to explain who I am and why I am calling, Carol catches on and describes the job and the requirements. I offer, a little too excitedly, that while I didn't major in English I did have some past high school teaching experience. (I neglected to mention the actual amount of experience consisted of a few days of substitute teaching at a local high school right out of college, and two entire weeks in 1984 teaching American history in England to European students on their way to a year abroad in the States as exchange students.) Additionally I do my best to sell the relevance of my long career managing a public school district's facilities and transportation departments. But even after my all-out bullshit sales job, I assume that the absence of an English degree will be a deal-breaker. Surprisingly, Carol remains interested and she enthusiastically encourages me to apply.

I did not know it at the time, but this initial exchange would turn out to be the most congenial conversation Carol and I were ever to have.

Even after accepting the job, and even after numerous assertions from various staff members in human resources that it was on the up-and-up and that I could legally teach in a California public high school, I didn't feel either at ease or legitimate until the last day of September when I received my first paycheck. I discovered later in the school year that I had been hired under the *State Provisional Internship Permit Program* (PIP). This program was set up to allow districts unable to find qualified teachers to hire, in an emergency, unqualified college graduates like me. And despite the name, I can assure you that there was nothing *internish* about the program the district offered me. There was no formal training. No mock teaching. No curriculum guidance. No help with lesson plan development. No nothing. Prior to the opening of school there was some ostensible instruction that was in no way appropriate to my situation. In essence, it felt to me as though the administration simply announced, "Hey Eric, here's the keys to your room. Whatever you do, don't lose 'em. And please make sure you take roll every period. Good luck."

Today as I reflect back on my first year of teaching, I

can honestly say that regardless of everything I have been through—the battles, the victories, the defeats, and the bureaucratic bullshit beyond belief—I am happy I took the leap. I wouldn't trade the last year for anything. While my journal hopefully offers as many lessons as laughs, it is neither a primer for first-year teachers, nor *just* another ubiquitous indictment of our failing public school system.

With teaching as a backdrop, my story at its core is simply a chronicle of one man struggling to survive, to make the best of a difficult situation and to get though life. It is the tale of my quest for a provisional fountain of youth and my effort to fight off the complacency and the *mundanacity* of middle age; a final arrow from my near-empty quill, airborne and heading straight for the rapidly approaching *vigor mortis*.

Quixotic?

For sure, but what the hell, you only live once.

Bring on the goddamned windmills!!

NOTE TO READERS

The bulk of this was written contemporaneously during the school year; however in an effort to provide background and additional clarification, I produced some sections shortly after the school year ended. I did my best to preserve the authentic, real-time emotions and feelings as they were occurring, hopefully capturing my metamorphosis from a bleeding-heart skeptic to a hard-boiled cynic.

I did change some of the names, not necessarily to protect the innocent or to spare feelings, but to protect myself from retribution. I described things as I saw them, and I encourage anyone unhappy with my depiction of events to write their own damn book.

Throughout the story there are numerous bureaucratic forms, observations, emails, letters and evaluations concerning my teaching. For some these may feel like impediments to the free-flowing narrative, and I worry that too much detail may bore, or worse, scare off some readers. So while they do play a critical part in my saga, feel free to skim or skip the lot of them. Readers are like snowflakes; no writer can please them all, and besides, do you know anyone who actually read all that whaling crap in *Moby Dick*?

I should also warn readers of my glib cynicism and my proclivity, some say obsession, for puns, absurd literary allusions, hyperbole, made-up words, self-amusement, false bravado, hallucinations, rambling observations, and my seeming inability to stay on topic. Combine these stellar qualities with my recent discovery of the effectiveness of teaching adages in helping students transition from the literal to the metaphoric and voila—*digression is the better part of valor.*

Up in the Morning and Out to School

I love to talk about nothing.
It's the only thing I know anything about.
—Oscar Wilde

[*Cue up opening musical theme to television's longest running drama.*]

In the educational system, the state is represented by two separate yet equally important groups: The educators who hand out the sentences, the students who do the time.

These are their stories.

[*Play ominous two-note theme allowing last note to fade...*]

Two things I never thought I would ever do, and that in truth never even entered my imagination—to be a high school English teacher and to be the author of a memoir––are looking more and more likely by the minute. Only a month after retiring as the Director of Facilities and

Transportation for San Lorenzo Valley Unified School District where I worked for the past twenty-four years, a brand-spanking-new career teaching high school English awaits me. At eight o'clock sharp on Monday, August 6, 2007, the first day of the rest of my life, I report for duty at San Benito High School in Hollister, California. And then, on August 20th, after ten days of in-service and preparation, school opens.

Here goes…

Friday - August 3, 2007

The job interview was the first critical challenge I faced in my prospective career as an educator. This full-time professional career opportunity came out of nowhere, and feeling I had nothing to lose, I did little to prepare for the interview other than trying to anticipate some of the questions I might be asked and dressing appropriately. The drive down to Hollister from my home in Santa Cruz gave me ample time to ready myself. I felt relaxed as I entered the beautifully renovated old school building, and bounded up the long ramp towards the human resources office and my first glimpse of the daunting adventure that lay ahead.

The interview: Three people and me sitting around a large oval table: the Carol Havisham from the telephone conversation, a seemingly pleasant woman around my age, Melanie, a pretty young English teacher, and the requisite suit, Pete Pecksniff, head of human resources. After the introductions and pleasantries I inquire about other possible openings, mentioning I might make a better social studies teacher. Carol replies that at this time they only have English openings, but that could change before school starts. Carol asks if I prefer to be interviewed for a potential social studies position, rather than the open English position. "Let's start with the English interview and if it goes bad we can switch." I reply.

After they read my resume, my serious shortcomings are painfully obvious to everyone. I have to say that I found this openly admitted lack of qualifications quite liberating. Everyone present was aware I would, by and large, be thinking on my feet—bullshitting to be exact.

Pretty Melanie asks the first question, "How would you teach English composition?"

I chuckle out loud and start with something like, "You may not believe this, but that particular question has never crossed my mind." I make a lame attempt to answer it, and then just as I thought I was a goner, Melanie throws me a lifeline and asks me a question about literary analysis.

I inquire, "What books might we be reading?"

Melanie lists the usual suspects, four or so I had read sometime in my life. I decide to use *The Great Gatsby* as an example, a book I read like a million years ago. I toss off an instant impromptu analysis alluding to everything I could remember (more so from the movie than the book): that green light, the notorious beacon of hope at the end of Daisy's dock, the mysterious large eye on the billboard, the decadence, the pretense. And to wrap up the analysis I compare Gatsby to Paris Hilton. They realize I am winging it and I think they are impressed with my answers. Pete the Suit mentions how amazed he is that I remember as much as I do. For a guy who has trouble remembering what he had for breakfast, I am pretty impressed with myself.

They go on to question me about teaching styles and philosophies of education. Carol asks an open-ended question about what I consider the essential fundamentals for teaching today's students. I begin my dissertation with the importance of connecting and engaging students, and then after a short ramble about finding subjects relevant to their lives, I generate on the spot, my as yet untested teaching philosophy. Improvising I coin the term *diversion theory*, and go on to define it as an attempt to fool or misdirect students into learning something before they know what hit them.

Melanie asks a question about poetry. I talk about using rap music to help connect students to poetry, and then jabber on about how I would love to try and use Dylan's music. Probably not a wise move, as it says more about my own interests than it does about the interests of contemporary students. Pontificating on the difficulties of teaching poetry, and by now feeling a little too comfortable, I mention how much I love Charles Bukowski. (For the unaware, Bukowski's work is brilliant, dark, raw and full of profane, pornographic, alcoholic ravings that are often blatantly misogynistic.) At once I realize my mistake, but from the blank looks on the three faces it is obvious no one has a clue who I'm talking about.

Carol ends the interview with a confusing question regarding grade distribution. She asks me to predict how my grade distribution might look at the end of the year. I have no idea what she's looking for so I ramble on about possibly grading on the curve, and conclude with how, in truth, I have no idea about my grade distribution in advance of actually teaching a class.

And then it was over.

Leaving the school I am feeling, despite the craziness of the whole thing, pretty good about my prospects for becoming a member of San Benito High School faculty; so what if I am unqualified, uncredentialed and have yet to take the *California Basic Educational Skills Test* (the CBEST). (I had always assumed that passing the CBEST was a mandatory minimum requirement to teach in California public schools. As with most of my other preconceptions about minimum teaching qualifications, I was wrong. During the interview I learned that, if hired, I would have a year to pass the test. Weeks earlier, in preparation for becoming a substitute teacher, I had signed up to take the CBEST on August 11.)

Thoughts bounced around my head as I drove home… The positives: *They liked me, they appear desperate and they do seem willing to train me…oh, and starting pay is like $48K …with my pension from my last job I will almost be a millionaire…*The negatives: *My competition is probably twenty-five year-old idealistic and energetic female English majors…it is a hellish commute...I am too old for this…and what the hell am I doing?*

The odds? I figure about even.

I get home, have a beer and then worry all weekend… *If I get the job can I really pull it off? I can't teach English…damn I wish it were social studies…the long commute will kill me…blah blah blah.*

Monday at about five I get the call. Carol offers me the job and asks me to come in the next day to sign the contract.

Fuck! I thought. *This is really happening.*

Sneak Preview

The next day I drive to Hollister to sign my teaching contract. After dotting all the i's and peppering Carol with questions that reflect my growing anxiety, she suggests I drop in on Melanie who is teaching a resource English summer school class across the quad. Carol tries to prepare me for the experience by explaining that while I will get some idea of what I will be facing in a few weeks, summer school is generally made up of the toughest and most intractable kids. She assures me my students won't be as difficult.

I take her up on her offer and apprehensively head for Melanie's room to get my first real glimpse of my future. It's a typical summer day in Hollister—meaning it's near one hundred degrees—and as I enter the class I realize for the first time the classrooms are not air-conditioned. Melanie is in front of the class going over a vocabulary worksheet as I slip into the hot noisy room and slink into a student desk in the back row. The class is made up of about twenty, mostly male students. While Melanie teaches and does battle with several boys, the aide sits at her desk in the rear of the room quietly grading assignments, seemingly oblivious to the situation at hand.

Things look precarious as Melanie is working to teach and to control two or three kids hell-bent on getting her off task. One minute she is discussing the word *anthropologist* with a willing student, the next she is trying to keep the whole thing from falling apart by tossing one disruptive kid after another outside for five-minute timeouts. Order is restored for a time, and then when a timeout ends and the malefactor reenters, chaos returns. Melanie remains outwardly calm the entire time.

One particular boy, a small, buzz-headed, grinning Latino, is a real asshole. His self-appointed mission is to make teaching impossible. If he doesn't want to learn then he will make certain no one else does either. (This boy will later become an important player in my story.)

I recognize several of the classroom management tactics Melanie was using in her attempts to control her students from my days long ago as a school bus driver: The *broken record* method where the teacher repeats over and over the direction ("Sit down John! Sit down John!") regardless of the student's ongoing protestations. And the mainstay of classroom management, *progressive discipline,* where the teacher begins with a warning and then cranks up the consequences as the problem continues until eventually the perp is sent to the office. The primary rule of this system is to never threaten anything you can't deliver on. Believe me, it is an easy rule to ignore in the heat of battle.

As bad as things were for Melanie—a very experienced resource teacher—when I got up to leave I wasn't disheartened at all. Apparently the old worksite adage, *Ten-percent of the staff creates 95% of all problems,* is equally applicable to the classroom. The experience was a real eye opener, and somewhat of a relief for me to see that total dominance or control is out of the question. I knew it wasn't going to be easy but I thought, foolishly perhaps, *I can do that.*

Not-So-Basic Training

Sunday - August 5

Tomorrow my new career begins with the first week of the *New Teacher Academy.* Wondering what my fellow recruits will look like—maybe a dozen mid-twenty-something recent college grads? Feel pretty sure I will be the oldest. House abuzz this weekend, homemade beer brewing, lots of people in and out including my twenty-six year-old daughter Lily, her boyfriend Pete, my brother-in-law Richard and my wife Mary.

Everyone has advice for me. Mary says whatever I do,

don't make the kids feel stupid—advice that made *me* feel pretty stupid. Richard, per his MO, asks tons of questions and doesn't listen to any of my answers, Lily's old friend Jerome suggests I just phone-it-in, makes anarchistic statements about the failure of our society to educate its youth, and then, without irony, asks me if there is any chance he could get a job at San Benito High School. Jerome, a part-time stand-up comic and the son of a university classics professor, is full of shit. This afro-haired Irish-Catholic boy and former *Peace Corps* volunteer works harder than just about anyone I know at doing everything he commits himself to.

Thus far, Frank McCourt's *Teacher Man* has provided the best insight into teaching high school English. Andy, my oldest friend, has been teaching high school English for over thirty years and has given me sage advice, offered to share some of his lesson plans, and even offered to loan me his extra Volvo for a few weeks until I can get around to buying a commuter car.

As you can imagine I am pretty nervous and really anxious to find out what classes I am actually going to teach and what my classroom looks like. Wonder if I can hide a futon or perhaps put an old couch in there so I can sneak a power nap during lunch, during my prep period, or after school on the nights when I have to stay late.

Yes, I do have my priorities straight. I am pretty fucking old to start over again.

OK back to the beer…

∞∂∾

Just discovered this *Hollister Free Lance* article published last week on July 31. The article might help illustrate the dire situation facing the district and the reason they were forced to hire *unqualified teachers* like me.

San Benito High School Fills 24 Vacant Teaching Positions

Despite a relatively high number of vacancies, high school administrators are encouraged they've hired nearly all the needed teachers. The school's human resources department is hoping to hire the last four before the end of the week so the teachers can be trained for the first day of school August 20.

"The recruiting is the difficult piece - and getting them to stay," Human Resources Director Peter Pecksniff said.

The school is still in need of a dance teacher, a business teacher, a Spanish teacher and one part-time position to fill roles vacated at the end of last school year, Pecksniff said. Pecksniff said he was pleased officials filled the special education, mathematics and science vacancies. Those roles are typically the most difficult to replace, he said.

To fill the special education positions, the school hired some teachers without full credentials, said Director of Student Services Carol Havisham. Special education teachers need credentials both in the subject area they teach and in special education, too. The need for multiple credentials has created a shortage of special education teachers statewide, Havisham said.

"We have to be creative because it's nearly impossible to get a staff of fully-credentialed special ed. teachers," Havisham said.

Despite some of the new staff not being fully credentialed, Havisham expressed confidence officials will make beneficial additions to the school. She's hopeful those teachers will like the school enough to stay and pursue their other credentials.

The high school will have a total of 28 new teachers this year. That turnover number is fairly high, even for a school of San Benito's size, Pecksniff said.

This high turnover has caused concern among administrators and teachers alike.

The high school teachers' union president, Clete Bradford, said it's worrying to see high numbers of new teachers leaving each year.

"We do seem to have a big turnover of teachers. We usually lose over 20 a year," Bradford said. "A lot of new teachers leave, and it's a concern."

To retain their new teachers, the high school offers new teacher-support classes, which all the new teachers will attend next week. It helps prepare the teachers for the school's culture and acclimate them to the environment, **Pecksniff said. "We expect them to jump high, but we say, 'Here's the springboard to get you going,'" Pecksniff said. "If you expect them to be good, you have to give them support."**

Guess we shall soon see how high they expect me to jump, how effective a springboard they are providing to jumpstart me, and most importantly, where will I land when gravity prevails.

Monday - August 6

Well I made it through first day of training with about thirty "new" teachers; new meaning new to the district.

UP IN THE MORNING AND OUT TO SCHOOL

Turns out some are veterans who have taught for over twenty years, and some are even older than I am. They come in all shapes, sizes and colors. Wonder who I am going to become friends with? It's funny how, when introduced to a large group of unfamiliar people, I quickly find some people annoying. (Of course some people, including my own loving daughter, quickly find *me* annoying.) But there are inevitably those assholes who think they know everything and make sure the rest of us know it.

We were told about lots of stuff from curriculum to technology. As they handed out a shitload of materials I discovered I would be teaching both 11th and 12th grade English. Damn! I was hoping to teach only one grade level so I would only have to develop one set of lesson plans. What the hell, *the best laid plans of mice and men.* (That novel is on the 11th grade reading list, by the way.) We were assigned our rooms and we picked up our keys; they gave me about a dozen. After leaving my last job with its seventy-five plus keys, I had assumed I would never have to carry more than four keys ever again.

I went to my room to check it out and discovered that the former occupant, a Mr. Pirl, had yet to remove any of his stuff. Right smack in the middle of his cluttered desk Mr. Pirl had inadvertently left me an omen, a half-filled bottle of *Pepto Bismol*—an image I am certain I will be recalling again and again throughout the year. Mr. Pirl, hoping to forestall the move and to remain in his room for one more year, stubbornly refused to clear his room out until two days before the start of school. This act of defiance prevented me from setting up my room until the last minute and significantly increased my growing anxiety.

Tuesday - August 7

Too tired to go into much detail now, so just a couple of things.

First: I learned that my resource students are not really expected to perform to "normal" state standards, and that they tend to crave routine so it is best to provide them a consistent daily schedule. It's a big relief to discover that I do not have to come up with a fresh, original act every day.

Second: Sally Smuts, an older (my age), experienced English teacher from Texas, is one of the people who annoyed me from the start. I just got the sense she thought there was only one way to teach English, her way. When she realized I was not a credentialed teacher, we got into a heated exchange in the library. Sally loudly proclaimed her distaste for the idea of non-credentialed teachers in the classroom. Not sure she understood that essentially she was telling me I didn't belong in the same program with her.

Not one to back down I said, "So you don't think Maya Angelou is qualified to teach high school English?"

"No she isn't, although I would let her talk to my class about writing." Sally shot back.

I mean I can understand her aversion to an unknown like me, but Maya Angelou?? I replied that there are thousands of horrible teachers with credentials, and thousands of excellent teachers without credentials, including college professors and elite prep school teachers. I honestly believe this woman would prefer a horrible teacher with a credential to a good one without. What a pompous, arrogant ass! I ended our exchange by telling her I looked forward to our having more provocative discussions over the years.

(This reminds me of a story I read recently. At one time Harvard was seriously considering hiring Vladimir Nabokov to teach literature; some pretentious pedantic professor of linguistics there wanted to know if the university was also planning to hire an elephant to teach zoology.)

Saturday - August 11

What a week!!

I am totally spent, not to mention stressed, scared and overwhelmed. I really never gave enough thought to how ill equipped I am to teach anything, let alone English. After an unimpressive and downright insufficient week of new teacher instruction, I now have serious doubts regarding the school's commitment to preparing me for the job. It's not like I pretended to be an experienced educator. They knew what they were getting and a little more support would be nice.

Resource specialists seem to exist in a netherworld, somewhere between regular education and the penal system. Most of the things they presented to the entire group of new teachers last week don't really apply to us, including little things like goals and benchmark standards for the regular curriculum! They don't actually say this in public, but in private they acknowledge that expectations for resource students must be "flexible and realistic". We are, more or less, free to do whatever we can to keep the kids engaged. Well that's great. But how about some realistic curriculum and instruction guides for new resource teachers?

As the days rush by there is more and more to do and I have less and less energy and less and less time to do it. I still have no lesson plans ready and I'm still unable to move into my room. Ok, done whining, oops—wait. I spent five hours of my penultimate Saturday before the opening of school taking the CBEST. It wasn't hard, just grueling, especially for someone who hasn't taken a test (aside from DMV and TB tests) in over thirty-five years. Almost certain I passed, although apparently it doesn't matter if I do fail my first attempt because, as I mentioned, the state gives you the entire school year to pass it.

August 14, Tuesday

Last week in a meeting with Carol and the three other new resource teachers we were handed some *Requisition Request* forms used for ordering classroom supplies and told to get them in as soon as possible. The only other advice we were given was to make sure we ordered everything we might need for the entire year because it is not uncommon for the supply budget to be completely spent by midyear.

Order everything I need?? Completely clueless about what supplies an English high school classroom needs, I went through the supply catalog item by item ordering whatever seemed appropriate at the time. The one item I was sure I would need—*Kleenex*—was not in the catalog. When I phoned the business office and asked about this oversight I was informed that the school does not supply *Kleenex*, and they explained to me that teachers either bought their own or asked for student donations.

When my order arrived in a half-dozen boxes yesterday I was stunned by my stationery stupidity. What the hell am I going to do with ten boxes of brass tacks, ten boxes of colored pushpins, and three wall-mounted pencil sharpeners? Oh, and to further illustrate my folly, I neglected to order any paper.

Thursday - August 16

I have been carpooling the last two weeks with Cassandra, a twenty-four year-old recent master's graduate in education. She and I—the cynic and the idealist––have had many interesting discussions as we share our excitement and anxiety about our first teaching jobs. It's refreshing to spend time with someone young, vibrant, and at the beginning of a promising career. Our conversations have not been limited to education; topics have ranged from religion to dogs. Cassandra is Persian and a practicing Baha'i, and she is often mistaken for Hispanic. (This easy to make mistake was made by, among others, me and the parents of Cassandra's Hispanic boyfriend.)

As far as job qualifications go, Cassandra and I complement one another. She brings a strong education background, including tenure as a student teacher. I bring lots of life experience. Cassandra is smart and eager and was actively recruited by the district. While I ain't dumb, my hiring was a result of sheer desperation. I have no doubts about her success. I am not so certain she feels the same optimism about mine. Cassandra's energy seems unlimited, evidenced by the fact that over the last two days, while I have been thrashing about attempting to pull everything together, Cassandra has been calmly calling and introducing herself to all 150 of her students' parents.

Saturday - August 18

Well, the bullshit is over.

Monday is opening day. The last two weeks have been the hardest two weeks of my work life. I have been working ten to twelve hours a day and the commute home has been miserable. My fifty-minute morning commute turns into a hot frustrating hour and forty-five minute trip home.

After a hard day this is a real killer. I arrive home crabby and tired. And worse, by day's end my back is burning. Pretty sure if I knew then what I know now I would not have signed up for this.

Every day for the last week the administration has promised me that Mr. Pirl's stuff would be out of *my* room by the following morning, and every following morning I expectantly enter my room and find his stuff still there. While the other new teachers are excitedly setting up their classroom and making them their own, I am stuck amid cluttered uncomfortable surroundings working feverishly, not necessarily effectively, on my maiden lesson plans. As the start of school nears, my anxiety is building. I visited some colleagues' classrooms to get some decorating ideas and poured over a book on effective classroom design. I never knew there were so many options and opinions about the optimal arrangement of student desks!

Finally, yesterday at about 10 AM, the last workday before school opens, Pirl's stuff is out of my classroom. When I see Pirl later in the day he apologizes explaining that he loved the room, he had been in for seven years, and he had hoped to forestall the move. Most galling of all to him was that the administration had refused to pay him to come in early to pack up his things.

Feng shuing for the aesthetically challenged... I spent a good deal of time yesterday scrounging up a battered old teacher's desk out of the large scrap pile in the maintenance yard. Working alone, without the slightest eye for interior design, I slogged away until after 9 PM putting my classroom together. Unable to obtain a lectern, I set the overhead projector front and center. After careful deliberation over the multitude of desk arrangement options, I settled on what I shall call a "semi-sunburst" pattern of six rows of four desks radiating out from my projector/lectern.

Per school requirement, I posted the *Baler Code*, Dress Code, Class Rules and a handmade sign stating *No Electronic Devices To Be Used In Class* in a prominent place next to the large whiteboard. I hung an assortment of posters around the room including two *Santa Cruz Shakespeare Festival* posters, a *San Francisco 49er Super Bowl XXIII* poster, and my favorite, a black and white poster of a young Muhammad Ali glaring down at an unseen, prostrate Joe Frazier with *Impossible is Nothing* emblazoned across the Champ's torso.

In one corner of the room, kitty-corner from the door, near the windows and under the watchful eye of a large wooden African mask, I did my best to create an inviting reading nook for my students. I furnished the nook with three comfortable chairs from home including an old wooden rocker whose creakiness could pose a problem. In hopes of creating my own comfort zone surrounding my desk, I hung some old baseball team pennants (*Brooklyn Dodgers, New York Giants, St Louis Browns* and *Boston Braves*) and some other pieces of personal memorabilia.

Oh wait; I almost forgot the piece de résistance. In the far corner on the bookshelf under a window sits a lone life form—a potted plant I won in a raffle at the staff luncheon earlier in the week. Owing to my gangrene thumb, and the fact that the nearest running water is about 100 yards away in the science wing, I'm afraid the plant's chances of survival are slim.

To these myopic eyes Room 230 exudes warmth and positive *chi*. I'll just have to wait until Monday to see how the critics react.

To date, the best advice has come from my freshly assigned mentor Sara, an enthusiastic thirty-something well-respected fellow resource English teacher. When I discovered my classes would not be the traditional fifty-five minutes in length, but instead would be a mind-boggling 100 minutes, I almost had a stroke. *"How the fuck would I be able to entertain and engage my attention deficit disorder laden classes for 100 minutes?"*

A quick overview of block scheduling as used at SBHS: Two years ago the district shifted from the traditional 6/55 minute classes a day to 3/100 minutes blocks a day with alternating classes every other day. Simply put, on *Red Days* students attend blocks 1, 2 and 3 and on *White Days* 4, 5 and 6. For the curious, the days are named for the school colors. Mercifully for me with my long commute, school starts at 8:50 and ends at 3:00. I will discuss the advantages and disadvantages of block scheduling throughout my journal.

Sara has many ideas to help me organize and fill out a 100-minute block. One simple recommendation is I do what she does with her classes and have my students spend twenty minutes a day doing *Silent Sustained Reading* (SSR)—time set aside for the kids to read quietly anything they want, more or less, and then to spend a few minutes writing down some thoughts in their reading journals; before you know it half an hour has flown by, spent on a worthy, standards-based activity. A corollary advantage of SSR is that it requires biweekly trips to the library. I accept Sara's advice without protest.

Ah, I thought. *Now all I have to figure out is how to use the remaining seventy-five minutes!*

The *New Teacher Academy* stressed the importance of discipline and rules, such as the school's no hat and no cell phone policies, at the expense of guidance with curriculum and effective teaching methods. There is so much essential information the school has neglected to provide, I am left with a sense of helplessness. One example: no one has taken the time to explain the variety of disorders my students have actually been diagnosed with, other than a casual aside that most of their learning problems stem from neurological processing disorders. What the hell does that mean exactly? I guess will just have to find out for myself.

The lengthy discussions about block scheduling were heavy on format and vacuous on content. We were given lots of advice on how to break the 100-minute blocks into manageable segments, and the proper nomenclature to use when referring to these sections. When it came to guidance and ideas on what to actually teach in each segment, we got nothing.

We were told to list the state standards addressed at the top of our plans and to break up our lessons into six phases: *Transition* (*Quick Writes*, poems, etc: 5 minutes), *Anticipatory Set* (SSR and *Journal Writing* in my case: 15 minutes), the meat-of-the-matter to be titled *Instructional Activities* (various teaching activity and modes: totaling 60 minutes), *Check for Understanding* (quizzes, rehash, etc: 10 minutes) and finally *Closure* (whatever). Although I realize I do not have even a minute of classroom experience to call on, I still seriously doubt any teacher's ability to have students complete an effective class-wide activity, even a short simple *Transition*, in five minutes.

Even with hours of instruction on structuring lesson plans, I was having trouble understanding some of the

THE ACCIDENTAL TEACHER

concepts. But after an intensive consultation with Sara, I managed to come up with my maiden lesson plan outlines for the first week of school. And at 9:30 the night before school opened I submitted (first year teachers are required to submit weekly lesson plans) the following to the Director of Instruction:

Subject: English 11 for the week of 8/20 – 8/25

	MON/TUES	WED/THURS	FRI
Standards Addressed	Reading 2.0, 3.0 Writing 2.2	Reading 2.0, 3.0 Writing 2.2	Reading 2.0, 3.0 Writing 2.2
Transition	Writer's Almanac NPR Poem	Writer's Almanac NPR Poem	Writer's Almanac NPR Poem
Anticipatory Set	SSR Writing	SSR Writing	SSR Writing
Instructional Activities	Pre-reading Activites For Mice and Men Class Discussion of American Dream Students Write Dream and share with partner Discuss Dreams: Define American Dream..Is it real?	Pre-reading Activites For Mice and Men Class Discussion of Depression Class Exercise on Problematic Situation of Mice and Men Work in teams and report back to class	Library Visit for Mice and Men Intro Worksheets
CFU	Summarize American Dream in relation to upcoming readings.	Discuss Depression in relation to Mice and Men	Go over worksheets

20

Closure	Homework:Ask parent or adult what their dream is/was. Write tn	Discuss upcoming trip to library for Mice and Men Intro	

Subject: English 12 for the week of 8/20 – 8/25

	MON/TUES	WED/THURS	FRI
Standards Addressed	Reading 2.0, 3.0 Writing 2.2	Reading 2.0, 3.0 Writing 2.2	Reading 2.0, 3.0 Writing 2.2
Transition	Writer's Almanac NPR Poem	Writer's Almanac NPR Poem	Writer's Almanac NPR Poem
Anticipatory Set	SSR Writing	SSR Writing	SSR Writing
Instructional Activities	Respect Class Discussion, Consequences Grammar Lesson	Reading Strategies Pre-read Vocabulary Begin reading short story Just Lather, That's All CFU along the way Write and answer questions	Library Visit Possibly continue story time permitting
CFU	Summarize and question about Respect	Foreshadowing and anticipating ending	

Closure	Homework: If you were the teacher what would your rules and consequences be	Discuss upcoming trip to library. Library etiquette	

Pretty thin I know, but because I am flying by the seat of my threadbare pants it is important I provide myself with a good deal of flexibility (a parachute might come in handy).

I'm beginning to feel like an alchemist from the Dark Ages. Doing my best to do the impossible.

[Once school began it quickly became apparent that planning my lessons a week in advance was impractical. Classroom planning is similar to conventional work place scheduling because at the end of the day what you actually accomplished looks nothing like what you had planned. After a few weeks I found myself outlining my lessons one day in advance and then refining them——mulling them over—the night before and finalizing them on my morning commute. I did continue to submit my weekly "plans" for several months until I finally decided during one really hectic week to see what happened if I failed to turn them in. Nothing happened, so I stopped for good.]

So here I am—the newly titled Mr. Mandel, English Teacher/Resource Specialist; my classroom #230 ready more or less; script prepared sorta, and me, as ready for the first day as I will ever be. Over the last two weeks I have been inundated with so much stuff that at times I thought my head was about to explode; way too much information in too short a time; too many theories, not enough practical support. Carol, the woman who hired me and promised to make sure I was ready for opening day, seems to have evaporated. She blows off a quick "Hi" in passing, and when I pester her about my lack of confidence in my preparedness, Carol falls back on her mantra, "Don't worry Eric. Your classes will be small and you will have an experienced teacher's aide to show you the ropes."

This situation is in some ways cathartic. I am beginning to get the idea they are going to watch me sink or swim, leaving me to rely entirely on my own devices. I originally had high hopes of success, but now I have lowered the bar and my new goal is two-fold: first, to make it through the first week without audibly uttering "fuck" in class; and second, to avoid being struck by a hard projectile directed at me by a student.

All that said, I am excited about Monday. I have seen my class lists. Four classes: two English 11's and two English 12's. Largest class is twenty, more boys than girls, more Latinos than Anglos. Sara, my mentor, knows many of my kids and gave me a quick tutorial on what to expect from whom, who not to sit next to whom, etc. While Sara has been a huge help, I realized immediately that our personal styles are almost diametrically opposed. Sara is super-emotive, wearing her heart openly on her tattooed sleeves. The kids love her and her enthusiasm is infectious. Me? Well I am more of a compassionate cynic and my mothering skills are rusty at best. I predict that after a few weeks of following her suggested lesson plans I will start to develop a teaching style of my own. I am confident I will be an effective teacher; just not sure how long it will take.

My primary concern now is finding a way to engage my students. There is a broad variance in the comprehension and performance levels of the kids, and it is going to be critical for me to slow down and figure something out within the first few weeks. I keep telling myself that all my years of experience supervising people, some of whom were bright and funny, some denser and stupider than humanly imaginable, will be invaluable in my new career.

I remember when I began my administrative career twenty-four years ago that it took me several years to realize how different people are in their abilities, their personalities and their adaptabilities. (I could tell stories about the many genuine and original psychos I have worked with, but for now I will spare you this particular digression.) Two things I learned quickly at my old job: not everyone is smart or even competent, and not everyone has a sense of humor.

Time to stop for now. I really am totally spent. I think I will take a nap.

Thirty-five hours and counting.

Oh boy, this is going be fun!!!

Class Schedule 2007/08
Red Days   White Days

First Block — English 12
8:50 –10:35

Fourth Block — English 11
8:50 –10:35

Second Block — Prep Period
11:00 –12:40

Fifth Block — English 12
11:00 –12:40

Lunch 12:40 –1:20

Lunch 12:40 –1:20

Third Block — English 11
1:20 – 3:00

Sixth Block — Prep Period
1:20 – 3:00

II

The Whiteboard Jungle

Call me Mr. Mandel...

Monday - August 20...The First Day of School

You know how it is when you are stressed and worried about some challenging upcoming event and your friends tell you to relax and everything will work out fine? And then how, despite their well-meaning advice, you go on stressing and worrying anyway? And then, of course, when the situation finally arrives, everything turns out fine just as your friends predicted? All that nervous energy and wasted time!

Well, my first day of teaching was a prime example of *the don't worry, don't wail* policy at work. What the hell was I worrying about? It could not have gone better.

I arrived at school an hour early and as I entered my room I smelled the inviting aroma of warm donuts. Bewildered, I heard a friendly female voice coming from the reading nook in the far corner of my room, "Good morning Mr. Mandel. Welcome. I'm Polly and I was assigned to be your aide for the year. I hope you like donuts and hot *chai*?"

Reeling from the surprise but elated, I walked over to Polly, a smiling thirty-something, stunningly attractive (almost as stunning as Sophia Loren in her prime) green-eyed raven-haired beauty, and introduced myself. We exchanged abbreviated life stories as we ate donuts (maple bars, my favorite) and drank *chai*. I learned that Polly graduated from SBHS in 1990 and currently is working on her BA degree in English and she has extensive experience working as an aide in resource English classes. She could not have been more helpful and she even offered to give me the trove of comprehensive lesson plans she has collected over the years. After hearing my story of woe about my lack of experience, Polly offered this simple but astute advice, "Because of your knowledge of American history you should develop a literature-based curriculum as it will give you a strong historical thread to build on."

I smiled and wondered if I had died and gone to heaven.

As the students straggled in, Polly introduced me to each one individually. The day got better by the minute, and the students seemed genuinely enthralled with their new teacher as I related relevant stories connecting the importance of English to their lives. Both classes were well behaved and eager to cooperate. One girl in Third Block even handed me a well-polished apple.

Sara dropped in during First Block to check on her fifty-eight year-old protégé, and she stopped by during lunch to tell me excitedly that I was doing an incredible job. She told me that she had never witnessed a teacher develop rapport with a new batch of students as quickly and effortlessly as I had.

THE WHITEBOARD JUNGLE

On my drive home I told myself not to let the early success go to my head as many serious challenges lay ahead. With Polly's help the day had been perfect. I wondered, *Is this a dream—a dream of synchronicity and perfection?* It certainly was nothing like my recent nightmares about the first day of school, the clichéd ones in which I forget my pants or can't find my room.

My performance was unexpected and unbelievable. Like Joe Montana during that final drive against Dallas, everything I tried worked. Or maybe like Hendrix at the *Monterey Pop Festival,* every note I hit was true. (In June 1967, a week after his coming-out party in Monterey, I saw Jimi at the Fillmore in San Francisco. He was third on the bill behind headliners, *The Jefferson Airplane*—although Janis subbed for an ailing Grace Slick the night I was there—and the Hungarian jazz guitarist Gabor Szabo. At the time, like most of the world, I had no idea what the *Jimi Hendrix Experience* was. The performance, in the idiom of the time, blew me away. I still can recall how for months afterwards I hammered his praises into any one who would listen. And to this day my right ear remains abuzz, albeit *pianissimo,* thank god. One more thing before I find my way home: tickets to the concert cost three bucks.) I was in the zone.

Ok, for real now...

There ain't no damn heaven. And the only zone I was in was the fucking ozone. My first day was nothing like that. None of what I wrote was true. Not Polly. Not the *Krispy Kreme* maple bars. Not even the red fucking apple. Nothing. And the only positive things I can say about my actual first day are that it could have been worse and I survived.

Got to school about an hour before the first bell. Felt

like a zombie, walking around in a trance, not sure what to do. Tried to get things organized. Tested overhead projector and bulb was out. Shit, just what I needed—I had planned to use it for several things. Wasted about twenty minutes scrounging for a bulb. The library was actually closed and I had to sneak in and take a new overhead projector because I had no idea where to find an individual bulb. I had planned to meet the students at the door, shake their hands, look them in the eye and welcome them to my class, but I was too busy scrambling. I met my aide for the first time two minutes before class and missed greeting most of the students as they entered the room.

First Block was pretty bad. No, wait, who am I fooling? It was really bad. Before class I assumed all the required first day housekeeping tasks (seating chart, intros and textbook pickups) would take up most of the class time. Wrong!! One hundred minutes seemed like hours, and I ran out of planned material with about twenty-five minutes still remaining. Went into an impromptu and error-ridden ramble about the history of communication from the beginning of time to now, and to top it all off both the district superintendent and the principal popped in during my bumbling mumblings. I also had a terrible case of dry mouth. I figured things could only get better with my next class. I was half-right.

It was about 100 degrees and muggy when, after my prep period and lunch, my next class, Third Block (juniors), began at 1:20. Sara and others had warned me that they were an ornery noisy bunch. And they were. There were lots of characters ranging from smart-ass gang bangers, skaters and metal heads to this lone, one-of-a-kind *Scene Kid* (a species of teenagers made up of *Scene Girls* and

Scene Boys), a new transfer fresh from Salinas with purple hair spiked out about 18 inches in two directions (must be a name for the style but I have no idea what it is). His name was Irwin, but as the class walked over to pick up textbooks Irwin told me he preferred to be called Zenebula. I said, "How 'bout I call you "Zen"? He said that would be okay.

Aside: In the course of the year, Zenebula was unable to explain to me what a makes a *Scene Kid* a *Scene Kid*. I found the following definition of a Scene Kid offered by a *Scene Girl* on Urbandictionary.com:

> Scene kid=boy/girl. usually seen wearing neon colors w/black, leopard and/or zebra print obsessed, hair colored at least 2 different colors and cut at different angles. male scene kids usually try to attain 500 friends on My Space and post pictures up of themselves making out with other boys, female scene kids just ADORE neon colored eye shadow and wear one thousand layers of eyeliner. hair of both sexes is usually parted to the side.

I am sure I will describe the kids as unique individuals in more detail once I get to know them. Anyway, the kids were hot and noisy as they tested the new teacher. They really worked at getting me off task. This group is going to be a challenge but I think I can make it fun.

I don't want to give the impression that today was a total waste. I actually enjoyed the sparring, held my own and may even have imparted some knowledge. I surveyed the class about reading habits; only two of the fifteen openly admitted reading a book for fun, and only three recognized the term *bookworm*. In an effort to challenge the kids and assess their critical and analytical abilities, I started my maiden discussion with the question: *Why do you think kids read less today than ever before?*

The discussion went well. It didn't take long for them to determine that the main reason for the drop in reading was the stiff competition it faces today from other forms of entertainment, from TV to the Internet. I nudged them further down that road by seeing how many activities they could imagine a teen 150 years ago might have engaged in for entertainment if stuck home alone with some free time. Right off the bat one eager girl named Gina made the point that there was much less free time back then and very few options for entertaining one's self. After some discussion and some prompting, the activities they came up with were reading, playing solitaire, drawing, playing music and watching the fire burn in the stove.

After class I asked my Third Block aide Rayna, a twenty-year veteran, "So how bad was I?" Rayna replied charitably that she had seen much worse and that it would get better and I would do fine. Nice of her.

Tomorrow I have my two other classes and they should go better; after all today was in a way just a dress rehearsal for tomorrow, and now I have two performances under my belt. We shall see…

Tuesday - August 21

Well I was wrong about my second day going more smoothly, it was miserable. Halfway through the day I began to feel like this is all a big mistake. My second class of the day, Fifth Block (seniors), was pretty bad. I kept butting heads with this kid, Jorge, who was doing everything he could to annoy me—ignoring me, laughing, not doing any assignments, being a distractive pain in the ass. After Fifth Block I spent over an hour with Sara, my mentor teacher, and it became obvious that while Sara will be a big help, the district has left me to fend for myself. Plus my role as caseworker for twenty-five students is, as I suspected, going to further tax my ever-dwindling energy.

Got home and was pretty dismayed. Lily did her best to encourage me but I was having trouble imagining any light at the end of any tunnel. Worked on some lesson plans and went to sleep dejected.

Wednesday - August 22

Today, my third day on the job, was much better. I had some activities planned, plus I was able to begin the twenty minutes of *Silent Sustained Reading* (SSR), and for the most part the students read and were quiet. One boy worthy of note: a red-headed junior named Rick, read a gun catalog that was nothing but pages and pages of descriptions and photos of hundreds of firearms. Rick tried to convince me the book was actually a biography. I wasn't buying. I mentioned to him that bio is the root word for living organisms. He argued that guns are alive. Another kid read auto parts catalogs and another, a pig farming catalog. I guess reading anything is better than reading nothing. Equally important, the quiet time is good for me and I read too in an effort to model for them. Led an icebreaker that had the students and their teacher sharing things about themselves, and before I realized it the classes were over.

Funny how distinctly different two classes can be; my morning First Block seniors are a pretty docile group, although a few seem engaged in the lessons; my afternoon Third Block juniors, as predicted by Sara, are a handful—

—loud and rambunctious with a smattering of some lively intellects. The hot afternoons are bad enough, add this hyperactive group to the mix and it only gets worse.

The kids definitely are testing me, but today I think I may have turned a corner with them; of course it could all blow up in my face tomorrow. Sara gave me some advice regarding this group—get a stopwatch, time all the distractions, then make the entire class stay after school for the total accumulated time of the disruptive behavior. It worked. After a few incidents I walked over to my desk, showed them the stopwatch and threatened to use it. They were pretty good for the rest of the day!

Remember how Carol promised me I would have an experienced aide? Well, unlike all experienced teachers, I ended up with a different aide for each of my four classes. At first blush this may seem like an advantage, but trust me, adjusting to four different women (to my knowledge there are no male aides) with unique attitudes and styles is no walk in the park. I found out later in the year that veteran resource teachers train, nurture and manage to keep the best aides for themselves, eventually developing a strong sense of ownership toward them. And who can blame them?

Going to lie down now…

Sunday - August 26

First week over. Way too hard, but I never uttered *fuck* in class, nor was I hit by a projectile of any kind, so I guess you could call it a success. Someone did steal my stopwatch. When the school day ended on Friday I was *so* ready to leave, go home and sleep through the weekend.

Thursday and Friday were *Picture Days* and I had to escort each class to the gym to have their ID photos shot.

THE WHITEBOARD JUNGLE

Turned out to be quite an adventure; whatever learning disabilities these kids have, their instincts for scamming the system and wasting time do not seem to be effected. On Friday some of my Fifth Block boys were taking way too long having their photos taken in the gym. Half the class was done with their photos in ten minutes. So off I went in search of the half a dozen stragglers, the usual suspects. I found them, each in a different line; each time one of them neared the front of a line, he would slide over to the end of another line. I actually admired their creativity, their inadvertent exploration of perpetual motion and infinite time-management; however they were not happy campers when I rounded the lot of them up, escorted them to the front of a line and stood there waiting while they offered their defiant smiles to the camera. The fact that my aide for that period was a no-show did not help matters.

After my initial week, some first impressions of a few of my more "interesting" student personalities:

Jeremy: a skinny, long-greasy-haired, lip-studded, high maintenance junior who begs to be the center of attention. Thinks he is a real player and everyone seems to know he is gay except him. Jeremy has an acute case of juvenile flamboyance and reminds me of Oscar Wilde, minus the wit and charm.

Tony Morales: a junior and an amateur boxer (his names even sounds like a fighter), who, during a class discussion about Michael Vick's treatment of dogs, claimed to raise fighting cocks for export to states where cockfighting remains legal. Tony is a welterweight (145lbs) and plans to be boxing professionally within a year. He does few, if any, of the class assignments.

Jorge: a seventeen year-old, buzz-headed, saggy-baggy-pantsed senior with a killer shit-eating grin, who does his best to entertain the class and get me off task. Has a terrible home life, lost his best friend to gang violence two years ago, and spends a lot of time at his friend's gravesite and writing *R.I.P.* on his book covers. Told me he hates to go home. Doesn't seem to enjoy school either. Pulled him out of class Thursday to have a little talk. Resisted looking at me when I talked. No idea how much of what I said reached him. When we walked back into class and his friends made *ooohs* and *aahs,* I realized it might not have been a good idea to "show him up" in such a public way.

Tomas: a sullen, brooding, quietly defiant senior and co-chaos-collaborator with Jorge. While Tomas is neither as animated nor as outwardly disruptive as Jorge, I have a strong sense he will be the more dangerous foil.

Gina: a gregarious junior drama-queen who eagerly participates in all discussions, too eagerly at times. The other day, after several inappropriate or just off-topic off-the-wall responses, I asked Gina to make sure in the future that she has a general idea what she is going to say before waving her hand in the air. She is entertaining, intelligent and seems to be one of the few students who has dreams and the accompanying desire to make an effort to reach them.

I think my frustration about my classes thus far is twofold. First fold, the wide variety of skills and interest levels; the fact that some students do sincerely want to learn, while others have no interest in learning and seem content to passive-aggressively undermine the class. And second fold, the fact that most have no concept of the future or how important being at least marginally literate will be to their success in life. They live entirely in the moment. And yes, I do realize most teenagers are in the same boat, but it is still frustrating as hell. I am thinking that, at some point, the kids who show zero interest in being in school should be removed in order to provide the more willing a positive learning environment. And while it took me less than one week to become so cynical, you must remember I did have a nice head start in this area. Next thing you know I will be advocating the return of corporal, if not capital, punishment.

Kidding...for now.

Who's who and who's what?

The first weeks were a discovery process, the age-old dance of teacher sizing up class and class sizing up teacher. As we go through our respective motions, our respective subtexts go something like this:

Teacher: *Who's going to give me trouble? Who's the class clown? Who has any real desire to learn? Who will be my favorites? Who's smart? Who's not? Who comes from a horrible dysfunctional situation? Who gives a shit and who doesn't?* And most important: *Will they like me? Will they think me cool or will they see me as just another annoying stupid obstacle on their forced march to finish high school?*

Students: *What the hell is he talking about? Is he nice? How old is he? Is he married? How much homework will he assign? How difficult will he make my life over the next ten months? How boring will he be? I wonder how much we can get away with in his class? Is he cool? I wonder does he smoke weed? What's with his goofy big ass smile? Does he really think he is funny??* And most important: *Does he think he is better than us? Does he remember how he acted when he was our age?*

Thursday - August 30

Been so fucking hot the last few days I have been wearing shorts and flip-flops to school. If they don't have the decency to provide air conditioning, I will wear as little as I can get away with. Today it felt like Malaysia, HOT and MUGGY. Why would a school located in an area where hot summer weather is the norm, a school that prides itself on demanding its teachers utilize every minute of class time effectively, not have air conditioning?? (Did I mention they expect teachers to provide their own fans?) With this oppressive heat, little if any educating is getting done.

Speaking of educating, for the most part things are getting better. The kids are connecting with me, more or less. I really don't seem to mind the active, resistant, fun-loving pains in the ass; it's the brooding, dark, passive-aggressive boys defying me with looks of disdain who could be my undoing. My Fifth Block seniors are real tough, and while these brooders eventually get around to doing a portion of the assignment, I expend excessive amounts of energy on them to the detriment of the two or three kids in the class who actually want to learn. I am tempted to just ignore the brooders and allow them to fail, or better yet, to wake-up and realize that, just maybe, graduating high school ain't such a bad idea.

Think I am going to work with Sara on the two hard-core cases, Jorrid Jorge and Toxic Tomas, and see if I can crack through their *hardassmotherfucking* shells. Today I went into Sara's classroom during a break. Sara was talking to Tomas, and he looked like a totally different Tomas than the Tomas who shows up in my class. He was open, looking eye-to-eye at Sara. He even looked at *me* when I was talking to him and may have had a hint of a smile. Sara has put a lot of work into Tomas and she is now the one teacher he trusts. Not sure he will ever warm up to a male authority figure, but I will keep trying.

Enough of that.

Spent time discussing the *American Dream* this week in preparation for beginning *Of Mice and Men*. Some things I learned about my students: They have dreams. Most of their dreams are close to the traditional American version with some interesting spins. While the majority want to make piles of money and have big houses with lots of cars, all Austin, a goofy, amiable, blond junior, wants is to go to Sweden and marry a hot Swedish girl. Cal, the lone black, wants to be a singer/songwriter, but plans to learn a trade so he can have a source of income until he actually makes it in the music world. Most of the girls want to marry rich and have kids, and the interesting thing to me is that they want sons exclusively. According to them, daughters are way too much trouble. Tony, the amateur boxer, says that in ten years he will be the middleweight champion of the world and have millions of dollars. Tony is emphatic that this isn't a dream, but a fact.

I explained to the class the traditional *American Dream*— —that no matter how poor you are if you work hard you will make it big. I then asked if they believed they would attain the dream, and almost without exception they said yes. For homework I had them question their parents about their own dreams, and ask if their parents felt they were living them. They reported that most of their parents were pretty disappointed with their current situations, but had hopes for their children. One exception seemed to be Jasmine, a sassy, pretty, wide-eyed Latina junior. Jasmine reported back that when she told her parents she hoped to attend UC Davis, they told her to just forget it, that she would never amount to much.

Friday - August 31

Today was a good day and I'm ready for the three-day weekend. Had the first rally of the year, two thousand screaming teenagers in a hot gym. A little like how I imagine a Hitler Youth Rally, minus *der fuher* and *der deutsche,* with loud earsplitting music and shrill oratories. The new teachers were introduced and I was escorted through the screaming throngs, a nubile cheerleader on each arm. Felt a bit awkward to say the least.

Later in the afternoon as my toughest class (Fifth Block) began, Jorge announces to the group, his voice dripping with sarcasm, that Mr. Mandel is a real *playah* and he knows this for a fact because he saw with his own eyes Mr. Mandel at the rally with a young hottie on each arm. Jorge, always the smartass, then goes on to accuse me of sexual harassment, declaring with an attitude, "An old man in his forties with an underage girl on each arm should be arrested for being a pervert."

"Thanks Jorge." I reply without explanation.

After that exchange, fearing the worst, I took my ba-dass class to the library. But things actually turned out fine. I worked hard to connect with both Jorge and Tomas. Left some books about tattoos at their tables and, lo and behold, Tomas actually started looking through them.

I notice Melody, a skinny, white, black-lipsticked poet *emo* girl-interrupted type reading books on witchcraft. (According to rumors, Mel used to be a lesbian until she became pregnant, and then she either left school to have a baby or had an abortion.) I approach gingerly and ask teasingly, "So Mel, you planning on becoming a witch?"

"Mr. Mandel, I worship Satan." she replies in all seriousness.

Okay I think, noticing for the first time a 666 tattoo on the top of each of Mel's meatless biceps. *This is going to be fun.* Oh, one more thing about Melody: because she is way behind schedule to graduate, she is in both my English 12 Fifth Block and my English 11 Third Block. This doesn't make my job any easier because I have to come up with extra assignments just for Mel to replace the duplicate *Transition* and *Quick Write* assignments I often use for both grades.

I notice Jorge eavesdropping on my conversation with Melody and as I leave Mel he calls me over. Jorge tells me, in all seriousness, how offended he is by Melody's tattoos and anti-god beliefs. Apparently Mel's blatant satanic worship had awakened the boy's long dormant Roman Catholicism. Pointing out that many people might be offended by the fact that he wears saggy pants down to his ankles, often with his ass sticking out, I explain clearly to Jorge that he might want to be a little more tolerant of others. He tries to argue that this is different. (He might have a point if fashion weren't more important than god to most teenagers.) I go on to lecture the group on religious freedom and tolerance. After my sermon I go in search of more books for my students.

Later, Jorge, in a transparent effort to both get my goat and show Mel up, asks me to help him find a book on God. This was the same Jorge who had, to this point, never shown any interest in either books or God, "Jesus or just God?" I ask.

"I don't care." he replies, and I send him off in search of *A History of God*, knowing he will reject it on its size alone. Jorge quickly returns complaining about the book

I recommended and asks if there are any books with pictures of God.

"Photos or drawings?" I ask chiefly for my own amusement. I tell Jorge if he does find a good photograph of God I would love to see it.

I do worry a religious war may break out in this class in the future. Later I sit down at the table with my bad boys and make an attempt to let them know I am a real person. I think it may actually have worked a little. We bullshit…I take…I give. They try their best to embarrass me with questions like, "Mr. Mandel do you smoke weed? You know, have you ever puffed the magic dragon?" Stuff like that. I recount stories from my teen years concerning old-school gangs and gang fashions from the Los Angeles barrio (Highland Park) where I grew up. Aware of his fascination with tattoos, I gently nudge Tomas about his ink artistry and am able to get him to open a little and tell me, relatively enthusiastically, about the Virgin Mary tattoo he designed and applied (it took 4 weeks) to his uncle's back.

Exchanged the following emails with Doug the Librarian after this first visit:

From: Eric
Sent: Friday, August 31, 2007 1:38 PM
To: Doug
Subject: Thanks

I do appreciate all your help and positive feedback during my Library visits this week. I actually think most kids found stuff to read that they are genuinely inte rested in. And thanks to the Library I had breakthrough of sorts with two of my most difficult students. The Library provided a neutral site that allowed me to spend some time sitting at a big table, actually talking to both of them about real things from god to tattoos, not to mention various decorated body parts. I actually noticed the two of them smiling, and a few times they looked me in the eyes.

It's a start.....And so it goes.

Eric

From: Doug
Sent: Friday, August 31, 2007 1:41 PM
To: Eric Mandel
Subject: RE: Thanks

I'm hoping we can do some projects together this year. I enjoy working with your students, and I especially enjoy working with you. You already have a rapport with your students that some teachers never get. Keep up the great job.

Doug
Library Media Teacher
"I have always imagined that Paradise will be a kind of library."—Jorge Luis Borges

Many around school consider Doug the Librarian a god. Sara tells me that the fact that Doug gave me his seal of approval is a big deal.

Feeling pretty good—for the moment.

Sunday - September 2

It didn't take me long to realize that each of my classes operates as an independent living organism, each with its own unique metabolism and personality. Blocks One and Four are subdued, even docile, while Blocks Three (Jeremy, Gina, Zen) and Five (Jorrid Jorge, Toxic Tomas) are outgoing and at times on the verge of mayhem. There are explanations of course, and the obvious ones involve time of day and gender.

First Block and Fourth Block begin at 8:50, while Fifth starts at 11 and ends at lunch, one hundred minutes later. Third starts at 1:40 and ends at 3:00. It is no secret that hunger, heat and after-lunch lethargy are all a teacher's adversaries.

As for gender breakdowns, First and Fourth are about 60% male; Fifth has one lone girl adrift amidst a sea of teenage testosterone, and Third has just two females, Gina and Jasmine, who seem to have no difficulty holding their own with the boys.

Readers might guess that as a self-described skeptic I have no trouble wading into the turbulent water of political correctness, so let me just say this: after fifty-eight years of life experience in group situations (to be completely honest I reached this conclusion when I was in high school with only about eighteen years of life experience, and since then I have never seen anything to change my mind), I have concluded that, in group situations, boys behave worse than girls.

And then there are the extreme cases of acting out––the Jorge's of the world. These students deflect attention from their intellectual shortcomings by challenging authority and disrupting the class. They'd rather be bad than dumb; in the coin of the teenage realm, being known as an asshole is far better than be known as a dumb ass. Ignorance is always a losing proposition, while swagger does have its rewards.

A subtler contributor to the different personalities of the blocks is the inadvertent tracking of students. For example, seniors whose poor performance requires they take a remedial reading or exit exam prep course that is only offered first period, would end up en masse in my Fifth Block.

In my classes there does not seem to be any direct correlation between academic performance and behavior. Some bright motivated kid, perhaps basking in self-confidence, can create as much havoc as the bitter failing kid who has perfected other ways to gain notice and/ or notoriety. Individual personalities have a significant influence on each group as a whole, as does the comfort level some kids feel when they have spent years together in school perfecting their team teacher-tormenting skills.

One thing is certain—it only takes a small number of marvelous miscreants to affect the overall atmosphere of the entire class. Tomfoolery—or in parlance of the day, *fucking off*—is contagious.

Saturday - September 8

All in all it was a pretty good week for me, pedagogically speaking. Besides learning the sophistic word *pedagogy*, which in today's educational techno-speak has come to mean the science of teaching (its noun form *pedagogue* interestingly, is defined as a teacher who teaches in a pedantic or dogmatic manner), I am also getting to know the kids better. While some remain incredibly difficult, I am developing a rapport with the majority and I have even learned most of their names. I had every student write a "formal" two-paragraph essay on one of five topics so I could use the essays as a tool to identify the weak points in their writing. It was eye-opening and refreshing. Some of the essays were quite good, some horrible, but most of them displayed a real willingness to express real feelings.

A few weeks back I had had the kids fill out a questionnaire, and we shared their answers to the question:

THE ACCIDENTAL TEACHER

Have you met any famous people? Defining *met* in its broadest sense; many kids had met some "famous" athletes and singers. And when they wanted to know my most famous acquaintance I scanned my memory banks. In my long life I have met a few famous people, but I narrowed it down to two biggies: Martin Luther King and Tony Hawk. As a boy I was briefly introduced to MLK in the early *Sixties* at a large civil rights rally in Los Angeles when King, accompanied by Paul Newman and Joanne Woodward, stepped out of a limo just prior to giving a speech. At the time I was pretty blasé about the whole thing. Tony Hawk I met several times through Steve, an old friend, who was once married to Tony Hawk's sister for a time in the early *Nineties*. (Steve, I might add, at one time was perilously close to becoming my stepbrother.) *Hmmm, which one should I mention?* Really a no-brainer. "Tony Hawk." I said. They were pretty damn impressed and they wanted to hear all the details.

As for the non-teaching part of my week, it sucked. Case managing is going to take a lot more time than I originally thought. And as I find my rhythm in the classroom, the case manager side saps my finite energy and time. Making things worse, Ethan Putzmire, the special ed compliance specialist and the person responsible for helping me with my casework, while dedicated and well meaning, is a dick. Ethan is a thin, hyper-fit jock in his early forties. He is also an assistant football coach for the *Hay Balers* and many boys call him Coach. Putzmire sometimes talks to me in a patronizing and condescending tone as if I am some dorky spaz trying out for his junior varsity football team. The other day, while Ethan was lecturing me on how to read an IEP (*Individualized Education Plan*: pages and pages of tests, pysch reports acronyms and arcane jargon), *I* inadvertently began calling him Coach!

I spent a good chunk of last week reducing IEP's down to one-page summaries—*IEP's at a Glance*—to send out to students' teachers; a real pain in the ass. I was supposed to have all twenty-four of them out by the end of the day yesterday. At four I was still working on them and decided to take my chances and wait until Monday or Tuesday to get them out. It won't surprise me at all if Coach Putzmire makes me do laps, push-ups and perhaps even a few wind sprints as punishment. Lucky for me resource specialists don't grow on trees, so even after this blatant act of insubordination I am pretty sure that for now my job is secure.

The Pretender

I'm going to pack my lunch in the morning
And go to work each day
And when the evening rolls around
I'll go on home and lay my body down
And when the morning light comes streaming in
I'll get up and do it again

—Jackson Browne

Tuesday - September 18

I need to run to Pilates, but I want to type this before I forget.

In class today, as the students were filling out job applications, Gina asked, "Mr. Mandel, how do you spell Marie?"

"Who's Marie?" I asked, assuming she was one of Gina's references.

"It's my middle name." she answered guilelessly.

Ok, back from Pilates. Haven't written in a while so I want to get some things down. Tony the boxer was promoted into a regular English class last week, Girl-Interrupted Mel has been missing for a week. Rumor is she ran off with some man. All in all things are going better.

Today I had my first meeting with one of the students I represent as a caseworker, Natalie, a pleasant bright senior in my First Block. After almost flunking out of school two years ago, Natalie earned straight A's last year and has been working hard to turn things around. She met with me to discuss requesting a transfer to the area's alternative high school (aka: San Andreas, the high school of last resort for losers, gang bangers and druggies). Natalie realizes she doesn't belong at San Andreas, but she is behind in credits and won't be able to graduate from San Benito on time. Apparently (this is all news to me of course), San Andres requires fewer credits, and if she were to transfer there she could graduate in June. Natalie got teary as she told me how lonely she has been since her parents moved the family from San Mateo to Hollister (the nearest place they could afford a house) last year. Her mom and dad are gone all the time; one brother works for dad while the younger siblings are still in San Mateo living with their grandmother. She has no friends at San Benito High and wants to graduate as soon as possible so she can get a job and move back to San Mateo to be with her boyfriend. It seems that behind every troubled student is some sort of dysfunctional home situation. Beginning to make sense. I pretended not to notice the tears as I promised I would help her examine her options.

After Natalie left I called her mother to schedule a meeting, and during the conversation (Mom was at work––she manages the family construction company), Mom suddenly starts yelling, "Get the fuck out of there!" at someone who is rummaging through the company dumpster. Mom yells at the intruder, apologizes to me, yells at the intruder some more and apologizes to me some more; after a few more *fucks* and *sorrys*, we eventually set a date for the meeting.

Tomorrow is *Back to School Night* and I will have an opportunity to perform my charade in front of grown-ups for the first time. Should be interesting.

Thursday - September 20

Yesterday was intense. I arrived at school before 8:00 and didn't get home till after 9:30, *Back to School Night* and all. It turns out Mel Interrupted did not in fact run away with some guy, worse—she's in some psyche ward. Mel is probably the brightest and definitely the most disturbed of all my students, and I really am pulling for her. More bad news—Jesus, an impish Hispanic senior who, with a sparkle in his eyes, enjoyed plying me with questions like, "Mr. Mandel, so do you do weed or acid? Come on, you can tell me!" was suspended for ten days, and now the school, unbeknownst to Jesus, is in the process of expelling him. Seems that sparkle in Jesus' eyes was not solely the result of the joy he derived from sitting in my class. At this time all I know is that Jesus was busted for marijuana. I will find out more details tomorrow when I attend his expulsion hearing.

On the way to school yesterday I decided to ditch my scheduled lesson and attempt instead to hook the kids with something I know really interests them—rap music. They all seem to have strong opinions about rap: love it or hate it. I can't count the times they've complained about the poems I subject them to (read by Garrison Keillor on *The Writer's Almanac*) as they go on and on about that great

American poet, Tupac. So with all this in mind, I drop *Of Mice and Men* for my juniors and a dry Colette short story for my seniors, and instead have them listen to a seven-minute NPR story about the current Kanye West/50 Cent feud.

I follow the story with a short class discussion and then I go over some really basic essay rules such as: don't use *cuz* or *cause* in place of *because*, or street language such as *sucks* and *asshole* when writing an essay. Oh, and always capitalize *i* and don't repeat the same thing over and over in different ways just to reach the required two paragraphs. I gave the following example of how <u>not</u> to write, *i hate Bush cuz hes a jerk. I relly don't like him. What an asshole.*

Most of them were eager to start, so I turned them loose. Off they went writing about one of two topics: *Who I like more, 50 Cent or Kanye West and why?* For the rap haters, I offered the alternative: *Why I don't like either of them.* Most wrote way more than required. There was lots of debate and arguing going on during the writing. Many of my students have a patience problem when it comes to expressing their thoughts and ideas—when an idea hits it circumvents the brain's edit lobe and spews uncensored from the mouth or pen, which may or may not be a good thing. On the whole this was by far my most successful lesson.

While I was teaching First Block, my best-behaved class, with Kanye's new album playing softly in the background, my evaluator/boss Carol showed up unannounced sat down at the aide's desk and began observing me. Deadpan and stoic, Ms. Havisham sat quietly taking notes on a clipboard for twenty minutes. Great timing. Lucky for me the boss showed up during my most creative and appealing lesson. Considering I had been teaching for only a month, I thought I did a great job with the kids; most important, however, will be Carol's perceptions. Her initial observation could become the defining moment in our relationship. And by the way, as I collected the essays a quick glance caught this gem of a topic sentence, *I hate 50 Cent, he is a real bastard.*

What the hell, I had a good time.

Back to School Night: Other than making for an incredibly long day, it turned out well. Met interesting parents of interesting kids. Jeremy showed up with his mom and dad. Jeremy was quiet, well, relatively speaking; he definitely takes after his mom. His dad is a macho construction worker type. Both Jeremy's parents emphasized I should call anytime Jeremy acts up. I replied, "Are you sure? If so you might want to be near a phone every other school day between 1:20 and 3:00."

They laughed.

Gina came with her mom and her little brother Giuseppe. Not sure where to begin or end. When Gina's mom started saying nice things about her daughter, Gina looked at her mom with disdain and told her to shut up. As Gina and family exited, Melissa entered smiling brightly with both parents in tow. Melissa is a talkative, opinionated, energetic junior with a mouthful of chrome. Earlier in the day she had begged me not to mention to her parents any of the stuff that she gleefully boasts about in class, like the time I asked about their weekends and Melissa bragged about staying out until three in the morning partying when the whole time her parents thought their little girl was upstairs sleeping like a baby. While Melissa squirmed nervously next to her parents, I kept her on pins and needles but said nothing about our secret. I figure her secrets are more useful to me for now if they remain secret.

I felt a little uneasy just before parents and students arrived when it suddenly dawned on me that I still didn't know all my students by name. I worried I might inadvertently call some kid by another kid's name. Thankfully that never happened, although just in case, whenever I had any doubt I avoided using names altogether. One couple came without a kid and introduced themselves as Rick Steele's parents. At that moment the only Rick I could think of was the gun-obsessed, obnoxious, opinionated redheaded Rick—the Rick who had taken it upon himself to become the arbitrator of justice in my class, continually calling me out for not being fair to other students. So when the Steeles asked how Rick was doing I replied judiciously, "He's doing fine in class. Rick seems to have no trouble sharing his opinions on just about anything with anybody who'll listen."

Dad gave me a puzzled look and replied, "That's great. Generally Rick doesn't say a word in class."

Immediately I sensed a problem; however I stayed the course. As soon as the Steeles left I checked my seating charts and realized that their Rick had in fact not uttered a single syllable this semester. Oh what the hell, for the time being Mr. and Mrs. Steele are going to be thrilled their reticent son is coming out of his shell.

Saturday - September 29

I've been at this for almost two months and feel like I am living in two entirely separate worlds that are isolated from one another by far more than the for-ty-five miles distance between them. After living and working for over forty years in a university beach town,

I now get up every morning before sunrise and, bad back and all, begin my morning commute. I head down Highway 1 along the coast through intermittent fog, exit onto a dangerous two-lane country road that winds through miles of fertile farmland and rolling hills followed by a short jaunt north up Highway 101. Next I drive through ten more miles of farmland—Steinbeck country—before I sneak onto campus via back roads that allow me to reach the school without ever entering the city of Hollister.

No family members or friends have seen the school; no one from school is even remotely aware of my Santa Cruz existence. Additionally, I realized the other day that I have been isolating myself on campus, staying under the radar. There are several colleagues in our little pod I feel comfortable with, and I do bump into other teachers occasionally and make small talk, but I tend to keep to myself, eating lunch alone in my room. I drive to school, do my job, get in my car and drive home.

While I actually enjoy the solitude and quiet of the morning commute, the drive home is a real grind. Most days when I get home I greet the dogs, the wife, head upstairs, turn on NPR, flop down on the bed and take a nap. It appears my obsession for seeking my comfort zone has led me unwittingly, to create a new parallel patterned existence for myself.

Brando, The Beatles, Cow Tippers, Gang Bangers and Aseismic Creeps

The city of Hollister is the county seat of ruggedly rural San Benito County. It is nestled at the base of the rolling foothills of the Gabilan Mountains on a river plain just off State Highway 156 between San Jose and Salinas, about ten miles east of Highway 101 and twenty miles inland from the Monterey Bay. Before 1970, prior to the growth boom, Hollister was a quiet farming town with a population of just under 13,000. Today, as the population nears 40,000, strip malls, box stores, and hordes of large housing developments, along with rapidly dwindling farmland, encircle the Victorian-era downtown area.

The demographic statistics, complicated by ambiguous classification criteria for whites and Hispanics, are confusing at best. According to the most recent census the racial makeup of the city is 59% White, 1.4% African American, 1.1% Native American, 2.8% Asian, 30% from other races, and 5.5% from two or more races. Fifty-five percent of the population is Hispanic or of ethnic Latino background. Go figure. It's probably safe to assume that the town is about equal parts white and *Hispanicish*. From my own observations, Hollister seems to have at its nucleus a large number of influential white, Hispanic and mixed-race families that have lived in the area for generations.

This once sleepy town, despite a strong jolt of caffeine and adrenaline from a tremendous growth spurt, is still far from becoming a mecca for local teenagers. Its relative isolation from urban centers limits the variety of activities available for teens to movies, shopping, partying, drinking, blazing and cruising. Its location does provide some unique diversions from cow tipping to serious off-roading at *Hollister Hills*, one of the largest vehicular recreation areas in California. A highlight for many teens is a day trip to the *Santa Cruz Beach Boardwalk*, or perhaps a shopping safari to the outlet stores in Gilroy, the uncontested *Garlic Capital of the World*. While there is gang activity, including gangbanging, drive-bys and other assorted murders, the gangs in Hollister seem to be small-town subsidiaries of their big brothers in San Jose and Salinas.

Arguably, Hollister's principle claims to fame, aside from the unauthorized use of *Hollister* as the brand name of the popular clothing line from parent company *Abercrombie and Fitch* (ironically, a look intended to evoke the *SoCal* surfing lifestyle carries the name of a relatively unknown cow town), are in the areas of geology and movie trivia. Hollister proclaims, along with two other California towns, Coalinga and Parkfield, to be the *Earthquake Capital of the World*. The *Calaveras Fault*, a major branch of the *San Andreas Fault*, not only bisects the city but also divides the *New Campus* from the *Old Campus* at San Benito High School. An added bonus for geologists—Hollister is one of the world's best examples of aseismic creep. Whatever the hell that means.

[Here is what the hell it does mean according to a Stanford website: *From San Juan Bautista to just North of Parkfield the faults in the San Andreas system are not ``stuck'': instead of moving only during major earthquakes, the usual pattern for faults, they continuously ``creep''. As a result of this creep, Hollister is being ripped in two, for the most part along a remarkably narrow zone running right through the middle of town.*]

For more than sixty years Hollister has been the site of an annual summer motorcycle rally. A riot that occurred at the rally in 1947 was the basis for the 1954 movie classic, *The Wild One*. The movie, starring Marlon Brando as the leader of the motorcycle gang *Black Rebels*, was banned in England until 1968, and when it was finally released there it was slapped with an undeserved X-rating. Speaking of England, *The Wild One* is also recognized as the origin of the moniker *The Beatles* (*The Black Rebels* rival gang). The movie includes one of the all-time great lines in Hollywood history:

"What're you rebelling against, Johnny?" asks Kathie, the town sheriff's saucy daughter,

"Whaddya got?" Brando's Johnny replies.

Sunday – September 30

Last week was tough, maybe my toughest yet, not counting my first week of course—lots of dreadful behavior from the usual suspects and a less than glowing observation summary from my boss. In general, a shitty week chuck full of little annoyances. I had to send Tomas and Jorge to the office and write misconduct reports. Then more casework crap, parent contacts, emergency meetings, truancy problems, behavior plans, blah, blah, blah. Jesus, as expected, was expelled for smoking marijuana. It turns out the boy he was puffing the magic dragon with was Josh, who also just happens to be in my caseload, which means yet another meeting on the horizon. And making things even worse, three of my four regular aides are out for two weeks for assorted reasons. This means I will either be teaching without an aide at all or with a substitute aide. More work for me, less consistency for the students.

The fun never stops.

Mel Interrupted, freshly released from the mental ward, showed up on Tuesday. Within minutes she had exerted her disruptive influence on the class. Two of Mel's many problems are an inability to self-edit and a total lack of propriety or shame. And while she does get her share of flack from her classmates, in her own way she provokes them and seems to relish the ensuing attention. As I was reading aloud a notice to the class from *The Daily Bulletin* (a dreary, tedious, redundant collection of warnings, club news, upcoming dances, sports crap and birthday greetings) about a meeting of the *Christian Fellowship of Athletes*, Mel, completely aware of the consequences, blurted out, "Mr. Mandel, is there anything in the bulletin about the gay and transgender club?"

As you might imagine, some took the bait, and off we went on a bumpy detour of insipid gay jokes and general *stupidness*. Mel seemed to enjoy herself. After assuring a gloating Mel that if there were ever any news about the club (it does exist) I would be sure to read it, I did my best to rein 'em in and cut the discussion short.

Here's the short version of what happened with Jorge and Tomas: Every day in every way they do their best to show me up and disrupt the class, ignoring my requests, making clicking sounds and stupid comments. Worried the kids smelled blood in the water I decided to clamp down. I was through trying to handle things internally—it wasn't working. So before class on Thursday I notified everyone I was sick of all the crap and from now on I was going to warn them once, send them outside after the second warning and to the office after that. *Three strikes and you're out.*

Los Dos Amigos took my words as a challenge. They were both gone within fifteen minutes. Tomas snidely egged his highly impressionable friend over the edge. Jorge's last act of defiance was, when asked for the third time to please put his water bottle down, to simply stand up and drop the open bottle to the floor. He went on to insist, in mock innocence, that he had done exactly as told. On the way to the office both boys ditched their escort and left campus. I followed up with the paperwork and called their parents, but I'm not hopeful it won't happen again soon.

It still astonishes me that I have two 12th and two 11th

grade classes, and that one class in each grade is good and one is horrible. I am willing to admit that the horrible 11th grade class (Third Block) with Gina and Jeremy, while challenging, can be amusing, but I can't think of anything positive about the *Fight'n Fifth*.

∽◌◌∾

Here is Carol's official email of my observation. My response will follow.

Re: Drop In
Date: 9/21/07
     Erik- I am going to give you some recommendations regarding the drop in I did in your class on Wed. 9/19. First, I am considering the drop in unofficial so that I can work with you regarding instructional techniques and then later I will do an official drop in.
     Your students were cooperative and followed your directives. There appears to be no classroom management problems which is very good for a new teacher.
     The idea of using the article/audio tape regarding Rap/HipHop was an excellent "hook"- motivating idea.
                    Recommendations:
     Transition: Should be a question that reviews the previous lesson **5 minutes only**
     Silent Reading – **No more than 15 minutes with an additional 5 for writing in a reading log**
     Next please model, using the overhead, what you want students to do. For your comparison essay, I would have walked the students through the process, step by step and written the essay on the overhead.

Start by helping the students organize with a simple chart listing similarities and differences between the 2 rappers. List on overhead as students give you the answers. Next ask the students for a topic sentence. Write it on the overhead; ask questions to help students improve the quality of the sentence. Ask students for 1 similarity. Have another student put in a sentence. Write on overhead and help students improve the sentence…. Follow the process for both paragraphs.

(See Sara Stasi. She can review the Shaffer writing model which is used in the English department. It is important that you follow the format as all our students have learned this process and it works. This whole process may take 30 minutes.)

Next I would have another article. Read and discuss as a class. Then have the students list the similarities and difference on the chalkboard. Ask different students for topic sentences orally. Then for some sample detail sentences. Then they are ready to write an essay independently. The following day, I would take sample essays and as a class read them. Discuss good points and guide students in making constructive suggestions.

Erik, it is very important that you model everything you are going to ask students to do, step by step. Also, please move your stool to the center. I'm sure that you did not realize that you called upon and addressed only the students on the door side where your stool was. These students happened to be primarily the Anglo students in the class.

I would like you to work with Sara to obtain some ideas and other strategies. I will be out next week, but the following week I would like to see you do a lesson using the recommendations I listed above. Please email me a day and time when I can see this lesson. Thank you.

Aside from the fact Carol misspelled my name even after my having corrected her twice, and aside from the fact a few of her recommendations were appropriate, the tone was disheartening and some of her points were completely off-base. Carol's implication that I have an unconscious preference for calling on Anglos over Latinos is total unadulterated bullshit. The class Carol observed was 13/15 Hispanic, and of the two Anglos one has yet to utter an audible sound this semester. Apparently Carol was judging ethnicity by skin pigmentation alone.

Carol is right about my needing to model more; however for this particular essay the kids were so excited and eager I decided to let them go for it with little prompting. Funny thing, Carol never looked at the end result, the essays. As for the *Silent Reading* — "*No more than 15 minutes with an additional 5 for writing in a reading log*" I was following Sara's model and I have no plans to change it.

Admittedly I have a lot to learn, but Carol's comments were too critical and lacked any sense of my situation. If anything they got my hackles up making me much less likely to heed her direction. I would prefer she provide more real support, like the opportunity to observe and learn techniques from other teachers or to attend workshops. I shared Carol's observation notes with Sara. Sara did her best to point out the few pearls among the swine. She encouraged me to stay positive and offered to help me prepare for the upcoming "official" *drop-in*. Overall the results of my first official assessment from my boss do not bode well for our relationship and are probably not a good omen for my future in education.

I don't want to end the entry on a sour note, so I will mention Cal, the only black kid in any of my classes and perhaps one of only ten in the entire school. Cal is a good student in my Third Block. Although eager and articulate, a processing disorder makes it difficult for him to organize his thoughts in writing. Thus far his essays have been written in outline form. Cal starts each paragraph in list form with TC (topic sentence) followed by two separate CM (comments, generally starting with "for example"), and then a C (conclusion). He is using an aborted form of the *Schaffer Writing Method* sited by Carol in her earlier email. My next step is to have him translate the list into normal prose form. Again I digress.

Currently we are reading *Of Mice and Men*, and in the upcoming chapter, Steinbeck frequently uses the word *nigger*. Although I wasn't too concerned because Cal and the other boys seem to tease one another with an open easiness about ethnicity, I thought it best to give Cal a heads-up. Cal and I talk about the issue for a while and we also discuss Steinbeck's use of *Negro* as the accepted term for African-American at the time. We have a nice adult exchange and the two of us joke about how even resource kids, with their distaste for reading, always seem to find the passages with sex and inappropriate language within seconds of being handed a book.

When we finish, Cal smiles, thanks me, shakes my hand firmly and leaves.

Monday – October 1

I saw an eye-opening statistic today: only 25% of San

Benito High School students go to college, junior colleges or trade schools. My surprise at this statistic illustrates how little I know about this school. My ignorance is catching up with me and it is time to do some research on San Benito High. What follows is a compilation of my findings.

San Benito High School is large, both in the size of the student body and in the size of the campus. The student body, along with the area population, has grown significantly in the last thirty years. In the mid-Seventies the school population was close to 1000 and today it is over 3000. This growth has led to major expansions of the physical plant. The sprawling campus covers many city blocks and is loosely divided into four areas. The *Old Campus*, where my room is located, is anchored by the beautiful main building designed by William Weeks and built in 1909. The other areas are of more recent vintage: the *New Campus* was built in the last several years and is separated from an older addition, which includes the *New Gym*, industrial buildings and funky 1950 barrack-style classrooms (the only structures with air conditioning) by a large, barren patch of ground directly over a major branch of the *San Andreas Fault*. The largest section of the campus consists of the football stadium, ball fields, large parking lots, the agricultural area including livestock yards, and the maintenance and transportation yards. The campus is actually located in two separate legal jurisdictions: The *Old Campus* is in the city of Hollister, while the other areas are in the unincorporated section of the county. As you might imagine, this can often lead to confusion during situations involving law enforcement.

The district boundaries are large, covering 95% of San Benito County. This sparsely populated county of 53,000 residents covers 1400 square miles (seventy-five miles north-to-south and thirty miles west-to-east at its widest point) and borders on five counties: Santa Clara, Santa Cruz, Monterey, Merced and Fresno. An interesting consequence of the district's considerable size is that over the years there has been an ongoing controversy over what to call the high school. And while it seems that the school was never officially named Hollister High, many old timers from Hollister continue to call it by that name. To this day some of the school's athletic uniforms have *Hollister* on them and the team's football helmets are emblazoned with an *H*. The battle rages on.

According to San Benito's *2006 School Accountability Report Card*, the student body is 53% Hispanic, 43% White, 2% Asian and less than 1% Black. California uses different race classifications than the US Census and makes a clearer distinction between White/Anglo and Hispanic/Latino. In spite of this I think this data is fuzzy at best. Race classification is self-selected, and in my experience with the students I have noticed that a great number are from mixed backgrounds, most of these including Anglo and Hispanic blood. Approximately 10% of students are classified as *students with disabilities* (ranging from severe to mild), and 20% are considered *economically disadvantaged*. While I could not find any official data on the racial makeup of the faculty, I estimate that among a faculty of 130, fewer than thirty-five are Hispanic. The support staff, on the other hand, is overwhelmingly Hispanic.

Academically the school is about average among all California public schools and when compared to high schools of similar socio-economic and racial makeup. The graduation rate of 93% for San Benito students is well above the state average of 85%. The district spends a little more than a thousand dollars per student above the state average. And if those stats weren't enough, take a look at how stats drive public education in California.

The *Academic Performance Index* (API) is all the rage in today's data driven education world. School boards and administrators focus on their API to the detriment of all else. This makes about as much sense as some grizzled old horseracing junkie standing in line at *Santa Anita*, nose buried in the *Daily Racing Form*, preparing to wager a good chunk of his Social Security check on some broken down gelding based solely on the nag's speed rating (equally as confusing a formula as a school's API) while ignoring all the other factors generally used in predicting a thorough-bred's performance. As a result of their myopic vision, both the school and the handicapper are more likely to fail than to succeed. The gambler's losses, while distressing, affect only himself and his family, while a school's miscal-culations can result in a tragedy of epic proportions—a generation of ignorance.

This data-driven frenzy has created a situation today in which our kids are drowning in information while at the same starving for genuine knowledge they can use to successfully navigate through their lives—a situation that administrators and politicians lost sight of a long time ago when they sold their souls for a variety of reasons that seemed to make sense at the time.

What is the API? Here is how it is described in the *School Report Card*: *The Academic Performance Index (API) is an annual measure of the academic performance and progress of schools in California. The API is a score on a scale of 200 to 1,000, with 800 set as the statewide target. Schools are ranked in ten categories of equal size from 1 (lowest) to 10 (highest). A similar schools API rank reflects how a school compares to 100 statistically matched "similar schools."*

Got all that?

Basically the API is the critical criteria for rating the school's performance and determining the school's level of success in "educating" its students. San Benito's state-wide API rank is 6 and its *similar school rank* is 5. As I mentioned earlier, about average.

San Benito High School District is in the relatively rare position of being both a high school and a district. And while the district includes adult education and other services outside of the high school, in essence the school and the district are one and the same. This makes for interesting overlaps in authority and management. There is a superintendent responsible for the district as a whole, and a principal responsible for running the school. The principal, who earns around $95,000, has job duties that are clear and obvious, but I have yet to find one person who can explain to me what the superintendent does to justify his hefty salary of $160,000, other than reporting to the board and facilitating board meetings. Labor relations are strained and faculty and management turnover is very high. This is evidenced by the number of new teachers— twenty-eight—that came on board with me this year, and by the fact that as the school year began, the district had a new superintendent, new HR director, and the high school had a completely new leadership team including a principal and three new vice-principals.

Moving on from the academic realm to the athletic field. Not surprisingly for a school located in an isolated town with not much going on, athletics are important. Football occupies a vaunted position in the school and in the surrounding area. Friday night football is a tradition in Hollister. There are a large number of alums in the area and on staff. The *San Benito Hay Balers* athletic teams (aka: the *Balers* or *Hollister*) are a major source of pride and entertainment. I personally believe that the role athletics plays in schools is overwhelmingly positive. Competing in sports gives a large number of students a reason to come to school and do well in class. My own son's incentive to attend classes and do well had nothing to do with academics. Simon tolerated the academics in order to enjoy the social aspects of school and for the pure joy of playing baseball and soccer.

As you can imagine, the importance of sports can be a source of conflict among faculty members. Priorities do get skewed. Sometimes it seems like every other male member of the faculty is a football coach. This leads to battles over scheduling, athletic eligibility, and the other added sports-related supervisory duties for faculty. Football homecoming, parades and athletic rallies all lead to truncated schedules and reduced instruction time. Some faculty members openly resent the attention and money athletics receive. Many kids also resent the whole jock scene. I heard bitching from both groups all year long. The two biggest sporting events of the year are the football homecoming game and the *Prune Bowl*—a fifty-year tradition against the *Balers'* archrival the *Gilroy Mustangs*. The *Balers* lead the series 29-21.

Campus Safety: The campus is well maintained and nicely landscaped. While San Benito High has a reputation for being a dangerous, gang-infested place, at no time during the year did I ever feel uneasy or threatened. I may be naïve, and though we were often on alert because of off-campus gang situations, I was unaware of any serious gang activity on campus, The school is hyper-vigilant in regards to student safety, spending money and working diligently to maintain a safe and clean campus. In what some might consider an extreme move, the school recently installed large picture windows in all the boys' restrooms in an effort to reduce graffiti, smoking and whatever. (Yes, there are doors on many of the stalls.) I don't recall seeing any graffiti on the campus during the year. The school is patrolled constantly by a predominantly female group of orange-vested campus supervisors, affectionately known as *Campos*. The *Campos* do a fine job of dealing with problems, escorting unruly kids from the classroom to the office, and keeping the campus free of intruders. The school's strictly enforced *no-hat policy* makes it easier to identify outsiders on campus. In addition, both the Hollister Police and San Benito Sheriff Department patrol the campus and make their presence felt when necessary.

Well I think that does it.

IV

Pissing in the Wind

Wednesday - October 3

I'm midway through the longest week thus far. Grades due, IEP's up the ass, and both tomorrow and the day after I have to stay late to do extra duties, sans extra pay, as required by contract. Tomorrow I have a 5:45 Girls Volleyball game, Friday at 6:45 the annual *Powder Puff* football game, next week two more extra duties, and then, mercifully, no more until my last one in April.

Today after school I went to a meeting to learn more about the *Schaffer Writing Method*. *Schaffer* is the proprietary writing system the school is pushing on all teachers. Without going into too much detail, the method uses a formulaic system in an effort to produce competent writers. *Schaffer* utilizes a complex system in an effort to simplify writing and uses terms such as: one chunk paragraph, *Topic Sentences* (TS), *Commentary* (CM), *Concrete Detail* (CD), and *Concluding Sentences* (CS). It involves using different color-coded pens: green for CM, red for CD, blue for TS and black for CS. The system probably works fine with regular ed students, especially if introduced early on like in sixth grade or so. However for resource kids who often have trouble just comprehending or even remembering simple instructions, it is a very steep mountain to climb. Some do have a general grasp of the method, while others are clueless even after being "taught" the system for three years. Combine all this with the fact that their teacher, Mr. Mandel, had never even heard the term *Schaffer Method* until seven weeks ago and has a natural aversion to and skepticism about formulaic methods, and the likelihood of his students mastering the system is basically nil.

I have come to realize, as I mentioned earlier, that special education's dirty little secret (one of many I will discover later) is that while we pretend we are teaching the regular curriculum to the kids, in truth the curriculum for resource kids is modified to the point that it no longer resembles the mainstream version at all. It would be far better for teachers and students alike if we openly developed a modified curriculum with realistic goals and cut the silly pretense (don't ask, don't tell) once and for all.

Some good news. Yesterday Randy, the school's new teacher specialist, dropped in to observe me while my students listened to *Of Mice and Men* on CD (the disc not the *Concrete Detail*). I was stopping the disc from time to time to CFU (*check for understanding*), but things went horribly wrong. I accidentally unplugged the CD player and had trouble restarting the story in the proper place. Some kids fell asleep on their books, and then *nigger* raised its ugly head several times and Jasmine, by nature very emotional, shouted, "This is racist and dirty shit and I refuse to read it anymore!" For added emphasis she slammed her book down loudly on her desk as Cal looked on uncomfortably.

PISSING IN THE WIND

I thought my lesson was pretty bad, but Randy sent me a nice note complimenting me on my teaching and commending me on my ability to sense the pulse of my students. Randy was probably lying to boost my diminishing ego. After all a big part of his job is to offer positive reinforcement. What the hell, it felt good.

Toxic Tomas and Jorrid Jorge were removed from my class for good today. Sara volunteered, with Ethan's support, to move the two boys into her 11th grade Fifth Block to prevent them from either failing my class or being kicked out of school for good. Technically I remain their teacher, but they will do their work in Sara's room next door. Unfortunately their absence will not solve all my problems. Sara and I discussed which of the remaining boys would step up to the plate and seize Tomas and Jorge's coveted positions as class assholes. We agreed on four likely suspects to fill the void and lo and behold, within minutes of Jorge's and Tomas' exits, Michael and Smiling Tony made their move. Both are trouble, but trouble with a smile—a real couple of knuckleheads. For some reason the smiles make it easier for me to tolerate the behavior. The other two candidates, Stan and Oliver, were gone today attempting to pass the state exit exam for the fifth time. It shouldn't take them long after their return to stake their claims to the throne.

Another Mel Interrupted story: Yesterday Mel tells me, like for the fourth time, that her eighteenth birthday is in exactly 32 days. She follows up the announcement with something to the effect that she won't have many friends to celebrate her special day with. I take the bait and ask her why, assuming Melody may have scared off her remaining friends because of her recent stay in the mental ward. Mel replies, "Well I am a vegetarian and a Christian.

All my old friends are Satanists and meat eaters."

"But Mel," I reply, "I thought you were a Satanist. That's what you told me in the library."

"Oh Mr. Mandel, that was a long time ago."

"Oh yeah, you're right, my bad Mel, like a whole three weeks."

Tuesday - October 9

As always, there is so much to write about and so little time or energy to actually put it in writing and be forced to relive it; the first time was hard enough. I have noticed that since I began sharing this with friends and family my narrative voice has evolved. In the beginning it was like an inner voice dictating to my fingers for no one's entertainment but my own. I just wanted to get stuff down before I forgot it. Now, with an audience, it seems I have, unconsciously at times, begun to write in complete sentences, shape the narrative, and fill out personalities to help readers imagine each unique character.

I decided to share my journal when I realized I was telling and retelling friends the same stories over and over. At first I shared it only with people who I knew would tell me they liked it even if they thought it sucked. And when these handpicked readers seemed to actually enjoy reading it, and some even began pestering me for the next installment, I decided to send it out to the more critical-and-less-likely-to-spare-my-feelings friends and family members.

Today during Fifth Block, while I introduce a short story by Sherman Alexie, a wonderfully funny American Indian writer, poet and filmmaker, the class is on the threshold of open revolt regarding the new seating arrangement, stupid rules and the like. It felt as though I was working in a storm with fifty-mile-an-hour headwinds blowing me further and further off course, or maybe it was more like the ringmaster of a three-ring circus. Sometimes I feel I am wasting my time, but just as things are falling apart something unexpected happens. Like today, as we finished the first half of the Alexie short story and Smiling Tony, the class clown and chief distracter—as opposed to two-fisted Tony— tells me he really likes the story.

Of course at first I didn't believe him, so I ask "You BSing me Tony?"

"No. I really liked it Mr. M." Tony actually sounded sincere and I really wanted to believe him.

When class ends, Coach Putzmire, the district's red tape and bureaucratic bullshit compliance specialist, shows up to go over the mountains of bureaucratic crap necessary to conduct a thirty-minute annual IEP. Incredible. Each IEP requires, at a minimum, twenty separate forms that are known by numbers, such as SELPA10 and SELPA 23D-1. (SELPA=*Special Education Local Plan Area*, area in my case being San Benito County.) If you were to count every available SELPA form for every imaginable situation the number would approach one hundred. By the time Ethan is done with his scattershot tutorial, I am more confused than ever.

Curriculum: Navigating without a map

Now that I am cognizant of the elevator load of readers who are following my adventure, it is probably a good time to discuss the curriculum I suddenly find myself responsible for delivering to my less than enthusiastic gaggle of students. Below are the courses of study for English 11 and English 12 as described verbatim in the official school

Course Catalog. If you were to take the time to carefully read these outlines an extra time or two, you would know as much as I knew when school began about the courses I was preparing to teach. These course descriptions, along with a few tips from colleagues, are all that I have at my disposal to build my curriculum, piece-by-piece, one lesson plan at a time, for the entire school year. It would be fair to say that my curriculum is cobbled together with equal parts good intentions, genuine creativity and basic bullshit.

English 11 Grade: Description: English 11 is designed to improve students' reading and writing skills and to create readers and writers through an in-depth study of the different genres of American Literature and the historical, cultural, and philosophical influences which shaped it. The course flows chronologically from the Native Americans through the Puritans, the Age of Reason, Romantic, and Realist periods, to the 20th century. Core work read includes such novels *as The Catcher in the Rye, Of Mice and Men, The Great Gatsby, and Bless Me, Ultima. S*tudents will continue their study of *Schaffer Writing Model* components and strategies beginning with the concept of weaving and concluding with sentence blending. These strategies are designed to retain the advanced skills of literary and linguistic analysis while increasing freedom of style and student voice. Students write a combination of critical and creative pieces based on the literature and using the writing process. Students also write an "I Search" paper and research, write, and deliver an informative speech. Independent reading is also a major focus of this course. Instruction, activities and assessment focus on the concepts and skills outlined in the California State Content Standards for language arts.

PISSING IN THE WIND

English 12 Grade: Description: Students in English 12 read novels, short stories, poetry, essays, and plays including: *Kitchen God's Wife, Antigone, Macbeth, and Things Fall Apart.* Through reading genres of both classic and contemporary periods, students gain an appreciation of the universal values shared by writers from different cultures. Students will continue their study of *Schaffer Writing Model* components and strategies beginning with the concept of weaving and concluding with sentence blending. These strategies are designed to retain the advanced skills of literary and linguistic analysis while increasing freedom of style and student voice. Writing is critical, analytical, and reflective in nature and based upon class reading and outside research. There is an emphasis on collaborative work and presentations relating to topics relevant to the literature.

Toward the end of the year I will provide the reader with a summary of what I actually taught in my classes. It should be interesting to compare the expectations to the reality—*intelligent design* vs. evolution.

Before I forget, I did pass the CBEST with a pretty decent score for an old man who hasn't taken a test in over forty years. Prior to the test I foolishly wagered a steak dinner with my daughter Lily that I would best her on the exam. I was counting on building a big enough lead in the vocabulary section to hold Lily off from slaughtering me in the other areas. Turns out there was no vocabulary section, so of course Lily kicked her poor dad's ass.

More Melody drama: One day last week, after many of my students had taken the *California High School State Exit*

Exam (CAHSEE: pronounced KC), we had a discussion and short writing assignment on the pros and cons of the CAHSEE. It was surprising how many students wrote that they thought it was a good idea, even though many would not get their diplomas because they were unable to pass it. Jorge reflected their feelings when he wrote that the test was a good idea because if a student fails it, as he has done six times and counting, it reveals how terrible the teachers are for "not teaching the right way."

When Mel comes in that afternoon she is ashen and in an agitated state. After the class finishes the writing assignment on the fairness of the CAHSEE, they share their opinions. Mel wants to read her paper to the class. That alone is not unusual because Mel seems to enjoy any attention she can get. I hold my breath and say, "Go for it."

It goes something like this: *I hate the exit exam. The people who wrote it are fucking assholes. They don't know shit. I hate the assholes who wrote it. Fuck the exam!!* And for a final flourish, Mel pounds her fist on the table.

"Mel, you seem to have strong feelings about the exam. Perhaps next time you can get your point across better by using less emotionally charged language. And maybe a few concrete examples would strengthen your argument."

I was waiting for her to spontaneously combust sometime during the remainder of the class, but she held herself in check. Later that day we were in the computer lab doing career assessments. Worried that someone might intentionally set Mel off, I kept an eye on her. She remained pretty quiet, but as the class was ending I asked what careers certain students were interested in and Mel blurted out, "Mr. Mandel, I wanna be a bartender, or a stripper."

"That's wonderful Melody." I successfully resisted following up with, "and besides, you have the perfect name for it." Abruptly I dismissed class.

School's over for the day and I breathe a sigh of relief.

After school, concerned about Mel's emotional state, I called Mel's caseworker Bruce (Mr. Pirl), the teacher who had left the symbolic *Pepto Bismol* on my desk before the start of school. I shared my fears with him as we discussed the situation. Evidently Mel had been having a bad couple of days centering on boys and former relationships, and was threatening to bolt again. It is a horrible scenario. Mel is going to turn eighteen in a matter of weeks and over the past few months has been living in a women's shelter with crack addicts. She is too near her eighteenth birthday to be placed into a foster home, because on the day of her eighteenth birthday, when she legally becomes an adult, she could be turned out onto the streets. Nice birthday present. Something is seriously wrong with a system that cuts off support to children while they are still in high school. How can we as a society, condone crushing any child's spirit—how can we just toss these kids away and then do our best to forget them.

Bruce was worried that when she turned eighteen Melody was planning to quit school immediately and hit the streets. He asked me to do everything in my power over the next two weeks to avoid upsetting her. I promised to do my best. Bruce, who is responsible for most of the school's emotionally disturbed (ED) students, is a caring guy who only wants what's best for the kids, but in this particular situation I feel he is fighting a losing battle. In my mind, Mel is pretty much gone.

Even after all Bruce's work, when Monday came Melody was gone and she didn't show up the entire week. Word on the street is she ran away again.

THE ACCIDENTAL TEACHER

No joy in Mudville

As for the CAHSEE (and also the STAR Test—I will give the STAR its due later) it creates more problems than it solves. Yes, it would be nice if all high school students were able to pass a test based on relevant standards that accurately assess their knowledge base, but many students, no matter how hard they work and study, will never pass the CAHSEE and thus will never earn a diploma. Up until this year, the state has granted waivers to resource students permitting them to receive a diploma without passing the test. This year there will be no waivers, and tens of thousands of students will not graduate in spite of the fact they have completed the required units and grades. I'm not sure how many of my seniors will be in that group, but I am guessing around 30%.

Aside from this calamity, the current emphasis on data-driven instruction and the importance of test results on a school's reputation have seriously affected what is being taught in schools today. Teaching to content standards is all the rage. The problem, as I see it, is that by putting so much time and effort into teaching what is tested for in the exams, the curriculum is narrowed and many subjects not on the test are totally ignored. For example, creative writing is nowhere to be found in the English curriculum, and social studies and the arts are sacrificed for more intensive study of the two major content areas in the exams—math and English.

In addition, teachers are required to explain to their students daily which standards they are teaching in each lesson. For instance (and I am making up the numbers and actual standards because I don't know any of them yet), while reading a short story we might be teaching to

PISSING IN THE WIND

Standards **2.0** *ability to understand a story*, **2.0.3** *the ability to analyze a narrative as to symbolism, etc* and **2.1.5** *the ability to coherently discuss theme and character development.* (I will post the actual standards soon and insert them below.)

What follows are the actual relevant standards that I later found. The real standards are even lamer than the ones I made up.

> **3.0** *Students read and respond to historically or cultur- ally significant works of literature that reflect their studies of history and social science. They conduct in-depth anal- yses of recurrent themes.* **2.2** *Analyze the way in which clarity of meaning is affected by the patterns of organiza- tion, hierarchical structures, repetition of the main ideas, syntax and word choice in the text.* **3.2** *Analyze the way in which the theme or meaning of a selection represents a view or comment on life, using textual evidence to support the claim.* And **3.4** *Determine characters' traits by what the characters say about themselves in narration, dialogue, dramatic monologue, and soliloquy.*

As I mentioned above, in theory I am required to ei- ther post the standards or explain them to the students. Yeah right, a real waste of time for my students most of whom have trouble retaining anything without prompts and over-teaching, and I suspect a problem for regular ed students as well. Imagine this: *Okay class, today we will be writing two two-chunk paragraphs on the upcoming Presidential Primaries. This lesson will address standards blah blah and blah. These standards, when met, will make you a well-rounded member of society with a fine intellect and an ability to lead a productive life with a minimum of difficulty...*

Mr. Mandel? What is a presidential primary?

THE ACCIDENTAL TEACHER

This is getting too long and I am hungry, but let me get in one last vignette. Last week I hosted a truancy meeting for one of my students. A school administrator requested the meeting because Ernesto, a quiet senior, was ditching school almost daily. Funny, when I checked my class attendance Ernesto had missed only one of my classes. Here's the deal: apparently Ernesto has been skipping Third and Sixth Block regularly. Both periods are after lunch and he has been leaving school during the lunch break and not returning for his afternoon classes.

During the meeting the administrator in charge of truancy discussed the consequences with Ernesto and his parents in Spanish, continually trying without success to get Ernesto to explain where he was going and what he was doing when he disappeared. The administrator even promised no further repercussions, he just wanted to know Ernesto's motives, assuming that once we knew the motives it would be easier to deal with the issue. Ernesto continued to stonewall, feigning not understanding (he is fluent in English and Spanish), mumbling something about how he didn't know what he did or where he went. Ernesto was obviously hiding something, and even after his parents tried to get him to open up, nothing. Without discovering the motive we came up with the following plan: both parents would escort Ernesto to his first class in the morning and return at the end of lunch to escort their son into his afternoon class. It is funny to imagine this tough macho Latino boy being escorted to class by his mommy and daddy.

After Ernesto left, his dad stayed at the table and revealed the real story. His son has a twenty year-old girl-friend who picks him up at lunch and drives him to her place for who knows what. Whatever it is, I am certain it is more exciting than his afternoon math proficiency class.

Thursday - October 11

Just finished adding actual *State Standards* to the above entry, and aside from the fact that I realized I had not the faintest idea how to spell *soliloquy*, I discovered the standards are a well-meaning effort at quantifying the unquantifiable. If only it were possible to educate all our students to such a lofty level. Here's one more that made me chuckle: *In addition, by grade twelve, students read two million words annually* **on their own**, *including a wide variety of classic and contemporary literature, magazines, newspapers, and on-line information.* Who's counting? When I asked Doug the Librarian how many words were in an average novel, he told me he had no idea. *My Space* could play a critical role in students' word counts, not to mention texting.

Two quick stories (never as quick as I intend them to be): Every day of *Homecoming Week* is some theme dress-up day. Tuesday was *Hippie Dress Up Day* so I decided to don my UCSC T-shirt, some of Mary's beads, and an old pair of granny sunglasses. Few students have dressed up so far, but most teachers have made some effort. Most of the theme days were duds (yeah I know!). So far only *Pajama Day* participation was actually visible to my untrained eye, with only females participating. That could change tomorrow, *Spirit Hat Day*, since all headgear is strictly verboten any other day of the year. I used *Hippie Day* as a springboard to get the students thinking about a group other than their own. I had them do a *Quick Write* on two topics: *What's a hippie?* and *Three good things and three bad things hippies have contributed to our current culture.* Some had no idea what a hippie was, while others were surprisingly well informed on the topic, probably because their parents had been hippies in the past. Good hippie stuff: music, tree hugging, fashion, drugs, sex, peace and love. Bad hippie stuff: poor hygiene, patchouli oil, tree hugging, fashions, music and drugs.

Second not so quick story: I have been trying to get the kids to look at things from different perspectives or points of view (POV). It is much harder than you might think. So I decided that for a week or two I would begin each class with an assignment in which they had to imagine themselves as some one or some thing, and then describe part of their day as that person or thing. As I showed them the first assignment on the overhead I was unsure of how it would go. But I have found that the more I do this job, the less I actually care about how they initially react to my ideas. In fact I am starting to enjoy tormenting them.

My first POV writing activity for them was to imagine themselves as a desk in our classroom. I prompted them with—*After a quiet and lonely night the bell rang and...* Following the customary chorus of whining, they actually got into it. Some wrote about the fear of being sat on by a fat kid, carved by a sharp knife or farted on (mentioned thrice in one class). Some wrote about boredom, and two girls in one class, Gina and Jasmine, wrote about the sensuality of it all, almost soft porn. Gina of course went on and on about the sensuality of fondling some cute guy's ass. Jasmine's was simpler and funnier, something like, *He was approaching me. My heart raced. I love to be sat on and to be rubbed and touched. I am firm and strong and love the feeling of warm strong hands on my cold legs.* Jasmine was too shy to read it to the class, but later when I read it to my other classes they pleaded for more. And when I told them it was written by a girl, the boys begged me to tell them her name.

PISSING IN THE WIND

Some other POV topics I assigned with varying results: *Imagine you are a mirror in the girls' restroom at SBHS, a high school English teacher, a campus supervisor,* and finally, *You are a parent of a difficult teenager—describe dinner conversation at home.*

I gave my students their first spelling test today. When I had passed out the actual list of words earlier in the week most of the kids had acted insulted that I was using such simple-ass words. (I had made every effort to use words they commonly misspelled on their papers.) I gave them ten words to study and then threw in an extra one during the test, a serious pet peeve of mine—*a lot.*

Only four students out of sixty spelled *a lot* correctly as two words. What's more, one of my aides, while grading the spelling test, kept insisting for all the class to hear that it *was* one word. I told the class that if they learned only one thing in school today, please let it be that *a lot* is two words.

While I am on the topic of spelling it might be fun to test your deciphering skills with the spelling turned in today by RJ, a dyslexic, hard-working senior with above average intelligence (RJ had the list of words to study for two days.):

frend langish iland file relle alot srfis coman breve sintest cafoley

Wednesday - October 17

Had a workshop in Sunnyvale today on effective techniques for teaching in block scheduling. And while San Benito has been block scheduling for a few years, evidently the practice is growing in popularity nationwide. When I started in August I didn't know enough about it to blather on about its benefits or complain about its shortcomings. In general it seems like a better plan than the traditional 6/55-minute periods that most of us grew up with. The major problem I am having, aside from filling the entire 100 minutes with quality teaching, is dealing with the long time gaps between a Thursday or Friday class and the next class meeting four days later. This is more than enough time for my students to forget everything they have learned, not to mention the problems *I* have remembering where I left off and whether I assigned homework four days earlier. Often I spend the first half of a new lesson repeating the prior one. One step forward, two steps back.

I was exhausted last Friday when I got home at 8:30 after my required home-side crowd supervision at the *Homecoming Game*. The experience was wet, cold and no fun at all, except for talking to some of my students. It is always more fun to see and talk to them out of the classroom setting. Two-fisted Tony, future World Middleweight Champion, who I had not seen since he transferred out of my class into a regular English class about two months earlier, came up to me at the game. He told me he was having serious difficulties in his current English class and was thinking about requesting to be put back in mine. I told Tony I would discuss it with his caseworker and his current English teacher and get back to him.

Anyway back to my exhaustion. When I finally arrived home I fell asleep immediately and had trouble crawling out of bed the entire weekend. During the workweek I expend every ounce of my dwindling energy while at the same time building up stress, and then on weekends my body just lets go. I woke up in the middle of the night on Friday and worried I was having a stroke because my legs were so tired I couldn't move them. But when Monday

morning came I was sufficiently recharged to begin another week. Eventually I hope my body adapts to all this.
I remember when I began my former career twenty-five
years ago; despite my youth, I was spent and exhausted
every night for the entire first year. As I became comfortable in my job, I realized the exhaustion was mental and
was due primarily to the uncertainties, the unknowns and
the need to prove myself.

News from the trenches. The Melody saga continues.
Rumors on the street about her running away were only
part of the story. Apparently, a few weeks back while she
was in Bruce Pirl's class Mel and another girl rifled through
Rosa's (one of their aides) purse and stole two credit cards.
That night Rosa, realizing her cards were missing, notified
her bank and discovered that the girls had run up quite a
bill at the local *Straw Hat, Target* and *Starbucks.* Hollister's
own Thelma and Louise were actually caught on video at
Straw Hat. When Mr. Pirl confronted Mel the next day she
acted embarrassed, apologized and abruptly disappeared.
Yesterday when I logged on to the school's attendance
program there was a note—*Melody H…dropped.* This time
it looks like Ms. Interrupted is gone for good.

I lost another caseload kid, PJ. Good thing for PJ.
Good thing for me. PJ's IEP meeting was yesterday, and
as his caseworker I was responsible for organizing it. This
included notifying all the parties involved and getting the
mountains of paperwork in order. While I am getting better at the process, I still have very little idea what all the
paperwork actually represents, not to mention what the
tons of acronyms stand for. At this point I am mindlessly
following directions and doing what I am instructed to
do: *fill this out, attach this to that, set meeting date, call speech
therapist, etc.*

THE ACCIDENTAL TEACHER

PJ, categorized as developmentally delayed (DD. nee: high-level retarded), is low functioning, maybe a 65 IQ, and because he is on independent study this year and does not attend classes, I had had no opportunity to meet him prior to the meeting. Until I actually met PJ he was little more than a file to me. I completed all the paperwork I could before the meeting, realizing as I filled it out it would be foolish for me to write goals and a transition plan for a kid whose abilities and goals I knew literally nothing about. The meeting was eye opening. PJ, it turns out, is a nice quiet sophomore who, because of his limitations, was continually frustrated in school last year. This caused him to act out numerous times and end the year with a discipline log five pages long; primarily due to these problems, PJ passed only one of twelve classes last year.

Prior to the meeting, and judging only from his file, I expected PJ to be a surly little punk. But nothing could have been further from the truth. I discovered PJ to be sweet and a little scared. While his parents expressed their concerns about his future as an adult, PJ's five-year-old brother played quietly at the table. According to his teacher Ann, the independent study thing was working out great for PJ. His dad, a burly bearded Latino self-employed tile setter, has been taking PJ to work with him every day, and although dad has to tell PJ many times, in many ways, how to do things, when PJ does get it he gets it for good and is an effective assistant.

Dad and Mom both wanted answers from the psychologist that do not exist. They had been hoping that somehow there would be a major breakthrough (a miracle perhaps) and PJ would all of a sudden be "normal". In spite of his disability, PJ excels well beyond expectations in certain areas. He has excellent spatial aptitude, and according to dad PJ sometimes figures out solutions on the job more quickly than the other workers. Because of these "gifts" his parents have trouble accepting the fact that their son can't overcome the areas he struggles in. The IEP team did a nice job explaining the situation; they encouraged his mom and dad to celebrate PJ's gifts and downplay his lower functioning areas. I sat there quietly taking notes. As the meeting was winding down Ethan announced, unbeknownst to any of us, that starting today Ann, PJ's teacher, would be his new caseworker. She is a resource specialist with a caseload of her own and has worked with PJ since second grade.

Everyone seemed relieved. My only question, to myself of course, was *Why hadn't PJ been part of Ann's caseload from the beginning?*

Saturday - October 27

Don't want to jinx anything, but things have been good. Last week was my best yet. But of course things can turn to shit on a dime, as evidenced yesterday when my mentor had a major meltdown in front of her third period class. It is a horrible group. I know because I once sat in on the class in awe as Sara maintained her cool, circulating deftly like a ringmaster in a three-ring monkey circus. Despite her heroic efforts at holding back the testosterone and ADD-laden tides, several boys refused to be throttled and continued their annoying and disruptive behavior. As I watched Sara perform, I thought to myself I could never have such patience in the face of such crap.

After her meltdown yesterday, Sara sat alone at her desk in a very quiet and very empty classroom. Unaware of what had happened, I poked my head in and unwittingly asked Sara if our lunch date was still on. By the look on her face I could tell something was wrong and Sara asked me to give her a few minutes. Ten minutes later Sara walked into my room and calmly inquired if I heard all the commotion from her room earlier.

"Nope,"

"How 'bout me sobbing loudly outside"

"No, Sara, guess I must have been too busy with my own clowns to notice anything else. What did I miss?"

She then calmly explains what happened…It was her problem boys, a heartless pair, and it all began when one of them said, "You are being pretty feisty today Teach".

Unable to control my enthusiasm, I break in with, "Wow Sara, did he really use the word feisty?"

"Jeeze Eric, you sound just like a real special ed teacher already, noting proper word usage in the middle of a shit storm." Sara goes on to tell me the boys just wore her down with continual disruptive and disrespectful behavior until finally she burst into tears and bolted out the door.

In the meantime, while Sara cried in the courtyard, back inside her classroom her longtime aide took over; she castigated the boys for being total jerks and lectured the entire class on how grateful they should be to Ms. Stasi for all her hard work, adding with a flair that Ms. Stasi puts her heart and soul into her job and probably cares more about them than their parents do. Fifteen minutes later a now composed Ms. Stasi returned to her class and took her place front and center. Circling the wagons, the other kids opened a can of whipass on the two perps.

By the time Sara told me all this she seemed pretty composed, primarily because she had just spent fifteen minutes on the phone with her mentor. We talked about the incident for a bit as she shared some personal stuff that made her more susceptible to relatively routine day-to-day shit. I told Sara that while I am quite positive I will never break down and cry in class, I have no problem imagining a scenario in which I totally lose it and go off in spectacular, career-ending style.

∽∾

That day during a journal writing assignment to describe a favorite place or a place you really want to visit, Josh, one of my favorite students, a gun aficionado, a funny, pot-smoking, future Marine who lives with his grandparents, turned in the following passage and asked me to read it to the class:

> The most beautiful place I have ever been was in a house that was perfect. The reason was because my family was together, and there was perfect peace. It was so great. I had finally known what peace had felt like. I had thought to myself how did things get so good when yesterday I was stuck in Hollister? But then I forgot about it and said it was just a coincidence. This truely was paradise, there was no war, fights or even disputes between each others thoughts or points of views. Hell I didn't even have anybody hating on me. What got me the most was my brother. He had been young. Young as in when he was 6. It was because when you are young you have your innocence. For when you get old, your innocence is lost....It was so great to see him again. I weeped with tears of Joy I didn't want to leave. But then I started to shake and I heard my name called....It was a dream...

THE ACCIDENTAL TEACHER

Godzilla vs. Rodan

I realize it is pretty unfashionable in the field of education to admit to despising particular students, but trust me most teachers have students they can't stand. With Jorge and Tomas gone, I now have two other boys that test my patience and my humanity. First there's Irwin, aka Zenebula, the spiked-haired, eyeliner-wearing, close-minded junior *Scene Boy*, who never misses an opportunity to offend others who think or look differently than he does. Early in the week we somehow ended up discussing CPR. During the rather tepid discussion Irwin blurts out that he would rather die than receive CPR from a man. As a reality check I ask what he would do if he woke up in a hospital one morning and discovered that he was alive only because a man had revived him with CPR.

"I would kill myself." he answers and fires back at me, "How would you feel if you had a heart attack in class and some sleazy boy gave you CPR?"

Resisting the temptation to sanction his suicidal urge, I explain that of course I would be thankful the boy had saved my life thus giving me the opportunity to continue doing what I love, teaching high school. Then, my memory is fuzzy on this—I either called Irwin a stupid homophobe or said his comments were stupid and homophobic. Undaunted, he continued to rant on about how unashamedly proud he is to be a homophobe. Hard to maintain my composure and remain civil to this boy.

And in the other corner, from the same class, is the reigning queen of drama, Jeremy, aka Flam Boy. He always complains when others call him names although he has no problem doing the same to them. Jeremy is super sensitive when slings and arrows come his way. His feelings are hurt easily and often, nevertheless Jeremy gives as good as he gets. Last week during a *Quick Write* on how parents might react if their kid were dating someone of another race, religion or social status, Jeremy boasted that his parents wouldn't care at all and he doesn't understand why anyone would. Turning the tables, he asked me how I would feel if my daughter dated a black guy. When I casually responded that years ago my daughter had gone to her prom with a black guy, Jeremy shrieked a high-pitched "Yuk!!"

There have been some campy squabbles between Scene Boy and Flam Boy that have reminded me of those epic fiery free-for-alls between the two titans of Japanese schlock cinema—Godzilla and Rodan. Although Flam Boy and Scene Boy generally despise each other, on rare occasions they get along like a pair of blissful bickering boys in a bathhouse.

My preliminary diagnosis of Jeremy is that he suffers from a common form of cultural schizophrenia—a condition in which one does the same thing to others that one complains about when it is done by others to them. During an assignment yesterday on favorite places, Jeremy wrote about a trip to Canada and commented, in writing and aloud, about how pretty Canada was and how nice it felt not to see a single Mexican there.

This racist comment was only one example of Jeremy's horrible behavior yesterday. He disrupted class from start to finish. When I finally told him that I was going to call his mother, without skipping a beat he replied that it wasn't fair, he was only behaving badly because he was upset that Luke had called him gay.

"Go ahead and call my mom. She won't get mad at me. She'll blame it all on you."

When I did call Jeremy's mom about twenty minutes after school let out, Jeremy already had had time to debrief her on all the verbal injustices I had allowed others to inflict on her poor innocent son. Jeremy had told his mom that I had let other kids direct *that word* (gay) at him and that was the reason he had acted up. At first Mom was defensive, starting with "Luke hates Jeremy because he hurts his feelings all the time," and emphasizing that she finds the use of *that word* highly offensive. When I explained that the incident Jeremy described had occurred at the end of class, and only after Jeremy ignored me numerous times, pranced around as I attempted to teach, used his phone and his *ipod* while we were in the library, and handed out candy swizzle sticks to everyone including Luke, Mrs. Jeremy was quiet for a second. A few silent moments passed and then I heard her screaming at Jeremy. I couldn't make out what she was screaming, but eventually she came back on the line, told me she would take care of things, said thanks, and hung up.

Ten minutes later Jeremy calls my voice mail and leaves an apology that includes a serious-sounding promise to behave better in the future.

A political dispute between teachers and the district erupted recently. Turns out San Benito High School has a new policy this year requiring teachers who fail more than 15% of their students to have a conference with an administrator. Not sure what that means, but most of the faculty is really pissed and there was a big protest at the last board meeting. Haven't heard how the meeting went, should know in a few days.

I was ignorant of the new policy when I graded my classes, and when I received my *Mark Distribution Analysis* in the mail I learned that I had failed 14.5% of my students, thus inadvertently avoiding another meeting with Ms. Havisham. Definitely a relief. I really don't need another issue to debate with her. Had we actually met, I am quite certain I would have reacted negatively to this new policy's not so subtle shifting of blame from student to teacher.

Here is my grade distribution by percentage for first grading period:

	As	Bs	Cs	Ds	Fs	GPA
All classes	17.7%	53.5%	25.%	6.5%	14.5%	2.35
"bad" classes #3	0	23.1	38.5	15.4	23.1	
#5	6.3	37.5	18.8	6.3	31.3	
"good" classes #1	25	50	25	0	0	
#4	35.3	29.4	23.5	5.9	5.9	

❧

Randy gave me a great tip the other day after observing my students shutting down as the end of class approached and noticing that their eyes were on the clock and not on me. He said, "Hey Eric why don't you move the clock from behind you to the back wall?"

I moved the clock. What a difference! Now why didn't I think of that?

THE ACCIDENTAL TEACHER

Grammar Gestapo

By now readers must be aware of my shortcomings in regards to teaching my subject matter. Additionally, my skepticism of and aversion to authority figures and the rules they create often come into play as I confront the illogic of English grammar, spelling and punctuation. My general distaste for elitist attitudes further fuels my hostility toward those who have taken it upon themselves to save the English language from itself. Despite my internal quarrels with these self-anointed grammarians, I can assure you that I am not an anarchist or a nihilist when it comes to language. Standards are essential in communication and nothing is more important for success in a society than the ability to communicate with one's fellow human beings. The English language is in constant flux, evolving as new words and idioms make their appearance; some disappear like beanie babies, some stick around like flies on honey.

Where the hell am I going with this?

Hopefully my reasons will be revealed shortly. Since childhood I have had trouble with spelling; to this day I have problems with certain words. For instance, for decades I had no problem choosing between *choose* and *chose* in my writing. Then suddenly, without warning, I found myself flipping the words, using *choose* as the past tense and *chose* as the present tense. It appears that at some unknown time in the past, for some inexplicable reason, I invented a non-existent rule in which *chose* is pronounced like *lose*. I didn't realize this gaffe until I began writing this book, and I have no idea how long I been remiss in minding my chose and choose.

And then there are the sudden discoveries—those

eureka moments of horror and realization that one has
been misusing or abusing parts of the English language
one's entire conscious life. Take last night for example: as
I was watching talking heads pontificate on the TV, one
head said, "If our government taxed the improper use of
the word hopefully we would be well on our way to paying
down the national debt." Being a novice English teacher,
I had no idea what the fuck he was talking about, but I
was pretty certain I was probably as guilty of misusing
hopefully as the next guy. Now I don't mean to bore, or
worse, insult those aware of the still-raging 150-year battle
over the proper use of hopefully, but for those like me
who are unaware of this grave life or death issue facing
our beloved English language, let me quote directly from
the 2000 American Heritage Dictionary:

> hopefully: ADVERB: 1. In a hopeful manner. 2.
> **Usage Problem** It is to be hoped [I hope; we
> hope:] "Marriage is a coming together for better
> or for worse, hopefully enduring" (William O.
> Douglas).
>   USAGE NOTE: *Writers who use hopefully as a sentence
> adverb, as in "Hopefully the measures will be adopted", should
> be aware that the usage is unacceptable to many critics, including
> a large majority of the Usage Panel. It is not easy to explain
> why critics dislike this use of hopefully. The use is justified by
> analogy to similar uses of many other adverbs, as in" Mercifully,
> the play was brief" or" Frankly, I have no use for your friend."
> And though this use of hopefully may have been a vogue word
> when it first gained currency back in the early 1960s, it has long
> since lost any hint of jargon or pretentiousness for the general
> reader. The wide acceptance of the usage reflects popular recog-
> nition of its usefulness; there is no precise substitute. Someone*

who says "Hopefully, the treaty will be ratified" makes a hope-ful prediction about the fate of the treaty, whereas someone who says "I hope" (or "We hope" or" It is hoped") the treaty will be ratified expresses a bald statement about what is desired. Only the latter could be continued with a clause such as "but it isn't likely." •It might have been expected, then, that the initial flurry of objections to hopefully would have subsided once the usage be-came well established. Instead, critics appear to have become more adamant in their opposition. In the 1969 Usage Panel survey, 44 percent of the Panel approved the usage, but this dropped to 27 percent in our 1986 survey. (By contrast, 60 percent in the latter survey accepted the comparable use of "mercifully" in the sentence "Mercifully, the game ended before the opponents could add another touchdown to the lopsided score.") It is not the use of sentence adverbs per se that bothers the Panel; rather, the spe-cific use of hopefully in this way has become a shibboleth.

What's a shibboleth?

SYLLABICATION: shib ·bo ·leth
PRONUNCIATION: shb-lth, -lth
NOUN: 1. A word or pronunciation that distinguishes people of one group or class from those of another. 2a. A word or phrase identified with a particular group or cause; a catchword. b. A commonplace saying or idea. 3. A custom or practice that betrays one as an outsider.
ETYMOLOGY: Ultimately from Hebrew ibblet, tor-rent of water, from the use of this word to distinguish one tribe from another that pronounced it sibblet (Judges 12:4–6).

Gosh darn. Seems like you learn something new every

day. And exactly what class of people do these nabobs think are misusing *hopefully*? To little old modest me, it seems the panel's use of *shibboleth* is itself a shibboleth, distinguishing these pedantic, sesquipedalian pinheads from the rest of us. Oops, sorry—my crass populism is showing.

However I think it only fair I share some contrarian grammarians' dissenting views of the proper usage of *hopefully*. *Merriam-Webster*, after a detailed summary of the debate, states unequivocally: *The second sense of hopefully is entirely standard.* *The New York Times* published an article by Ethan Bronner in 1999 that begins:

> For years, language purists have rent their garments over the use of the word hopefully to mean "I hope," as in, "Hopefully, that will never happen again." Such use, they assert, arose in the rule-smashing 1960's. For many, it was and remains a sign of the decline of civilization.
>
> But now comes Fred R. Shapiro, associate librarian at Yale Law School, using a powerful new computer tool called JSTOR that permits detailed searches of thousands of issues of scholarly journals back to the 19th century. And, lo and behold, the use in formal English of hopefully to modify a whole sentence goes back easily to the 1930's. He has found dozens of examples before 1960, including an 1851 citation that starts, "Hopefully, not to say, certainly, in that time . . ."

October 31 – Wednesday

It's Halloween and time for a somewhat spooky student story:

James, a tall thin bespectacled Third Block senior, is an interesting character. This admittedly racist, anti-Mexican, half-Mexican, truck-loving, cowboy-booted walking contradiction, enjoys challenging me and his classmates. Earlier in the year during the essay writing session on Kenya West and 50 Cent, James had no trouble sharing with the class his disgust for black music. In an attempt to draw him out I ask, "So James exactly what type of music do you like?"

"Country." he answers quickly.

"And who's your favorite artist?" I ask, expecting to hear Toby Keith or some other popular, patently patriotic singer.

"Kinky Friedman, Mr. Mandel. Have you heard of him?"

Are you shitting me? I think to myself. I'm almost rendered mute by his response. James may be the only kid in San Benito County to even know who Kinky Friedman is. For the uninitiated, Friedman is the controversial singer-songwriter who fronts *The Texas Jewboys* and specializes in political satire. The 2006 Texas gubernatorial candidate's hits include *They Ain't Making Jews Like Jesus Anymore* and *Get Your Biscuits in the Oven and Your Buns in Bed.* Recovering from my initial shock I continue, "Yes I've heard of him. What is your favorite song?"

"My favorite song of all time is not by Kinky, it's by David Allen Coe."

Jeeze, this boy is full of surprises this morning. Coe, another non-household name, is considered by many to be the best Texas songwriter ever. "Which song, James?"

"Oh I can't say it in class."

My curiosity piqued I ask James to come up front and whisper the title to me. James struts up and softly says a little uncomfortably, *"Nigger Hatin' Me."*

I'd never heard of the song (turns out the lyrics are, even for the initiated, pretty shocking), but I know enough about David Allen Coe to explain to James that the song is satire and that Coe is using it to expose the stupidity of racism.

"I don't know what satire is. I just like the song because it says what I feel." James unashamedly replies.

I try to explain satire to James, but I realize I am in a no-win situation so I tell him we can talk about it later.

Ah, the perils of satire.

Despite his dumb-shit views, I think that James is a good kid. He is the son of the only male campus supervisor, and he gets along smilingly with his peers regardless of their race. He loves his truck and works two jobs to help finance its maintenance and beautification. He works late and often comes to class ten to fifteen minutes after the bell with a coffee *grande* and sweet roll in hand. Depending on his work schedule, sometimes he falls asleep, sometimes he doesn't. Depending on my mood, sometimes I wake him, sometimes I don't.

V

The Best Laid Plans

Sunday - November 11

A lot has happened since last I wrote; nothing earth shattering or catastrophic, just lots of starts and stops. I seem to have achieved a rhythm and balance, not quite stasis, more a precarious stability. Pretty close to the half-way mark, finals in a few weeks and first semester ends before Christmas break. Hard to believe I have made it this far. I still feel like a charlatan, but all things considered, a reasonably competent one.

Where to start: Teenage love drama? More testing horrors? My boss and her attitudes?

Let's get the boss and her attitudes out of the way. Over the last two months, ever since her informal surprise drop-in during my Kenya West vs. 50 Cent lesson, Carol's negative observations about my teaching have been persistently eating away at my self-confidence. So last week I decided I needed to sit down with Ms. Havisham before the upcoming formal observation and find out exactly what she expects from me, Carol Havisham is nothing like I thought her during our initial contacts. I have always considered myself pretty good at reading people, but with Carol this has been impossible. She never smiles. Gives lots of useless advice. Offers no genuine support for her new teachers. Not respected by her staff. I often get the sense Carol is just riding out the final few years before her retirement.

I called her office on Friday morning and made an appointment to see her that afternoon. I show up for my appointment and after the required pleasantries cut to the chase. "What are your expectations for me my first year?" She rambles on for a bit and then eventually gets to her point and tells me she wants me to basically connect with the kids and teach them effectively.

Hello? That is what I thought I was doing!

I share my frustration and my fear that she is expecting me, a neophyte, to do what other more experienced teachers have failed to do—teach my juniors and seniors to read and write to "acceptable" state standards. Carol mumbles on, spouting platitudes intermixed with "tips" on teaching. Then for the umpteenth time, she mentions the need for me to push my students harder, to work on their higher level thinking skills, and to teach more complex lessons. Of course when I ask for more specifics on what I should actually teach, Carol is unable to provide them.

My initial reaction is to be a smartass and ask sarcastic questions like: *So Carol, how far would you like me to go? Shall I teach them about the ablative absolute, the difference between proclitic and enclitic associatives, or perhaps between the hypotaxic and parataxic?*

Instead I simply ask her for some higher-level lesson ideas. After a halting hesitation she answers unflinchingly, "Maybe for starters you could work on adverbial clauses, prepositional phrases and complex sentences."

THE BEST LAID PLANS

By the end of our meeting I feel more insecure and unsure of what the hell she expects from me than I did before the meeting. As I am leaving she tells me she'll be doing a formal drop-in observation soon.

At that point I decide I'm not going to fret her upcoming visit. I'm not going to spend hours preparing some slick lesson plan to have at the ready for the moment my stone-faced supervisor, clipboard in hand, graces my classroom with her presence. When she makes her appearance I will plod on as if it were any other day and teach whatever I have planned.

We finished reading *Of Mice and Men* in both my English 11 classes last week. Last Wednesday afternoon in my Gina, Jeremy, Zen class (Third Block), as we are reading along to the Gary Senise narration of the final chapter on CD, Randy, the crew-cut mentor teacher who has been observing me and plying me with positive feedback, walks in clad in his traditional garb—red gym shorts, gray *Hollister Football* t-shirt, and whistle hanging from a red lanyard around his neck. After a friendly nod he sits down at an empty student desk. Randy enjoys *Of Mice and Men* and often participates in our discussions, enthusiastically sharing his views with the class. As he settles in I pause the disc and tell Randy his timing is good because, if all goes well, we will be finishing the novel today. Senise's narration is dramatic, and the kids are glued to his every word as it becomes apparent that something really bad is going to happen to Lenny.

The class is rapt when suddenly, out of the corner of my eye, I notice Jasmine stand up and walk out of class without explanation. Not wanting to break the spell, I ignore her untimely departure. Moments later her boyfriend David stands up, approaches me with a worried look and whispers, "Mr. Mandel, can I go get Jasmine? She's crying."

Shit, I think to myself, *just what I need right now, teenage love drama.* "Okay go get her. But hurry back, I don't want either of you to miss the ending."

We read and listen for ten minutes more. Still no David and Jasmine. The class is enthralled and eager to find out how the book ends. I decide to walk over and ask Randy (my aide was sick, again) to please check on the forlorn lovebirds. Randy leaves to go find them as the book marches to its climax. Just as George is describing their dream to Lenny: *the farm, the cows, the rabbits, the alfalfa and living off the fat of the land,* just as George lifts the Lugar to the back of his best friend's head, Randy enters quietly with the two lovers in tow. They both stop at the door and begin noisily rifling through the trashcan.

I pause the disc, walk over and ask, "What the hell are you doing?"

Both look up at me smiling. Jasmine explains, in tones of quiet desperation, that they are looking for the necklace David gave her: a miniature *Oakland A's* jersey with the number '3' on it. David wears a matching one. Apparently the two are huge fans of *A's* third baseman Eric Chavez, opting to use the Chavez jersey as their badge of undying love. It seems Jasmine, after a spat with David, angrily tossed her love logo in the trash on her way out the door. *Is this really happening?* I ask myself. *Of course it is.* I tell them to sit down and look for the necklace later.

When we finally do finish *Of Mice and Men*, Gina, with tears in her eyes, sobbingly and loudly blurts out, "This is the stupidest book I ever read. I hate it!" I mention to Gina that the fact that she is so emotionally upset might actually contradict her conclusion.

This brings me to another digression: Gina, Jasmine and a few others get so emotionally involved in fiction, whether in print or on the screen, that they lose all perspective. While we were watching a *Discovery Channel* video reenactment of the *Salem Witch Trials* Jasmine, not realizing the people in the film were actually actors, asked in all seriousness if the Puritans in the movie were still alive. Gina, an actress in her own right, came to class last week excited because of all the rumors that Dumbledore, the wizard in the Harry Potter stories, was a closeted gay. Of course I'm not complaining—most students would rather suffer some unspeakable humiliation than read a book for fun—at least they are reading!

Back to *Of Mice and Men*. After a heated discussion about love, mercy killing and the shattering of the *American Dream*, class ends, and as the kids leave they continue to argue. At one point just before the bell I kicked Zen/Irwin out of class because he was being an ass. (A few days earlier Zen refused to take his sweatshirt hood off in class because his spiked hair had flattened. In accordance with school policy I made him remove the hood. After taking it off, Zen, his hair flat for the first time all year, sat sheepishly like a teen girl with a giant zit on her nose.) As he was leaving, the still protesting Zen let out an annoying whinny, "Mr. Mandel, you're just jealous because you can't get a *Scene Girl!*"

[Refresher on *Scene Girls* from the words of *Posing Scene Slag* on urbandictionary.com:

Omfgzz hi, my name is posing scene slag. First off I just love to pretend Im bisexual because everyone else does and I cant be individual or different. Every morning I put crap such as ribbons in my hair because

its so emo. See emo is popular so Im emo. But when
goth is the fashion again Ill be goth. Anyway after that
I spend hours backcombing my hair so it looks like
a giant bunch of pubes. After that I meet all of my
"friends" who I actualy bitch about constantly behind
their back because Im a two faced slag. I also have to
wear leopard print shoes like everyone else along with
drainpipes that were actualy normal fitting jeans from
when I was 7. See Im an anorexic STD carrying whore.
Then I have to flirt with everyone because I think it
makes me look popular but I just look like a slag. Then
I have a sip of cider and pretend to be pissed so that
can be an excuse for fucking everything in sight. When
I get home I have to edit my *myspace* and write shit
like "Im a fucking bitch deal with it" while listening to
taking back sunday and panic! at the disco. Oh and of
course all of my pictures involve me in nothing but my
underwear so everyone can see my fat wobbly ass and
my flat chest.   All my friends are Scene girls.]

Safe to say that *Scene Girls* aren't really my type.

The next day I got a nice note from Randy commending
me on the lesson and on how well I handled all the distractions. Later that day I notice David eating lunch outside my
room, crow feathers dripping from his chin, wearing a pink
t-shirt with little hearts that reads *David loves Jasmine*.

That same day, while my other junior class (Fourth
Block) is listening to the end of the Steinbeck novel, who
should walk in, black notebook in hand? Yep, you guessed
it—my boss, Ms. Carol Havisham.

She sat herself down and observed my Fourth Block
juniors read and listen to the final ten pages. For Carol's
benefit as well as my own, I was tempted to stop the CD

at a few key points just to show off my skills at facilitating high level class discourse. I decided instead to let the kids, who were all pretty engrossed, read/listen straight through to the bitter end. Also, I was worried that my timing was off and that the bell might go off prematurely before the climax. Thankfully, I had sufficient time after the CD/ novel ended to present a few ideas for the students to ponder before the next class. I did make sure, with the boss watching, to ask the darkest-skinned person in the room, Maria, what she thought of the book. Haven't received Carol's observations yet, should be interesting.

Some rewarding and interesting things have happened over the last few weeks. On Monday during SSR, Redheaded Rick, the kid who from day one exhibited an obsession with handguns, Rick the inquisitor and self-appointed arbitrator of justice who questions just about everything I do, the same Rick I had mistakenly described as the outspoken son to the wrong set of parents at *Back to School Night*, was diligently reading a book. Rick sat with his back to the class in the creaky old rocking chair I had brought from home, making it impossible for me see the book's title. When class ended Rick approached and asked if he could take the book home.

"Sure." I say enthusiastically without knowing what book it was. Rick hands me the book so I can take the card out and have him sign for it—*The Collected Poems of Sylvia Plath.*

Bobby, a somewhat devious, light-skinned Hispanic slacker with a badly bleached Harpo Marx hairdo, missed two weeks of school about a month ago. Rumors at the time were that Bobby was either in the local juvenile hall or on a family vacation in Mexico. About ten days ago Bobby asked me what he could do for makeup work for the time he was absent. I asked him where he had been for the two weeks.

"Juvie." he said.

"Write about it." I replied, assuming I would never see anything from him.

A few days later Bobby hands me about six pages of poorly pencil-scratched prose. When he notices my confusion as I struggle to decipher his writing, he asks if he should take it home and type it. Realizing that if I give it back there is a good chance I will never see it again, I think, *Ah what the hell,* and say, "Please do." I hand the story back to him.

The following day Bobby did not have a class with me, nevertheless, true to his word, he shows up during lunch and with a grin and hands me a neatishly-typed narrative entitled: *My Two Weeks Behind Bars. Story by InfamousZ Bobby Boy.*

It was surprisingly good. It began:

It was a cold boring saturday afternoon. I was sitting home all alone watching TV wearing blue jeans, a light gray O'neil shirt with my favorite white hooded sweatshirt. I'm bored out of mind and it's 4:45pm. I decided to call my friend Jesus thinking ill go over to his house and kill sometime. He answered I asked "Hey whats up man what are you doing? He said "Nothing watchin TV." Then I said "is it cool if I come over right now? Then he said, "Yeah go for it." Then I said "Okay but I feel like walking so ill see you in an hour. Then he said "Huh alright but its hell-far though. Finally I said. "Okay laters."

I grabbed my cousin Pricilla's IPOD and began my long walk of 5 miles to Jesus's house. I put on a song I liked and walked out my door. It was a fresh feeling day and the sun was dim. As I passed my neighbors house I saw my 1985 "PIMP" Astro Van that my uncle gave me for free because I got it running. It was my project van I had been taking to my autoshop class and it was starting to run great. I had just put new brake shoes and machined the drums that Friday. As I kept walking I thought about new ideas and how to make my van better or the "SHAGGIN WAGON" as my friends called it. The reason for this is because I had an old mattress in it before. I also had a little mirror disco ball that I had bought at the flea market for $1. As I walked across the street the streetlights came on and I remembered looking up at the sky, my face and hands feeling nice and fresh. I was enjoying the view the sky was pinkish, the mountains green along with the trees...

Okay, it ain't no Shakespeare, nor no Steinbeck, but until this point *InfamousZ* has been more or less invisible and has shown zero interest in writing or self-reflection. The story went on for a few pages describing in garbled, colorful prose his arrest for hitting a cop with an egg in retaliation for the cop unjustly having his beloved *Shaggin Wagon* towed for expired plates. Bobby watched me like a hawk as I read it quietly to myself. He puffed up like a peacock when I told him it was really good. I asked if I could read it to the class and he eagerly said yes. It was entertaining, funny, compelling, and chock full of descriptive scene setting. I knew the class would love it. I planned to use it as a "hook" to get them to create their own narratives

For once something I anticipated came to pass: Bobby's story worked. The next day Bobby gloats as I read his story to class. They listen. They laugh. And then I turn them loose with: *Write about something that happened to you, good or bad, something you still think about...if you get stuck, embellish* (I had to define embellish and decided to change it to *exaggerate or, better yet, just lie*) *and make things up. Work on descriptions. Make it interesting.*

After a few questions like *Do we need to have a topic sentence?* I said, "No rules. No *Schaffer*. No format." Off they went. Jimmy, a handsome eighteen year-old Hispanic man-child and popular campus hip-hop dancer, asks if he can write about losing his virginity at fourteen. I gulp and say, "Sure, but no porn please." Later, when I peek over Jimmy's shoulder, I am relieved to see he is writing about the first time he played *Pop Warner* football. Most have no trouble getting started, but Oliver, who I know at one time was a good baseball player but got bored with it as he got older, is having a problem thinking of what to write about. "Why don't you write about that time in *Little League* you dropped a pop-fly ball in the outfield and cost your team the game?"

Surprised he replies, "Hey, how did you know about that?

"Every boy has a story like that, Oliver." He was impressed with my ESP, and off he wrote. Turns out, Oliver wrote about performing a particularly difficult skateboard trick for the first time. It got real quiet. They wrote and wrote, pages and pages. It was wonderful. I hope to have them peer-edit their work and then go to the computer lab and type their narratives. A few kids didn't want anyone to read their stories because they were too personal. The following day I used the *Shaggin Wagon* for a hook in my other senior class and it was equally effective.

Time to introduce another Rick—Rick, the master of the non sequitur. Non Sequitur Rick is a hyperactive, funny, incredibly imaginative senior, and a major pain-in-the-ass class distraction. Despite serious challenges, Rick has become an excellent guitarist/song writer and impresses me often with his knowledge of obscure Dylan lyrics. He suffers from a severe case of ADHD. Sara shared a story his mother told her that illustrates Rick's perspective on our world. Every morning his mom gives him simple instructions to make his bed. And no matter how many times she shows him how to do it, nor how much time she gives him to do it, the end result is always the same: Rick proudly calls his mom into his room to show what he sincerely considers a well-made bed. To Mom it appears to be a sheet pulled sloppily over a bunched-up pile of blankets and pillows in the center of the mattress. He is one of only a few of my students who use self-deprecating humor. "Hey Mr. Mandel, how many kids with ADD does it take to screw in a light bulb?"

"No idea Rick, how many?"

"Hey guys let's go for a bike ride."

Rick has stunned me several times with his quick, imaginative responses to my questions and to my essay and transition topics. About a month ago I had a *Quick Write* topic on the board: *Write about a favorite place you have ever been or a place you really want to visit.* I got the standard stuff about Hawaii, plus the heartbreaking dream from Josh, and the Mexican-free-Canada paragraph from Jeremy. But Rick wrote that he loved to go to Creamyville and have his favorite ice cream. I asked him where Creamyville is?

He answered without missing a beat, "It's in Coleville, near Santa Cruz."

"Nice try Rick." I told him. "No such place exists."

"Yes it does." Rick insisted with a big grin.

When I assigned the personal narrative and told the class to embellish, I just assumed Rick would go somewhere interesting. Rick wrote a stream of consciousness vignette about the time he and a friend decided to go to

Starbucks looking for some party girls. At Starbucks they find two hot, freckled-face party girls drinking mango juice and eating slaw. After some small talk, Rick talks the party girls into flying with them to Bosnia on *Jet Blue* to make their fortune by cornering the petroleum jelly market. The quartet arrives after an eight-hour flight and immediately proceeds to corner the petroleum jelly market. Their goal accomplished, off they go to meet David Bowie at the *Fifth International Bosnian Rock Festival...*

Sunday - December 2
This mass email arrived in my inbox at work Friday morning. I do no not know Michele:

From: Michele
Sent: Friday, November 30, 2007 10:56 AM
To: Administration; Staff; Classified
Subject: **Out-of-Control Teacher**
I have received some news that is very distressing and I would like some help. Some students came to me, upset from a scene they witnessed between their teacher and a student. The teacher, while circulating to check homework said to a student " Did you use your brain when you did this? Why are these all wrong?" The student answered, "Maybe it's because you're a bad teacher!" The incident escalated to the point of the teacher pointing a finger inches from the student's face and yelling "I will rip you to shreds if you ever embarrass me or disrespect me like that again". The girl then left the class.

The students asked me "Can a teacher do this?" I was at a loss – I told them to go talk to the principal. Certainly we have all had students complain to us about other teachers and it's always difficult to deal with but this took me by surprise. What would have been an appropriate response? What advice do you have for me or this teacher who will certainly read this?

My first reaction as I began to read was *Shit, is this me?* But when I got to *I will rip you to shreds if you ever embarrass me,* I realized with relief that it wasn't. The more I thought about Michele's tactic of sending a mass email out to ALL school employees, including cafeteria and maintenance staff, the more I realized what a bad idea it was. Aside from the fact that instead of addressing the issue at hand she might be starting a raging firestorm of hysteria, and aside from the fact that she assumed the students were telling the truth, the worst consequence is that I will now constantly be looking around wondering who the actual asshole is; even worse, others will be looking at me wondering the same thing.

Michele has the luxury of knowing who she is pointing the finger, while the rest of us are left in the dark, forever wondering the identity of the alleged out-of-control teacher. The fact she kept it gender neutral and that it involved homework probably means we can eliminate PE teachers and shop teachers. Gee thanks Michele… *And since you asked for my advice Michele, deal with it more professionally next time, confide in your colleagues, take it directly to the principal and leave the rest of us out of it.* Sounds more like a vendetta than an appropriate response to me. Still debating whether to actually reply to her email. It came as a big relief to discover that, after reading the *Out of Control Teacher* subject line, both Sara and Liz feared it might be about them. It's refreshing to learn that even veteran teachers maintain a modicum of insecurity.

❦

A few weeks ago, as I was talking to Gina about her spelling and the problems other students were having with their spelling, she blurts out, "Everyone in this class is dixlesic Mr. Mandel."

Stifling a chuckle, I mutter softly to my aide, "I guess that says it all?"

Over the last month I have been experiencing more and more problems with Zen/Irwin. His self-righteous homophobia, his insensitivity to others, and his general hostility to everyone in class, including me, has been getting on my nerves, becoming unbearable even. I decided to use his wish to be called Zen as a carrot.

At the beginning of class I notify him I will be happy to call him Zenebula whenever he is behaving appropriately; however, when I need to reprimand or correct him I will call him by his real name—Irwin.

This strategy works for about ten minutes, and when Zenebula crosses the line and I call him Irwin he retorts, "Only gay people call me Irwin."

When I tell him he's going to the office, Irwin can't resist an exact replay of the last skirmish that got him in trouble. Getting the last word as he leaves he says, "Mr. Mandel, you're just jealous because you still can't get a *Scene Girl*."

"Get some new material Irwin." I reply as Irwin disappears out the door.

Later that day I phone Irwin's foster mother to report the incident. Foster Mom was genuinely upset and told me that lately Irwin, after spending time with his mother, has been acting out a lot. And then irony of ironies, Foster Mom informs me that, just the other day, Scene Boy reported several boys to the principal, complaining self-righteously that they had called him gay; and now these boys are facing possible suspension for hate speech.

Now it's time to introduce to my story another worthy character: Vanessa, a cute, perky, foulmouthed, and perpetually tardy junior. Vanessa does have her somewhat endearing side: even as I am chastising her for the tenth time, she continues to faux-flatter me with, "Oh Mr. Mandel you are my favorite teacher. Why you hating on me?"

When I ask how she treats teachers she doesn't like, she just smiles and jabbers on. Vanessa can't seem to control her hyperactive mouth. I am aware that there are troubles at home and with boys. It is obvious that Vanessa, like Mel, relates to many males in a provocative manner, all flirty and smiley. And like Mel, Vanessa is a walking talking time bomb. A few days ago, an hour or so after a particularly bad day in my class, Vanessa was busted at lunch for being falling-down drunk (she blew a .12) and was suspended for three days. Although Vanessa shows no interest in any academic subject or any sign of ambition, she continues to insist that she is going to be a pharmacist and at this point sees no need for a fallback career plan.

While I am on the subject of female students using their nubile sexuality on male teachers, I should mention Jasmine. Jasmine too often tells me in front of the entire class that she loves me, and she continually attempts to hug me. I do my awkward and uncomfortable best to shirk off both these advances. Thankfully, her boyfriend, David, is usually present. Sometimes I feel way too old and unprepared to deal with this stuff.

Then there is Luke. He does his work half-assedly at best, complains about everything, calls everyone and everything "gay", and then bitches and moans when I give him a C- on his *Progress Report*. When I explain to Luke that he needs to control his mouth and behavior, he simply offers the excuse that it's not his fault that he has so many friends in the class he loves to talk to. Sometimes I get the sense that many of my difficult students, in spite of their continual complaining about how boring English is, are having too much fun in my class. In fact some have told me straight up that, while they hate school, my class is the one class they enjoy. Scary.

Special Needs Administrators

Think I feel an uncontrollable urge coming on to bash Coach Putzmire, Ice Queen Carol and Melanie. I am beginning to look at the three of them as a humorless, arrogant, special education troika. They rarely smile, are always issuing edicts, and rarely, if ever, have anything valuable to say. Neither Carol nor Ethan has once complimented me on anything. That makes me insecure at times, but it helps to know that other teachers have similar complaints about them.

Ethan especially has been pissing me off lately. He makes no effort to make me feel like I know what I am doing. Ethan has watched me facilitate several IEP's and has yet to say anything even marginally validating such as, *"Nice job, Eric."* Every educator, even a single-minded high school football coach, knows that positive reinforcement and a few words of encouragement can go a long way toward developing loyalty and team spirit. Almost certain Ethan thinks me an idiot, and for the first time real doubts are beginning to creep into my head about being asked back next year.

Another member of the special education junta is Melanie, the same Melanie who was on my interview panel and who I introduced at the time as Pretty Melanie. She looks a lot like the lead singer of the *Dixie Chicks* Natalie

Means, minus the electric personality and smile. Attractive she remains. I can't count the times I have heard references to her rack, mostly from females I should add, but as far as being of any assistance, there is nothing there; *all that glitters in not gold.* (I would be astounded to discover that *there is gold in them thar hills.*) In her role as the Division Chair of Special Education, Melanie has, on paper anyway, significant responsibility for helping new resource teachers and I had anticipated she would be one of the people I could turn to for advice, but aside from a few perfunctory phone calls in the beginning, Melanie has been all but invisible.

Nydia, oh Nydia, say have you met Nydia? The one bright spot at the special ed office, and the only staff person to make me feel welcome from the beginning, is Carol's secretary, Nydia. (I often wonder what she thinks of the Ice Queen.) Nydia always greets me with a smile and a big hello, asks how I am doing, and tolerates my pathetic attempts at speaking pidgin Spanish. Knowing I have a bad back, anytime I need to deal with heavy items Nydia offers to help, or goes out of her way to have someone from the maintenance department pick up the stuff and deliver it to my room. Aside from the kids, Nydia is the best part of my job.

Last week was tough. It was *Survey Week* for me. As part of the annual evaluation process my evaluator, that would be Carol, comes in at different times for thirty minutes every day over an entire week in order to observe a variety of my teaching techniques. I knew in advance which classes she was planning to observe, I just wasn't sure exactly when she was coming. Sometime during those blocks, grim faced Carol, clipboard in-hand, was going to pop in and head directly for her post at the aide's desk.

As you may recall, Carol had done a *drop-in observation*

of me several weeks back as the class was finishing *Of Mice and Men*. A few days after that observation she summoned me to her office to deliver her formal evaluation report on that one official *drop-in*. It went more or less as I had assumed it would; Carol basically said I was doing okay, offered her typical not-so-good advice and had me sign the evaluation. There are three options for the observer to check at bottom of the evaluation: *Meets or Exceeds Standards, Needs Improvement, or Does Not Meet Standards and Needs Remediation.* Her Majesty checked *Needs Improvement*, which of course is true. As a former supervisor who has evaluated dozens of new employees, I realized she was not going to give me anything too positive this early on. She probably feared that if she gave me a positive written evaluation and then later decided not to rehire me next year, I might just throw her good words back in her face.

When I used to evaluate employees I always assumed new employees needed improvement and generally gave them a *meets standards* evaluation. I graded them on a sliding scale, factoring in that they were new to the job and it would be unfair to expect them to be totally proficient from the get-go.

Before I left her office I asked Carol to give me a general idea of how she thought I was doing relative to others in the past with no experience. Carol feigned thinking for a moment and said. "You might not believe this Erik, but I've seen worse. You're probably right in the middle."

Thanks, Bitch! I thought and left.

Survey Week: The Ice Queen Cometh

Despite my previous protestations to the contrary, I diligently spent substantially more time on my survey week lesson plans than on any of my earlier plans. For my seniors I planned to use an authorized *New York Times* lesson plan on expository writing based on a *Times* article about how certain retail stores risk legal action by hiring good-looking, young, hip kids, regardless of experience, to work as *sales ambassadors* and walking billboards to promote *The Look* in their stores. It seemed a good choice. I could build on the lesson by incorporating a variety of teaching modes, such as organizing and ranking magazine ads in small groups and modeling the steps in writing an essay.

For my juniors I planned a multi-phased lesson on persuasive writing directly out of our as yet unused American literature textbook. The lesson plan was about the use of emotional argument, and centered on a fire and brimstone 1747 sermon by the Puritan minister Jonathan Edwards entitled *Sinners in the Hands of an Angry God.* I would use overheads, handouts, and two short films to try and get the students engaged. I had my doubts about both plans, but I didn't have the energy to come up with anything better.

Monday arrives. Fourth Block (juniors) begins. About fifteen minutes in, as my juniors are watching a short film on the Puritans, Carol appears. I get up from the student desk where I am sitting to watch the film, approach Ms. Havisham and hand her, per her earlier request, the week's lesson plans for both English 11 and English 12. Without the slightest indication of interest Carol takes the plans, turns around, heads for her observation post and quietly settles into her catbird seat. When the movie ends, I lead the class in a somewhat heated and disjointed discussion on religion and the birth of our nation.

The students know even less than I had anticipated. Most think the original colonies were either in the Midwest or on the West Coast. I prompt them with the *Boston Tea*

Party, and when I ask if anyone knows anything about the *Mayflower*, one of my more difficult boys raises his hand and answers. "How stupid do you think we are Mr. Mandel? The *Mayflower* was one of Columbus' ships."

After Carol leaves, the class wants to know who that lady was and if she ever smiles.

"That was my boss, the Director of Special Education, Ms. Havisham. And although I am sure Ms. Havisham smiles, I have yet to see it with my own eyes."

Oh well...

The next day Carol comes into my senior Block One class immediately after I discover a note under some books in the back of the class. The note was apparently written sometime earlier, and as I glance at it I make a snap decision to read it aloud. We are in the middle of a lesson on narrative writing and some of the students have written really good stuff. I am thinking the note might offer comic relief, and give an example of both the effective use of narrative writing and the potential dangers of passing notes in class. The note:

> first girl writes: *About a week cuz he ended up goin for someone better looking than me.*
> second girl responds: *The guy in front of me likes you. You should go for him.* ☺
> first girl again: *No he don't. He's in my U.S. History Class. I asked him before if he liked me. He said hell no.*

I point out to the class that every word is spelled correctly and that *first girl* used the correct *than*. They seem to enjoy the lesson, but of course I have no idea what Carol is thinking. Just before leaving, Carol calls me over and asks when I am going to give her my actual lesson plans because the ones I have given her apparently do not reflect what I am teaching. I assure her the plans are accurate and then add that it might be helpful if, while I am teaching English 11, she looks at the plan clearly marked *English 11 Plan*, not the one marked *English 12 Plan*.

Wednesday, another glitch. I have the *Times* lesson plan all set, agenda and relevant state standards posted. But when class starts I notice at least half of the kids are missing, the smarter half. Turns out they are on a field trip to a local junior college, and of course no one bothered to notify me in advance so I could plan accordingly. I don't want to start a two-day lesson with half the class missing. As I am wondering what to do, we have the first fire drill of the year. After the drill is over, I gamble that Carol will not turn up until the last half of the block, and I take the class to the library for twenty minutes to buy myself time to come up with an effective Plan B. When we return to the classroom I have them do a pre-reading activity for *The Look*; I hurriedly scribble some *Quick Writes* on the board: *What stores you do shop at for clothes? What look are you trying to project, and if you had lots of money would you shop at different stores and change your style?*

Carol comes in as they're doing the *Quick Writes* and heads straight for her post. Having learned from past mistakes (hers, not mine), I approach immediately to explain the field trip situation and also to let her know I am more or less improvising and that she should ignore the posted agenda. Then I walk around class checking the *Quick Writes*. Later in the period, with Carol still observing, we discuss the legality and ethics of hiring someone based on their appearance. I ask one of the cool guys the hypothetical question, "If you are managing a *Gap Store* and you have one opening for a sales person, and this really hot, sexy blonde girl with no work experience comes in and applies for the job, and later I come in with twenty years of retail sales experience and apply for same job, who would you hire?"

Without missing a beat Cool Guy replies, "I would hire you."

I laugh. I glance over at Carol and I think I can detect the beginning of a smile.

The following day when Carol comes in I am reading *Sinners in the Hands of an Angry God* to the class. I have a sore throat and feel like shit. I read the sermon aloud and do my best to make it interesting, but the kids are having none of it. Every time I stop reading and ask them to tell me what's going on (*Check for Understanding*/CFU), all I get are zombie looks. I'm dying on stage. I plow through the sermon and do my best to spark something. Still nothing. Eventually I finish the sermon and as I am clumsily going over catchy vocabulary words such as *wrath, salvation and deliverance* on the overhead projector, Carol slithers out.

Stuff happens...

It could have been worse of course. It always can. There's my son Simon's recent work experience that puts my bad day, and many other bad days, in proper perspective. Simon recently graduated from his dad's alma mater, UCSC, with a psychology degree, and moved to Spokane with his old high school buddy Paul to get away from his hometown. He got a job as a special ed aide in an autistic classroom. (Another aside: both Simon and I got jobs in public education when we were twenty-two. I never left. Like most parents, I have higher aspirations for Simon.) Since he started working about five weeks ago, I talk to

Simon almost daily on my drive home. We talk guy stuff, discuss sports and compare our days. He likes his job and enjoys working with the kids. The people he works with, mostly middle-aged mothers, love him. His explanation for this is simple supply and demand: "I'm a stud with a degree in psychology who loves retards."

The kids are a challenge and some have to be restrained several times a day. The ratio of aides to students is almost one to one and the kids have to be watched every second. Some kids can be well behaved and mellow one minute and then, without warning, go ape-shit—biting, hitting and scratching. Sly, an eleven year-old, non-talking autistic boy is Simon's biggest challenge. Sly loses it often. He's double-jointed which makes it even more difficult to restrain him and get him into the time-out room—a tiny, windowless, carpeted room that the staff uses when a kid needs to be isolated. A few weeks ago during our daily phone conversation, Simon told me about his particularly shitty day that went something like this: Sly was having a bad day. He was put into the time-out room for about ten minutes, and when Simon went to check on him he found Sly naked with shit all over himself. Shit shrapnel on the walls and the carpeted floors. Everywhere! Sly was holding shit in his hands, laughing hysterically.

My son has never been comfortable with other people's bodily functions, so this scene was particularly disgusting for him. Eventually the aides and the custodians got Sly and the room cleaned up. Because Sly had never demonstrated this particular behavior before, and not wanting to reward him by sending him home, the teacher decided to keep Sly in class. Bad idea. Within thirty minutes—an encore—a fresh torrent of shit—another shit storm. Simon told me he never realized one person could produce so much shit in so short a time. Simon did survive, did not quit on the spot, and in fact returned to work the next day as if nothing had happened.

So, while I will most certainly continue to complain about my situation, I am almost dead certain that I will never have a day as shitty as Simon's.

Sunday - December 15

Yesterday during lunch I am alone, sitting at my desk listening to NPR, quietly eating some barely edible, frozen, Asian chicken noodle concoction, trying to relax before the arrival of my drama-queen-laden Third Block. All of a sudden the door flies open and in barge a burly sheriff with a smallish Latino boy in tow. The cop, without a word or nod of acknowledgment, pushes the kid against the wall and frisks him. Both he and the boy seem relatively calm as he has the boy empty his pockets and backpack. The sheriff then asks the poor kid if he knows why he decided to frisk him.

"Because you're a cop?"

"No." The sheriff explains in a fatherly manner, "I went after you because when you saw me, you took off running. That's usually a sign of something wrong, son."

As the bust is going down I continue eating as if lunchtime busts in my classroom are routine. When the cop discovers a baggie with some drugs, questions the boy, and then starts putting him through some kind of sobriety test, I realize I need to pee pretty bad and that lunch is almost over. I get up and walk right past the pair and out the door. When I return five minutes later they are gone.

It appears I will survive the first semester. Finals are next week and then I have two whole weeks off. At times it does seem to be getting easier and less stressful, but it is still hard. Just when I think I have a handle on things, something else gets slopped on my already over-laden plate. Like a call from Ethan telling me, matter-of-factly, to set up a meeting right away to deal with some emergency with one student or another. Speaking of meetings, Ernesto, the truant Romeo with a twenty year-old lover, was referred to the district attorney last week for a final truancy hearing. He is being expelled at the end of next week and will finish his stellar educational career at the notorious San Andreas campus.

I still haven't heard a peep from Carol regarding the weeklong survey observation of my teaching that she completed over three weeks ago. I am a little worried because Carol is usually anal about timeliness and getting all her legal ducks in a row. Wondering if she wants to spare me a bad evaluation until after Christmas? We shall see.

A confluence of three of my least favorite people occurred Thursday evening at the gym. After napping and some moderate drooling on a yoga mat in my room, I report to the gym at my allotted time of 6:15 to serve my extra-duty as scorekeeper for the girl's JV basketball game. As I enter Carol is leaving, and I ask her which administrator is working my shift so I will know who to report to. Carol tells me with a touch of disdain that it's Pecksniff. She snarkily adds that he is always late for his supervisory duties. One thing Carol and I agree on is that Pete is a prick.

Pete eventually shows up. When I get to the scoring table to take my position, I find two people on their knees under the scorer's table trying to plug in the mike for the PA system. Lo and behold, one of the bodies under the table belongs to none other than Sally Smuts. Apparently it is my lucky night, and I will have the pleasure of spending the next ninety minutes sitting next to Ms. Smuts, the bitch from teacher's training who told me to my face that I should not be allowed in a classroom. (Earlier in the day this same Ms. Smuts sent out a mass email to the staff complaining about seeing her name misspelled as Ms. Sluts too often to think it an accident.)

I say hi, and then take my place on a stool, just inches away from my nemesis. Within minutes Sally makes it quite clear that she has played and coached basketball, and therefore has the right to question the 30-second time-keeper, the refs, the coaches, and lowly non-credentialed me. I just sit there quietly taking it all in and smiling to myself. At one point the *Lady Balers* lead 20-7, only to be outscored 28 to 1 before eventually losing by 15 points. Several times during the rout Sally goes apoplectic over some minor miscalls (i.e. the proper place to put the ball in play after an offensive foul) by a hardworking pair of loveable, aged, frail referees.

The next day during lunch the phone rings. It's Carol. It is important to note that to this point Carol has never called me, other than for specific business related information, and that she never engages in small talk. So when I recognize her voice I assume she is phoning to set up a time to discuss my evaluation.

Nope, that's not it.

"So did Pecksniff ever show up last night?" she asks me right off.

"Yes." I answer.

And before she can hang up I can't resist asking, "So you just called to check up on Pete?"

"You betchya." she replies and then quickly hangs up.

VI

Born to Ruin

Saturday - January 5, 2008

I made it!!!! I survived my first semester as a teacher and I brought over 93% of my students with me. On one hand I still feel I am pretending to be a teacher; on the other I think my students are learning something, not certain what exactly, but something.

During winter break I've been lying low hoping to revitalize my vanishing verve for the second half of the season. Mary and I just got back from several days with friends on the rugged North Coast at *Sea Ranch*. Stayed in an incredible house on a bluff overlooking the ocean. Weathered a spectacular storm that reminded me of those ominous scenes from vintage Vincent Price movies of a rickety old Victorian house on a cliff above a raging angry sea, waves crashing as lightening illuminates the black and gray night sky. We lost power for the last two days. It was fun, and I tried to avoid talking about my job or even thinking about school matters, although I did schlep over a hundred pounds of books and materials with me in the unlikely event I chose to start work on next semester's lesson plans.

School starts Monday, the materials remain in the car and I have yet to plan a thing. What, me worry? I have all day tomorrow to plot my next term.

The last several weeks of school were action-packed and ran true to form. I started preparing my students and myself for finals. By "law" the final must count for at least 20% of a student's final grade. I was worried about many of my students failing the test and consequently failing my class. I looked over a few other teachers' finals from last year and tweaked and customized them to suit my style, emphasizing the stuff I covered and eliminating the stuff I neglected.

I talked to my students ad nauseam about the importance of organizing their notes and going over the vocabulary words. We went over sample questions. I provided a study guide and spent two entire class sessions breaking down *Of Mice and Men* into the simplest form possible by making a flipchart that included the novel's themes, characters and vocabulary. And then, against my natural instincts but with encouragement from Sara, I decided to make failure all but impossible for anyone willing to put in thirty minutes of study time; I made the final an open-book test and allowed my students to use all their notes, books and textbooks. The only book I banned during the final was the dictionary, though in retrospect this restriction was gratuitous.

A few weeks before the final I sent a letter home to the parents of students in danger of failing offering my help to any of their kids who were willing to make an honest effort. In addition I discussed the importance of the final with each student facing an F, emphasizing how easy it would be for them if they just organized their notes and studied for about half an hour. And for the two weeks prior to final, I did my best, every day, to impress upon them the importance of turning in missing assignments. I certainly wasn't expecting an overwhelming response from the letter, so I wasn't surprised when I heard nothing.

Well, almost nothing. At 4:15 on the last Friday before finals week, as I was preparing to head home for the weekend, I heard a knock at my door. (I generally lock my door fifteen minutes or so prior to leaving so I can spend a few minutes without interruption preparing my escape.) At first I ignored the knocking, but it went on unrelentingly. Leaving the safety of my desk, I approached the door. The door is windowed, but the top half is covered with posters to provide some semblance of privacy. Catching a glimpse of two boy-legs clothed in black denim, I deduced that both belonged to William, one of my most lethargic and straight-out lazy students. For a moment I was tempted to step back and continue ignoring him until he went away, but of course both my undying dedication to teaching and my innate curiosity got the better of me.

I open the door. William waltzes in like he lives there. "Oh, Mr. Mandel." Referencing my letter home to his parents, William continues in a most fraudulently sincere and earnest voice, "I never knew you tutored after school. I need some help on the final and my parents want me to find out what work I am missing so I can do it over the weekend."

Bullshit! You jiving little pain in the ass!! I think to myself, but say instead, "William, I really wouldn't mind helping you, but isn't it a little late to come asking? And besides I'm on my way out the door."

After some discussion and some pathetic pleading

on his part I give in, print a list of some of his twenty-two missing assignments, give him another list of twenty vocabulary words, and because there is no dictionary (or any books for that matter) in his home, I loan him a dictionary for the weekend. William promises to get all his missing work to me by Monday morning. He assures me repeatedly that he does this every year—waits until the last minute, works super hard the last weekend, and ultimately passes all his classes.

I wasn't buying any of it. I was certain William wouldn't do any of the work and would consequently fail the class. I would be happy just to see my dictionary again. Monday morning comes and goes, no William. Later in the day, I see him outside and ask him about the missing work. He gives me a line of bullshit a mile long about how he has done most of it, punctuating his story with hand gestures and grimaces, "You know how it is Mr. Mandel, when you have all this work to do all at once, all the thinking, all the pressure, and how confusing it all gets."

"Oh William, you mean like your head feels like it is about to explode?"

"Exactly" he replies with a tight little smile and then disappears around the corner.

A few days later William shows up for the final without the missing work, his notes, my dictionary or a pencil. For five points I rent a pencil to William and the half-dozen others who also forgot pencils. (I mean how hard is it to bring a pencil?) Despite the rented pencil, William fails the final and the class.

Speaking of lazy-asses. Calculating that a zero on the writing section will not adversely affect their overall class grade, neither Non Sequitur Rick, the boy with the amazing imagination but no interest in succeeding in school, nor James, the anti-Mexican, half-Mexican cowboy smart-ass who thinks himself brilliant because he passed the exit exams, bother to attempt the essay portion of the final. Not for the first time both were mistaken. Rick's C+ fell to a D and James's B- to a C-. But for them, as for many others, a passing grade is a passing grade, happiness a D-. Rick and James, two middling fish in a pint-sized puddle.

Mr. Mandel's skepticism rolls on, inexorable and unfettered, towards its final stop—total complete unapologetic cynicism.

Sunday - January 6

Beginning to seriously wonder about my priorities. School starts in less than eighteen hours and I am working on this journal instead of my lesson plans. But I want to relate some stories about grade deflation, my colleagues, English Department meetings, *The Crucible,* and finally, of course, my students, many of whom I have come to love.

Grades: I have noticed that there are two types of students: those who strive to do well, and those that just want to pass the class, get the five units and avoid having to take the class again. Those that want to do well tend to do well. They ask questions, and if they get confused they ask me to explain things in terms they understand. And then there are those like Non Sequitur Rick and Cowboy James who are just thrilled to avoid an F. I never realized until "becoming" a teacher how relative academic goals actually are. In a way it makes perfect sense. The students that do go on to attend college start fresh. The other kids aren't going to set the academic world ablaze, consequently their high school GPA's have no impact on their futures. The exit exam's importance and the difficulties it presents these students give them one more excuse to not give a shit, to bide their time until they turn the magic eighteen and are free—free at last.

Pod mates: My classroom is located in a quiet corner of the main campus within a small, shabbily constructed Mediterranean-style pod consisting of four poorly ventilated rooms. I find the location pleasant and cozy, and I get along well with my pod mates, as we all seem to share a quietly defiant attitude towards outsiders. My fellow pod mates are Sara, Liz, a tall, incredibly longhaired, funny no-nonsense resource social studies teacher, Bryan a fellow non-credentialed resource teacher (Bryan teaches chemistry next door to me in a room with no running water, let alone lab equipment), and finally Catalina, an attractive, ex-*Baler* cheerleader and "regular" Spanish teacher who returned to teaching this year after a ten year hiatus spent at home with her young children. Cata is one of the few colleagues I feel comfortable sharing my frustrations with on a regular basis.

English Department meetings: Where to start? Unbeknownst to me I was supposed to be attending at least one of the two monthly meetings of the English Department. Someone may have actually mentioned that fact, but either I didn't hear it or I just flat out failed to file the information in the proper slot. About a month ago I attended my first and hopefully my last English Department meeting. I had assumed that the purpose of these meetings was to share information, network, and of course to bitch and to let off steam about how those at the top make our jobs more difficult. The English Department is the largest department at the school and has a reputation for being its most divisive. While the other departments are noted for getting along, the English Department is noted for internal strife and a general atmosphere of sexism, ego and bullshit. There are many sub-groups in the department based on gender, teaching style, politics, jock-ness and professional hubris.

I slid into the meeting with my smug air of outsider who-doesn't-give-a-shitness, and with every intention of just sitting back and enjoying the fireworks. However I was disappointed. Initially the exchanges were mundane and far from entertaining, and quickly degenerated into a petty banal pissing contest. The agenda seemed to consist of two items: what going-away gift to get the custodian, and whether to expand the current number of annual student English Department awards. Regarding the first item, after about fifteen minutes of discussion it was decided the department would give the custodian a gift certificate for some amount to some store somewhere.

The next item, as you might guess, was more prob-lematic. Currently the department presents one annual award to the most deserving English student in the entire school. The question on the table was whether to main-tain the status quo or to expand the number of awards to one per grade level. The first few speakers thought it was a good idea to increase the number of award recipients, and just when I thought it was going to be a slam-dunk, an annoying and pedantic guy began his remarks with, "I hate to be the contrarian."

And with that I thought, *here they go.* And off the contrarian went, into a long diatribe about how everything in the whole world these days is watered down, and to increase the number of awards would make them meaningless. I was thinking to myself, (you're nuts if you think I was going to get involved in the actual discussion) *Wait, there are 3000 students taking English, can't we find at least four deserving students among the bunch?* The battle raged on for twenty-five minutes more until the facilitator, frustrated and fed up, finally tabled the item for a future meeting. As the discussion wound down, I tried to make myself as small as possible before silently slipping out the door and heading home.

The Crucible: The curriculum for 11th grade includes this Arthur Miller parable drama, literally about the *Salem Witch Trials*. It was Miller's transparent but effective attempt to use the trials as a metaphor to condemn McCarthyism and the accompanying anti-communist show trials of the *House Un-American Activities Committee* (HUAC). This fact was problematic for me as the teacher. Should I treat the play simply as literature and use it to discuss early American history, or should I delve into the symbols and metaphors Miller used to reflect the evils of the *Red Scare* and the obvious parallels to the present? As an American history major I love all this stuff, and also I have a strong personal connection to this time. I was raised in a cauldron of fear, self-righteousness and rabid patriotic hysteria as my dad was caught up in the dragnet and was called to testify by HUAC. (He did the honorable thing and refused to testify by taking the Fifth.) I realized, however, that I would have my hands full just getting the kids to comprehend the literal dialogue and historical content; teaching the historical metaphor would entail more pre-reading activities and preparation than I had time for.

So what did I do? I lamely attempted both, and as is usually the case when trying to do too much with too little, I did neither justice.

I became pretty disheartened during my initial attempts to develop background knowledge for the play. Most students had no idea where Massachusetts is, and when I asked them about the original thirteen colonies, some thought

BORN TO RUIN

they were on the West Coast. We discussed religious persecution and the irony of the Puritans leaving England to freely practice their religion, only to persecute and kill those who disagreed with them once they arrived in America. I told them that Arthur Miller, a true nerd, married the hottest sex symbol ever, Marilyn Monroe. We read the first act aloud, which was pretty fun, although I had a hard time stifling Gina as she changed her accent with every sentence, neglecting to actually match her emotions to the tone of the dialogue. One girl wanted to play every female part. During one class I made the mistake of playing the part of John Proctor in a scene where Abigail (Gina) tries to seduce him—very uncomfortable to say the least.

The students enjoyed *Crucible*, the movie with Daniel Day-Lewis, which I choose to believe was because they had read part of the play first. The best teaching moment in the lesson happened by accident, and helped me drive home the psychological phenomenon of witch-hunts and mass hysteria. I was trying to explain the effects of peer pressure on individuals when my aide Vera raised her hand. She proceeded to tell the class about some murders that had occurred in Hollister in the mid 1980's.

A body was discovered one morning on campus near the library. Other bodies were found in the area. There were rumors at the time about Satan worship, witchcraft and animal sacrifices. Before the murder, three pigs had been slaughtered in the high school Ag Yard and their blood splattered all over campus. During the investigation a hippie type was arrested. The local press mentioned that he had some kind of altar in his house, and while he was in jail a mob burned his house down.

Eventually the police discovered the murders had been committed by a fifteen year-old SBHS student and that hippie man had had nothing to do with the crimes. The kids were enthralled. It was surprising how few had heard the story. You would think that news of a student being stabbed on campus would resonate for decades.

Being the experienced—almost five whole months under my belt—and, in my mind, brilliant educator, I recognized what an effective educational tool the story could be, and even fantasized—for about five seconds––about motivating my classes to write a short play based on the true story. I checked the facts of the case online and discussed some lesson ideas with Doug. Aside from the competency question—regarding both students and teacher—and the hard work required, I worried that because the murders were so recent, scars and raw emotions might still remain in the community. Nevertheless, I took the story and ran with it.

The next day as I recounted the grisly murder in a rather dispassionate matter of fact tone to another of my classes, I noticed my aide Linda tearing up.

Shit. What should I do?

I stop my story and ask Linda if she is ok. Linda asks for a minute to compose herself, and then delivers, from her insider's perspective, an account of the crimes. It turns out the girl murdered on campus was Linda's best friend and she was planning to get married soon. Linda was going to be her maid of honor. It was then that I realized just how deep and how fresh the scars and emotions were.

You never know where you're going to end up, especially when you have no idea where you're going.

Two quick kid stories:

Gina: Not sure I mentioned this earlier, but Gina is a big girl. Almost every day when Gina enters class and sees me finishing my lunch, she says, "Mr. Mandel, are you going to finish that?" and begs me to let her have it. At first it was kind of charming, but then I realized her mom must have her on a strict diet and she must be foraging food throughout the day.

Oliver: This hyperactive, bouncy senior just can't sit still. Oliver has a hard time understanding how anything he does can possibly be annoying to others. He has a toy chest full of nervous tics. We have a comfortable relationship that comes to a head every once in a while. Oliver often finds himself unconsciously spinning his notebook on his finger. In the beginning of the year this really bugged me, but I got used to it and decided it was better just to live with it than to try to replace it with some less annoying energy-burning alternative. Sometimes he just gets up and toddles around the classroom playing with things—the thermostat cover, the pencil sharpener. or whatever attracts his nervous fancy. One day I told him if he didn't sit down I would have to childproof the room. That didn't seem to have the desired effect on him. *Ok focus Eric, get back to the story of Oliver spinning notebook.* Suddenly Oliver, decides to upgrade the act and begins spinning a large pillow in place of the usual black notebook. The pillow spins in place for a few seconds and then flies across the room. I tell him to pick it up and not spin the pillow again. He picks it up.

Minutes later, totally unaware of his own actions, Oliver is spinning the pillow again. Abruptly I tell him to go outside and fill out a *Behavior Reflection Sheet.* You know the drill, #1. *What I did wrong,* #2. *What rule I broke,* and finally #3. *What I will do to avoid the behavior in the future.* Oliver goes outside and returns five minutes later with his *Behavior Reflection Sheet* still blank and loudly insists he broke no rules. Then, busting at the seams to prove his point, a gloating Oliver leads me to the posted list of class rules and asks me to show him the rule prohibiting pillow-spinning.

I explain to Oliver and the class that while there is no specific rule stating *No spinning of pillows in class*, there are general rules that cover the act of pillow spinning, such as being respectful and not distracting others. Oliver isn't convinced. So I tell him and the class, "I don't see any rule prohibiting throwing a hand grenade into the classroom and killing everyone either. So Oliver, does that make it right?"

Eventually after some more give and take, Oliver begrudgingly fills out the sheet; about fifteen minutes later, his frustration finally over its threshold, Oliver lets out a nice stream of pretty serious profanities that I assume are directed at me. (I generally employ the *umpire rule*—I will give you a warning if you swear non-specifically, but if you direct the expletives at me, *you're outta here*.) When I confront Oliver he pleads over and over that he was calling his best friend Stan an asshole, not me. Stan confirms this, over and over, with, "Mr. Mandel, he called me an asshole, not you!"

By now, sick of the whole thing, I order Oliver to get out and go to the office, adding as he is leaving that I am going to write a misconduct and call his mom. Hearing this, poor Oliver can't resist the last word.

"Fuck this shit! I am going home."

Grant me the serenity to accept the things I cannot change....

Monday - January 21

The longer I do this journal thing the harder it gets. It seems to get stale and less interesting as the veneer of newness wears off. The more comfortable I get at this teaching gig, the less my external antenna receive and perceive stuff as note-worthy. What was once funny, unique or eye opening now seems routine and mundane. It appears I have morphed from an outsider to an insider. Not a fully entrenched insider, but an insider nonetheless. I could show off my rusty old history major chops by citing Alexis D'Toqueville and discussing in depth the advantages one has in viewing a society from the outside. But I will spare you those pontifications for now and get back to what's most important, the story.

Energy, or more precisely the lack of energy, is another principle reason this is getting more difficult. Although it has been just over a year since my back surgery, I still don't feel anywhere close to a 100%, and I probably never will. I arrive home tired, stressed and in pain in spite of the prescribed pain meds and stimulants. But here I am. Enough about my tribulations, let's get to my trials.

Lots has happened since second semester began on the seventh of January. Melody came back, made a dramatic exit, and then came back again; my nemeses, Jorge and Tomas, returned to my classroom after a two months respite with Sara; Tony, future middleweight champion of the world, returned after an unsuccessful foray into the regular English world; Ernesto, the truant Romeo, was sent away for good to the area's alternative high school. Coach Putzmire is starting to grow on me; Priscilla, the school psychologist, is emerging as a real piece of work; and I finally had my long-awaited evaluation meeting with Carol.

More Melody Mayhem: This particular Girl Interrupted seems to have evolved into the centerpiece of this opus. When Mel disappeared for the second time a couple of months back I was certain she was gone for good. As you may recall, the former Satanist and freshly reborn Christian ran away after being caught stealing two credit cards from an aide's purse. A few days after her getaway—freshly reborn—Mel became an adult and was free to make her own decisions. I foolishly assumed that returning to school was not likely to be one of them. While I was hectically racing to set up my class for the first day of the new semester, I heard a familiar voice over my shoulder, "Happy New Year Mr. Mandel. I'm back."

I froze.

My initial instinct was to stand perfectly still, hoping the sound and the body accompanying the sound might vanish; but realizing I had no other option, I turned around. There she was—Mel in her latest transformation—short bleached hair, a too revealing t-shirt, too much mascara, and a look of pure innocence. And while I was relieved to know she was okay, I was seriously apprehensive about her negative effect on my classes. With Jorge and Tomas returning to Fifth Block, the environment would be perilously close to nuclear. Jorrid Jorge and Toxic Tomas were volatile enough on their own without the flammable additives of Mel's shock and awe performances and their accompanying emotive explosive expletives.

It didn't take Mel long to reintroduce herself to the class, maybe seven minutes. Before I share Mel's latest odyssey I should describe her first bombshell. For the opening *Transition-Quick Write* of the new year I had the students to do several things: explain what they think *resolution* means, list their new year's resolutions if they have any (most didn't), and finally guess the most popular resolutions in the country. Initially most, as usual, are at a loss for words, but not Mel. Never shy or unwilling to share her darkest secrets with the whole world, she raises her hand. I call on her and hold my breath. She says something like, "I have four resolutions: the first, by January 1,

BORN TO RUIN

2009 I want to get stoned like over 200 times, second, by June 2010 I want to get my GED…"

As Mel basks in the phosphorescent glow of her first successful detonation of 2008, it takes me a good ten minutes to get the class back on track.

The first writing assignment after the break was the clichéd, but always entertaining, *What I did for my winter vacation*—with a slight twist. I have them list everything they can remember doing during the break, then I ask them to transform the list into an interesting narrative.

Mel's list:

Movies (theaters)	watched TV
job applications	on My Space
learned Spanish in Hispanic rehab	read 2 books
registered to vote	smoked cigarettes
	and much much more

As for her narrative, it was dramatic and relatively well written. To avoid self-incrimination, Mel cleverly wrote in the third person:

> On October 5th, Serenity left school and ran away to Fresno. She was getting high off crystal meth, pot and smoking cigarettes. She'd get really tired a lot (**Yes!!!**) after staying awake 5 to 6 days a week. She got kicked out of her friend's house. After Serenity left, she ended up in a Spanish speaking rehab. She had nowhere else to go.
>
> The people were teaching Serenity to speak, write, sing and understand Spanish. She left the rehab 18 days later, and smoked rock, snorted coke and drank liquor. She went back to the rehab after a week and a half.

THE ACCIDENTAL TEACHER

The rehab people told Serenity she would come back. Serenity didn't believe them at the time, but here she was, at their door, yet again. Serenity fell in love with a guy at the rehab. His name was Jesus, nicknamed Chewy. She loved him a lot. He would buy flowers, food, clothes and more for Serenity. She thought it was real, but dreadfully was mistaken. He took advantage of Serenity and she was so hurt she almost killed herself with a string (sic) around her neck.

Serenity's mom picked her up and took her home. She was angry that Serenity had begun smoking cigarettes. When they were home, Serenity began to date a past love. He broke her heart by leaving her for another girl, telling Serenity that, she got drunk and cheated on him with a male and a female. They were beginning a new relationship, and Serenity fell in love with another friend from the past. His name was Jonathan. They'd known each other for a year and a half already. Later on Serenity thought she was pregnant. She was devastated because it was with Jonathan, the one she cheated on Ryan (her boyfriend) with. Serenity got a test, and it was negative. She wasn't pregnant. Relieved, Serenity began to try finishing school. She was thinking of her son, Adam. She missed him so much, wishing she had him back.

The day Serenity got a bunch of applications done, she printed out a ritual. Serenity was doing a ritual to commit to Satan, her higher power. Everyone thought she was crazy because she worshipped the devil. But really no one saw that Serenity was really looking for someone or something to help her find strength, to help Serenity learn how to be an individual. She was lost, lonely, depressed, angry and happy all in one. She was mixed up, And the reason she went back to school was so she wouldn't have too much time to think about it, or to get into trouble. Serenity was trying to find peace over her vacation. She was trying to start over. And now, back in school, Serenity has a chance to do just that.. The End

When "Serenity" asks me to read her story aloud to the class I react quickly with, "Maybe later, Melody."

The next day as the class walks to the computer lab to practice writing resumes, Mel and I talk. She tells me she joined a girl gang a few days earlier, but for some reason her mom, with whom she is now living on a trial basis, is pissed. Apparently Melody is the only white girl in the gang and her initiation rite consisted of getting beaten up by the other gang members. Curious. I ask some questions. *Why did you join? How are girl gangs affiliated with boy gangs?* Questions like that. (Turns out they have a relationship similar to the one sororities have with their sibling-like fraternities.) I try to give her some fatherly advice. Whenever I do talk to Mel alone she seems receptive and willing to listen. I think it is pretty safe to assume that this girl probably hasn't had many healthy relationships with men. I share my concerns about her well-being. I point out that her volatile nature, and her apparent need always to be the center of attention, run counter to her desire to avoid conflict and finish high school. As we near our destination Mel asks what I thought of Serenity's story. I try my best to be diplomatic, but being the laugh whore I am, I just can't resist temptation. "Mel, you are a wonderful writer and poet and you should keep working at it, it could be your ticket out. As for your story, some people spend their entire lives searching for true love, but look at Serenity, that girl was able to find love three times in less than two months!"

She smiles and laughs. Thank god she appreciates my twisted humor.

Melody struggled her first week back, had several of her patented outbursts, ditched some classes, and by week's end I was concerned enough to call her caseworker, Bruce Pirl the *Pepto Bismol* Man, to suggest moving Mel out of my Fifth Block to his more closely supervised classroom. (Mel is also in my English 11 Third Block, but her drama queen style seems to be a good fit with that group.) Bruce and I agreed the move would be best for Melody and for everyone else. We decided I would tell Mel about the move after the weekend. Late Friday afternoon as I was getting ready to go home I got the following confidential email from Bruce:

FYI- 1/11/08   MOM LEFT MESSAGE THAT MELODY TOOK SOME PILLS AND IS IN "ICU" IN THE HOSPITAL. SHE FIGURES SHE WILL GO TO A MENTAL WARD AFTER SHE GETS OUT, SO SHE DOESN'T KNOW WHEN SHE WILL RETURN TO SCHOOL.

Nice way to end the week. I was worried about the girl most of the weekend, but on Monday when class began, there she was as if nothing had happened, grinning like the Cheshire Cat, eagerly awaiting her first opportunity to wreak some havoc.

Los Dos Amigos: Toxic Tomas y Jorrid Jose. Things were so much better after the departure of Jorge and Tomas it should come as no surprise that I wasn't looking forward to their return. In their absence the class had reached a sort of stasis; not perfect, not even good, but tolerable. I talked to both boys during finals week in December and told them I would give them another chance, but they were on thin ice and I had no plans to put up with any of their shit.

With Melody's return I knew someone's days were numbered, I was just hoping they weren't mine. Tomas was fine, relatively; he didn't do much work, but he was quiet. Jorge, on the other hand, was the same old pain in the ass; showing off, making sure he got the last word, and overreacting to my directions in his brainless literal way. For instance, when I asked him to stop drumming his pencil on his desk and put his pencil down, he dropped it dramatically on the floor—an homage to the bottle-dropping behavior that got him kicked out of class the first time.

Later when I confronted Jorge about his actions and mentioned that he needed to pass my class in order to graduate, he said, "No big deal." Unbeknownst to me Jorge was already resigned to that fact and that he would be coming back for a fifth year. *Shit*, I thought, *if I can't hold his diploma over his head, I got nothing.* Later when I called Jorge's mother and described su hijo's behavior, mama replied curtly, "I'll tell his dad." Then hung up before I could get another word in. Jorge's not going to be around much longer.

It turns out Tomas is leaving at the end of this week, when he turns eighteen, to go into adult ed. Evidently Tomas can graduate with a GED through adult ed after completing just one more class. If Tomas stayed at SBHS, he would have to finish both the current semester and the fall semester. A no-brainer. Now, if only Jorge were so practical.

THE ACCIDENTAL TEACHER

All dressed up and nowhere to go

One more story. Roberto, a small engaging sad-eyed Latino junior, has spent most of his life in foster care. Like many of my students, Roberto has no idea what constitutes appropriate behavior. From time to time he will just blurt something out, and when sad or frustrated he has no trouble revealing his grief to the entire class with earnest warnings like, "I am too sad or hurt to do any work today, so Mr. Mandel, you may want to leave me alone."

The first day back from winter break, as the rest of the class is busy, or apparently busy, working on their vacation lists and narratives, Roberto just sits there doing nothing. I approach him cautiously and see only three words on his paper: *I AM SAD.* Roberto explains to me in a whisper that his dad died over winter break and he misses him and he is sad.

I have Roberto follow me to my desk so we can talk in private. I tell him to forget the assignment, but if he wants he can write about his dad. Roberto tells me that he didn't actually know his dad well and hadn't seen him for a long time. It does seem these kids have had more than their fair share of tragedies. And people wonder why so many of these kids fail at everything they try, except maybe getting into more trouble.

A few days later, minutes before the start of class as I am trying to finish my lunch, Roberto comes up to my desk, open cell phone in hand. I tell him to close the phone and put it away. (The school's zero tolerance policy for cell phones, *ipods* and *mp3's* in class mandates that teachers confiscate the devices on sight and send them to the office where they must be retrieved by a parent. Needless to say, this dude don't abide unless a student refuses to put a device away or brazenly texts or listens to music after being warned. The faculty seems to be evenly divided between cell phone Nazis and the rest of us.) Roberto tells me in a soft but proud tone, " Mr. Mandel, you have to see this picture I have on my phone."

He then holds the open phone right up to my face. There, in living color, is a picture of a well-dressed, middle-aged beatific Latino in serene repose inside an open, satin-lined coffin. I am almost speechless but manage to ask, "Is that your dad?"

"Yes," he replies with a smile and a real sense of pride.

Roberto snaps his phone shut, turns around, heads to his desk and waits for class to begin.

And the courage to change the things I can...

Sunday - January 27

A couple weeks back, right after we returned from vacation, Carol sent me an email summoning me to her office on the following day for our long awaited evaluation conference. I showed up in her office apprehensive and anxious. Carol and I do not see eye-to-eye on much of anything. I've been in a state of frustration since my first evaluation because of her failure to identify which standard she is measuring me against—a new inexperienced non-credentialed neophyte, or an experienced veteran teacher?

I have found Carol to be long on advice and short on support. Although I have never felt intimidated by her, the fact that she waited over a month after the actual survey before calling me in for our meeting had me wondering if my evaluation was so terrible that she had intentionally waited until after winter break to avoid ruining my vacation. In retrospect that seems silly, as Carol has yet to display a scintilla of sensitivity to me or my situation. I have heard lots of things about Carol, most of them derogatory and reflecting her overall cluelessness and total lack of people skills, the latter despite years of management experience including as the director of counseling. One English teacher recently told me he called Carol *The Crazy Lady*. (I assume not to her face.)

With all this in mind, entering her office I was pretty much ready for anything. And anything, more or less, is what I got. Carol and I exchange pleasantries for a few minutes and she actually asks how I am doing. And just as she hands me her formal written evaluation, her cell phone chimes. Carol reaches for her purse. I assume she is going to fish out her phone and turn it off; I mean no administrator would take a routine phone call during an important meeting with a new employee, right?

Wrong.

Carol fumbles in her purse for her phone, pulls it out, opens it, and precedes to have an intimate ten minute chat with her twenty-something son who, from what I can tell from where I sit, wants his mommy to send money, like muy pronto. As Carol chats with her boy I just sit there pretending to be invisible and using the time to read over my evaluation. (I do seem to be getting better at the pretending thing.) Finally Carol hangs up, looks over at me and picks up exactly where, in her mind, we left off.

Her report, while generally fair, is off the mark in certain areas, and I find several of her comments especially aggravating. First, Carol disapproves of the amount of *Silent Sustained Reading* (SSR) I provide my students and wants me to increase direct instruction time at the expense of SSR. We go round-and-round on this topic. Carol tells me SSR is not an efficient use of precious instructional minutes. I argue that reading in class is essential for these kids because most have no books at home. When I back up my position by pointing out that both Sara and Doug the Librarian maintain that daily reading is critical for resource students, Carol responds with a shrill, "Of course Erik, what do you *think* Doug would say?" And then cackles for good measure, "He is a librarian for god's sake!"

Realizing I am not going to win the book battle, I move on to my second complaint—her charge of racial inequity. During her initial drop-in several months back, Carol nailed me with an erroneous observation that I was favoring whites over Hispanics. At the time I had decided to ignore the issue and not bother to point out the fact that the class she observed was almost entirely Latino, and that many kids Carol assumed were white were in fact Hispanic. I had decided instead that in the future, when she showed up, I would make certain to direct most of my questions to the brownest faces, and that is exactly what I did. It's ironic that the first time in my teaching career I consciously use race as a criteria I do so to combat Carol's belief that I may subconsciously be a bigot.

In her own words off her official evaluation form:

STANDARD I – Engaging and Supporting All Students in Learning

- Connecting students' prior knowledge, life experience, and interests with learning goals.
- Using a variety of instructional strategies and resources to respond to students' diverse needs.
- Facilitating learning experiences that promote autonomy, interaction, and choice.
- Engaging students in problem solving, critical thinking, and other activities that make subject matter meaningful.
- Promoting self-directed, reflective learning for all students.

RATING: NI

During the first semester of 2007-08, Mr. Mandel has increased the time devoted to engaging learning activities during each block. During the survey observation, he planned for three or four learning activities within a 100 minute block. Approximately half of the activities were teacher directed and were about 50 minutes. Daily lessons began with a transition followed by silent sustained reading. During direct instruction, Mr. Mandel addressed key vocabulary, provided modeling for writing paragraphs on the overhead, played an audio tape for <u>Mice and Men</u> and led classroom discussions.

> Mr. Mandel utilized higher order thinking questions during classroom discussion. In general, he took responses from volunteers. <u>These volunteers were primarily white males. The Hispanic males were seldom called upon and appeared to be disengaged. The discussion regarding personal styles centered on typical white middle class teenage preferences. When indicating the stores where students shopped, Hispanic males listed "D" mart and K mart.</u>
>
> RECOMMENDATIONS:
> 1. Increase the amount and types of teacher directed learning activities within each block.
> 2. Create a system, e.g. student names on cards to ensure that each student is called upon an equal number of times during each block
> 3. Work on incorporating differing cultural perspectives into your lessons. This can be done through selection of literature & articles, video clips, guest speakers...

Needless to say, after reading the evaluation (most disturbing comments are underlined) I am pissed, but I do my best to remain calm and address her points in a firm and respectful manner. After explaining to Carol that most of the kids I called on were in fact Latino, (I did make certain to call on everyone in class during one of her visits), Carol finally admits that perhaps she wasn't speaking about race per se, but rather in socio-economic terms.

Fuck! I thought. *So I'm not calling on enough poor kids? Does she mean what she says? Does she have trouble distinguishing between race and status? Is she just flat out nuts?*

I then ask if maybe she is actually differentiating by skin pigmentation and not by race. Carol hems and haws, eventually copping to the explanation that what she actually meant was that I was unconsciously avoiding calling on the gang-banger types. For once I am at a loss for words, almost. Not once during my teaching have I ever actually thought to myself, *ese vato is a gang banger, I'd better avoid this pendejo.*

After more rambling, Carol describes two specific dark-skinned Hispanic males that, according to her, I ignored; moreover, she adds that I may actually have embarrassed them with my typical middle-class-teenager biased questions regarding shopping preferences. Carol asks me if I am familiar with *D-Mart*, and when I shake my head no she explains that *D-Mart* is a cheap store just one step above *Goodwill.* I can only assume that by asking them about their shopping habits I had, in Havisham's mind, inadvertently embarrassed the boys.

I realized then the two boys she was thinking of were Hector and Eduardo; two super-quiet, intensely shy Latinos that I have to pry words out of, one syllable at a time. (Later when I relate this story to Sara, she laughs and says something like "I have never ever been able to get Hector to say anything.") If Carol had actually read the lesson plan I was using she would have realized that it was, in fact, a critique of the white middle class biases she was accusing me of perpetuating.

And that was not all. Despite my low expectations of Carol, I was nevertheless astonished when, after acknowledging her racial identification faux pas, she did not offer to rewrite or drop that part of my evaluation. (I have since learned that Carol's hypersensitivity to issues of diversity may be rooted in the fact that her two adopted children are Guatemalan.)

Moving right along, I then made the mistake of asking about my chances of being rehired in June. She told me that, because I have no credential, the district is required to advertise every year for my position and the three other positions filled with non-credentialed (PIP) teachers. According to Carol, while it is uncommon to replace a teacher who is doing a good job, it can happen if a qualified teacher applies for one of the jobs.

"I don't like this any more than you, but my hands are tied by the *No Child Left Behind* mandate to reduce the number of unqualified teachers. I just want to be honest with you Erik. It could happen." (Of course I checked later with my one reliable source in HR, and though what Carol said is technically true, it rarely happens that a competent, non-credential teacher is replaced.)

I felt like I had been poked in the stomach, not stunned, but shaken. Back in June when I was hired, Ms. I-want-to-be-honest-with-you Havisham had given me the distinct impression that, as long as I did a good job and made progress towards obtaining a credential, I would be offered a job next year. By now the conversation was becoming surreal and I decided to bite my already scarred tongue, cut my losses and get the hell out of her office.

Her Summary Comments were pretty much on point, aside from the equity bullshit of course:

> **SUMMARY COMMENTS OF EVALUATOR:**
> These comments may include commendations for performance exceeding standards.
>
> New to the teaching profession, Mr. Mandel has had a steep learning curve. Despite this challenge, he has demonstrated growth in the areas of lesson planning, lesson delivery and the implementation of state standards. Key components of classroom management are in place with his students following procedures and teacher directives. Daily lessons contain three or four learning activities with two, sometimes three – teacher directed. Areas for focus and improvement continue to center around the need to increase pacing, the amount and level of standards based curriculum addressed, implementation of a variety of effective instructional strategies, implementation of strategies which address equity issues and the meeting of IEP compliance issues.

and the wisdom to know the difference...

After sharing the entire report with Sara, I decided to respond in writing to the equity issue. Last week I sent Carol the following sugarcoated sycophantic email:

Carol,

Thanks for all the work and constructive comments you provided me during my latest evaluation. I do appreciate all the help you have given me and in general I feel your comments were fair and accurate. However, I would like an opportunity to reply to the "equity" comments you made under Standard I. I did discuss the issues with you in person during our meeting, but

I think it is important I address my concerns in a more formal manner.

Could you please send me an electronic copy of my evaluation so I can reply to my area of concern?

Thanks.

Eric

When Carol emailed me requesting a Monday meeting to discuss a "remedial plan" for me (I would have preferred the term *improvement plan*) and made no mention of my request for an electronic copy of my evaluation, I emailed her another request immediately. Ten minutes later the electronic copy arrived along with a curt *Here it is*. I am curious and apprehensive about tomorrow's meeting. Initially I worried that my official written reply to her evaluation might worsen things between us, but I decided, *What the fuck! I am a big boy. I can take care of myself.*

I am tired, cranky and hungry, but I don't want to end this entry on a downer. Speaking of unqualified teachers and credentials and stuff, enter Sally Smuts, my foil from the *New Teacher Academy*, the woman who thought Maya Angelou wasn't qualified to teach high school English because she doesn't have a valid California teaching credential. Ms. Smutts is an obnoxious know-it-all who has a not so subtle way of letting you know what a wonderful teacher she is. Well, I have been working with Sally on some English Department stuff, and while I still find her as annoying as hell, droning on and on about her asshole ex-husband, she is also very entertaining.

I was even beginning to wonder if I had been wrong early on when I had decided Sally was a horrible inflexible bitch of a teacher, but I soon learned that there was no need to worry. On Friday I mention to Sara in passing what an odd person Sally is, and Sara surprisingly comes back with an out-of-character, "I can't stand that bitch."

I laugh...

Sara is one of those positive nurturing people who can always find a good thing to say about almost anybody. Sara went on to tell me how earlier in the fall students circulated a petition to get rid of Ms. Sally. I smiled broadly and asked why she hadn't shared this precious nugget with me before, adding that from now on she must make every effort to keep me current on all the juicy school-related gossip. After all, Sara is my mentor and knows I am keeping a journal; shouldn't it be part of her duty to furnish with me with more grist for my mill?

Anyway, it is a relief to have my initial judgment validated so unequivocally.

Despite the fact that we have totally opposite styles and outlooks, Sara and I get along well. While at times she comes off as a hypersensitive PC type, she is a wonderful teacher. A fellow UCSC grad, Sara is more progressive and open-minded than most of the faculty. More importantly, despite the fact she is in her mid-thirties, she loves Van Morrison. Musical taste to me is critical in calibrating a person's cool quotient. (But one does need to use caution when equating musical taste with overall intelligence. I have heard vicious rumors, that President Bush loves Van. Enough said.) I loaned Sara a copy of Charles Bukowski's *Love is a Mad Dog from Hell.* Sara told me some time ago that she had attempted reading Bukowski during college and had hated him.

"Too sexist and misogynist for you?" I asked.

"I guess," she replied, "but I am willing to give him another try."

"Bukowski objectifies everyone, including himself."

BORN TO RUIN

A few days after loaning her the book, Sara admitted liking some of Bukowski's poems. Maybe it has something to do with the fact that she has lived a little since college, or maybe it has more to do with me telling her that Bukowski was an exceptionally ugly hunk of flesh.

A disclaimer before I bid good night: While many of the educators I write about are assholes and some are incompetent, every educator I have met thus far cares about the students and is doing what he or she thinks—in accordance with their abilities and the myopic rules and regulations they are saddled with—is best for the kids. And almost without exception my fellow teachers have been helpful and eager to share teaching ideas with me. Several have gone out of their way to assist me with the multitude of problems I have been facing this year.

There, now I can sleep tonight.

One final thing: I swore in front of the kids for the first time last week. That it took this long may come as a surprise to some readers as I am so free with my *fucks* and *shits* in these pages, but I do work hard at compartmentalizing my personas. Two kids, Tony the boxer and David, Jasmine's boyfriend, were goofing around making gang signs and snide gang comments while I was trying to read *The Great Gatsby* to the class. (Remember the book I used in my job interview to show off my literary criticism skills? Green light, pitfalls of fame, Paris Hilton and stuff?) I got pretty frustrated at their shenanigans and blurted out, "Just cut out your stupid gang shit!"

"Ewwww Mr. Mandel, you just swore." And then to rub my face in it, "You said shit. shit, shit."

I did my best to downplay the whole thing, but some of the kids thought they had me, and a few even teasingly threatened to turn me in. Sensitive serenity-filled

Melody could not resist the opening and took a cheap shot. Because I had reprimanded Melody many times for her inability to string two sentences together without dropping the f-bomb, s-bomb or any other explosive expletive, I knew what was coming. "Mr. Mandel how can you expect me to improve my language when you set such a poor example?"

"Well Mel," I reply, "just think how much more effective your swearing would be if you only swore in class once a year."

I wasn't too worried about being outed, but to play it safe I decided not to send any kids to the office for misconduct for the rest of the day—no matter how deserving—just in case they decided to use my profanities as a bargaining chip in negotiating a reduced sentence. Actually, losing control and swearing felt damn good. Shocked them and me for a second. I am sure it will happen again, if they keep me around long enough.

VII

Evaluation Row

Saturday - February 2

My remediation meeting with Carol last week went pretty much as I had expected. She prepared nothing in advance, and I sat quietly as she crafted an impromptu improvement plan to assist my development as a teacher. It was quite remarkable to observe Carol's mind in action as she struggled to formulate her ideas and to translate those ideas into words, eventually producing a plan that fit her nebulous vision. Carol wrote as she thought out loud, and I was uncertain whether she was expecting feedback or simply talking to herself. Her finished document, in outline form, detailed how she saw me improving my direct instructional skills and using the hundred minutes of classroom instructional time more efficiently.

It is clear to me now that Carol and I do not share a common point of view on what works best in the classroom. To be honest, I am not even sure we share a common language. I feel strongly that some of her ideas are actually detrimental both to my students' education and to my own development as a teacher. It is becoming more and more apparent that Carol has not spent significant time in the classroom recently, and it wouldn't surprise me to learn she has never taught a resource class. The Ice Queen's expectations are far too ambitious, and if I implemented them I would be setting the kids up for something they already have too much experience with—failure.

Now mind you, this is the same woman who earlier in the year, in response to a question from me about grading resource students, begrudgingly explained that if she were teaching and she had one student who worked hard and was cooperative but because of limitations was unable to earn a C, and another student who was too lazy to turn in class work and was disruptive but because of innate smarts aced tests and scored high enough to get a good grade, she would probably give both of them C's regardless of their actual point totals. It seems she wants me to develop a challenging curriculum that pushes my students beyond their limits, and at the same time she wants me to customize my grading system to fit each individual's perceived capabilities.

Talk about mixed signals!!! What is a poor boy to do?

Talk about ironic!!! I wonder why Carol doesn't evaluate me on a similar sliding scale. I try hard, turn in all my work, do everything asked of me, but because of limitations and a lack of teaching experience I am unable to perform at the same high level as my "highly qualified" colleagues.

One concession Carol did make was to drop the "diversity" issue, a small victory. Oh, and she did tell me Ethan had said I was doing a great job with my IEP's. After consulting with colleagues, my current strategy for dealing with Carol's plan is to go through the motions of

EVALUATION ROW

adhering to it, and to have grammar worksheets at the ready in the event she does pop in this month as promised. In the meantime, I will work seriously on the areas I am weak in, especially writing instruction. In spite of my hostility towards my boss, I do honestly want to be the best teacher I can possibly be.

Before I left her office we discussed how my students are doing on the exit exam (the CAHSEE). This is the first year that exemptions will not be granted *en masse* to the tens of thousand of resource students in California who will not have passed the exam by the end of their senior year. Currently more than 60% of the seniors in our resource program have already passed the exam. I made the mistake of telling Carol I thought that 60% was pretty good. She let me know that she will not be satisfied until we reach the goal set by the board, that 70% of our resource kids pass the exit exam. Carol then went on to rant about how (super-affluent) Los Gatos High School had already exceeded 70%. I resisted bringing up the obvious differences between our student populations, differences that easily explain the higher scores. I have learned it is best when dealing with Carol to constrain my comments. I kept my mouth shut, grimaced a tight-lipped smile and left.

Carol's evaluation would be even more frustrating and disheartening if not for the positive feedback and support I get from my students and colleagues. For instance, a few days earlier, David (Third Block) told me that I was one of his favorite teachers. "Top ten," David said, "going all the way back to 6th grade." Not bad for an old man who, in truth, is basically improvising. I know that most of the kids like me, but I'm not sure of my effectiveness as a teacher—of how much my students are actually learning.

They do seem to be enjoying themselves—too much at times.

Yesterday I had a heart-to heart with Randy, the mentor teacher who drops in almost weekly to observe and give advice. Randy thinks I am doing a great job for a new teacher, with or without a credential, and feels I am a real asset to the school. It is becoming less likely by the day that I will be offered a contract for next year, and it may have nothing to do with my performance. The state is facing a massive budget shortfall and the school may need to cut more than a million dollars from the budget. The entire faculty received letters last week explaining the dire situation and asking for volunteers willing to reduce their work schedule 20%. The district is offering volunteers a continuation of their benefits at the current 100% level. I am guessing that the non-credentialed teachers, and that includes me, are going to be the first ones released when layoffs begin.

Losing the job is not the real bummer for me; I never really expected to have an honest to god teaching job. The real bummer is realizing how much better my teaching would be next year, and how much easier the job would be with a year's experience under my belt. And then there is the expertise I have picked up in the areas of special ed rules, mandates and paperwork, and the skills I have developed in dealing with challenging personalities—and I am not talking about just my students.

Now some student news: Dark brooding Tomas turned eighteen early last week and immediately left school for the greener pastures of adult ed. I will not miss Toxic Tomas. I never did figure out a way to make it work. Toward the end Tomas sat quietly drawing and doodling, speaking only when he felt the urge to criticize me for

EVALUATION ROW

something I said that did not meet his supercilious standards. Sidekick Jorge remains, but hopefully his days of tormenting me are numbered. Lately I have begun tightening the screws: writing him up, calling his parents and sending him to the office at least once a week. So far Jorge seems oblivious to these threats and consequences.

Serenity Melody is gone for good for the third time. When her mother called her counselor to alert the school that Mel had once again run away to Fresno, the counselor explained to Mom that eighteen year-olds don't technically run away, they just leave. As bright and interesting as she was, her antics and the constant disruptions were exhausting.

The last time I saw Mel she came into my afternoon class ten minutes early in a manic state and could barely contain herself, "Mr. Mandel, I am so happy today. I just found out two guys really like me. It could get complicated, but they both are totally hot."

My mouth full of *Trader Joe's* strawberry yogurt, I mumbled something while Mel rambled manically on until, mercifully, other kids began to appear. I don't mean to sound fed-up and lacking in compassion, but the girl finally just wore me down. I can honestly say that regardless of how entertaining or tragic her life has been, I don't want to see her walk into my class again.

A large portion of my male students are into metal music and they dress and act the part: skinny boys, both Latino and Anglo, in metal-head fashion rigor: black jeans and black t-shirts with the name of some metal band I have never heard of emblazoned across their chests. A few actually play in bands. Most of these boys seem to be fascinated by violence. The other day when the class was in the library, one my metal-boys, Miles, a contrary and

163

somewhat paranoid musician, sat alone at a table reading *Psychology Today*. I approached his table and began quizzing him about things he likes to read; favorite books, his interests, stuff like that. (I do my best during our biweekly library visits to find anything that might interest my least enthusiastic readers.) Miles' initial reaction was defensive, as if it were an inquisition, and he demanded to know why I was asking him such personal questions.

Miles eventually relaxed during my interrogation and opened up enough to tell me that his band *DFN (Damn Fucking Nomads*—Miles and his band-mates evidently think that nomads is a synonym for Arabs), plays metal and country fusion. The only book Miles willingly admitted he ever enjoyed reading even a little was *Lord of the Flies,* mainly because of the violence and the killings. After some further resistance and more denials, he also copped to reading some Stephen King novels.

I sense an opening and move quickly. I head for the shelves and return minutes later with *Helter Skelter,* the brutal and fascinating account of the *Manson Family* murders. If Miles wants violence, I am going to fool him with some decent and complex character-driven literature disguised by a gift-wrapping of blood and terror. I hand him the book, ask him to give the first few pages a try, and if they grab his attention, to check it out and read it for extra credit.

A few moments later dark thoughts begin to make their way into the paranoid recesses of my brain. *Am I encouraging deviant behavior? Am I feeding a beast that could turn the as yet still innocent Miles into a mass murderer?* My instinct is that reading is so important to these kids that the risk is worthwhile, but to play it safe and cover my rookie ass I decide to check with the expert-in-residence, Doug the

Librarian. I share my concerns with Doug and his initial response is "Of course it's ok, I have the book in the library after all."

"Yeah," I reply, "but I am the one who actually took the book off the shelf and handed it to Miles."

Doug half-jokingly agrees that perhaps that puts me in greater legal jeopardy than he if Miles were to go off on a brutal murder spree.

"Just tell me I did the right thing Doug. You're the expert"

"You did fine, if that makes you feel better."

"Oh now I feel better. I just transferred most of the weight off my shoulders onto yours."

Needless to say I have mixed feelings the following day during SSR when I notice Miles intently reading *Helter Skelter,* and it appears he is already more than halfway through the book. In all seriousness, the crucial point to both Doug and me is that these kids read something; anything is better than nothing. Numerous studies show— —despite Carol's adamant antipathy toward SSR—that the availability of reading material in the home is a strong predictor of a child's future academic achievement.

Back in the library, I am sitting at a table just shooting the breeze with Luke, a bright, uncooperative lazy junior, and three other less-than-stellar students. The conversation somehow turns to my grading policy. Throughout the year Luke has constantly inquired about his grade, primarily because he is concerned about remaining academically eligible to wrestle, and wants to avoid being grounded at home. His goal is to maintain a C or C+. Luke is a lot like a binge eater; he waits for his grade to sink to a D and then decides to gorge himself by binge catching-up on most of his missing work. Then, when his grade reaches the desired level, Luke stops feeding his brain as abruptly as he began. Once again I digress. Luke wants to know how I calculate grades, so I explain my grading rubric and other stuff Luke could not care less about. In response he opines that I never assign any real work and have no real system. He claims that really my grading method is to look at the students and guess what grade they would get if I actually assigned real work. To protect what is left of my reputation I protest just enough; Luke, however, might be closer to the truth than I want to admit.

Thursday – February 14

The Digital Divide...I am competent in computer basics, but when I accepted this job I worried that in the hyper-tech world of education I might lack the tech savvy to keep pace with my peers. As it turns out there was no need to fret. While the district enthusiastically supports standards-based data-driven instruction, it is seriously lagging in its support for that other popular educational advance—the extensive use of modern technology in the delivery of instruction. San Benito High School classrooms are furnished with the following four technological tools: a telephone, a computer for teacher use, a whiteboard or blackboard, and an overhead projector. Televisions, VCRs, DVDs, and a minimal number of LCD projectors are available for checkout from the library. That's basically it. Oh and one more thing, there is no school-wide intercom system. This limits intra-campus communications to emails, telephones, messengers, smoke signals and the beating of drums. The majority of teachers procure their own technological tools including LCD projectors, televisions, VCRs, DVD players, and laptops to use with LCD projectors. To my knowledge, the only electronic smart-board that exists on campus is kept in the library and is used primarily for board presentations. Because I am able to share a TV-VCR-DVD cart with two other teachers, I am luckier than many. And although I have access to a colleague's LCD projector, I do 95% of my communicating by mouth, body language, whiteboard and overhead projector. I guess you can consider me old-school by necessity.

The reliance on technology varies greatly among the faculty, and the attitudes about its use mirror those of society at large. The younger teachers tend to embrace all the latest tools with ease, while their older colleagues tend to resist adapting for as long as possible. Two examples that illustrate the extremes: Brandon, an eager twenty-something first-year social studies teacher fresh out of a master's program, uses Microsoft Power Point for all his lessons; John, a grumpy sixty-something veteran chemistry teacher, resisting the advent of computers 'til his last breath, refuses to use email and still does his grades by hand. I fall somewhere in between. I rely mainly on overheads and the blackboard, occasionally using more high-tech tools from a laser pointer to an LED projector. My major contribution to modern classroom technology at San Benito High was to use my maintenance and supervisory background to befriend the maintenance crew, thus avoiding the lengthy bureaucratic requisition system, and have Sara's, Liz's and my antique chalkboards replaced with—those wonders of technology—whiteboards. When I originally told Sara of my back channel plans to get the whiteboards, she told me that she had been trying to get one for over two years and advised me not to waste my time. The afternoon the whiteboards arrived both Liz and Sara were surprised and thrilled, and from their expressions of gratitude you would have thought I had parted the Red Sea.

Saturday - March 1

Brief update re: *Havisham v. Mandel:* About two weeks ago Carol showed up unannounced during Fifth Block, my worst behaved group, that lovely group of lost seniors, some angry, most hiding their fears behind the thinnest veneers of macho bravado. I wonder if Carol even noticed that the class she was observing was 100% male testosterone, as the poor lone female was absent that day. Oh yeah, to make things worse, dark brooding Toxic Tomas had returned that day after a failed one-week stint in the not so green pastures of adult ed, to dance once again with his amigo Jorge in their volatile, incessant, *ese vato* tango.

As Carol entered I was standing in front of the class reading from *A Parrot in the Oven,* a fictional coming of age novel set in Fresno in the late 1970's, about Manny Hernandez, a smart, out-of-place, fourteen year-old Chicano and his dysfunctional family. (During our last meeting Carol had asked to see a copy of *Parrot in Oven.* When I handed her one, she fanned through it for a few seconds, and then offered her snap judgment based solely on type size and word length, proclaiming, "This is 9th grade reading level at best." Thankfully I was too annoyed at the time to point out the ineptitude of her remark.) I have to admit that the boys were remarkably well behaved while Carol was there. With Carol present, we finished a chapter about Manny and his mother taking his sixteen year-old sister by city bus to the hospital after her miscarriage. As the Ice Queen made her exit I thought to myself, *all things considered, that went pretty well.*

After Carol's departure I commend the class for behaving so well, and Oliver informs me there is no need for me to sweat it when "your boss lady comes to check up on you". According to Oliver, the kids all know the game and how to play it. Oliver then reveals a tried and tested plan they hatched with a teacher last year, a certain notorious educator who eventually got fired for, among other things, giving the kids money and letting them climb out the window during class to go downtown. The plan worked something like this: When Mr. P was being observed by his evaluator as he led a discussion and asked the class questions, every kid would enthusiastically wave his or her hand. The students who knew the correct answer raised their left hands, while the clueless ones raised their right.

"Brilliant" I reply to Oliver. "But what happened when there were no left hands raised?"

He laughs. Hey, Oliver got my joke. All is not lost. They are learning something.

It's a shame the way she makes me scrub the floor...

Two days ago I received Carol's classroom observation evaluation in the school mail. Boss Lady reamed me pretty good for a variety of failures, among them neglecting to teach to the state standards, and failing to develop students' higher thinking skills. As incompetent as I think Carol is, this particular observation startled me. I never imagined anyone, even Carol, would judge an entire lesson based solely on a small slice of observed instruction. Also, I thought that for the twenty minutes she was in my class the kids were on task and that the lesson accomplished both of the criteria she named.

If Her Majesty had had the decency to talk to me before writing her evaluation, I would have explained how everything she observed was tied to a larger assignment. The class had been following Manny's character development, citing and charting quotes from throughout *A Parrot in the Oven*, and working with literary terms such as interior monologue, action and dialogue. By the time the class completed the novel, they theoretically would be able to write a high level essay, incorporating the author's methods of developing the protagonist. But Carol never asked.

Next week I have some meetings planned with Sara, Doug and Jennifer, the administrator in charge of new teachers, to discuss my "situation". I realize I am involved in a battle I can't win, but at this point I see no option but to fight on. If I lose my job due to budget cuts I will understand. I mean, duh, I am second to last on the seniority list. However if I get fired for incompetence because of this crazy lady and her unreasonable expectations, I will be pissed. I plan to go down fighting.

When I shared my recent evaluation with Sara, she told me she thought the criticism, even considering the source, amazingly narrow-minded. Sara went on to confide in me her earlier serious concerns for my mental well-being during my first two or three weeks on the job. She had expected me to bail at any moment from all the stress generated by the intensely steep learning curve I had faced, combined with my frustration around the lack of meaningful administrative support. In reply to Sara's revelation and concern, I did confirm that my mental state had been pretty fragile during those intense weeks;

however I told her, as bad as things were, not once did I seriously consider quitting.

A side note regarding Carol's recent observation: Randy, the perennially gym-shorted mentor who has the responsibility of observing and advising all new teachers, observed me teaching essentially the same lesson (re: the miscarriage) that Carol had observed a day earlier. Randy had nothing but good things to say about the lesson. Granted, the lesson Randy observed was far more interesting, mainly because Jorge was fully engaged in trying to one-up the fictional Manny by boasting to his classmates about the night a few years ago when his sixteen year-old sister gave birth in *Technicolor* reality, right smack in the middle of the kitchen. (Jorge added that the long lasting gross-out effect still makes it all but impossible for him to eat in that room, and that his sister got married last weekend in Las Vegas with the help of an Elvis impersonator.)

I really am trying hard to keep the Carol sections brief, but it seems my seething fury consistently trumps my desire for brevity.

Moving on to my caseload and the last batch of IEP's I completed in February. Due to my lack of foresight, my choice to concentrate on teaching, and my *procrastinatorial* nature, I got myself into a precarious situation—I had five IEP's scheduled over an eight-day period. Actually it wasn't as bad as I had originally feared, and now is a good a time to shed some light on these five kids who are a fair sample of the various types of kids, who end up in resource programs.

Before I go into details, a little primer on IEP terms and practices. My caseload began with twenty-five students. (I think I have lost three or four due to expulsions and other events.) About half I know well because I have them in my classes. The state requires districts to hold formal IEP meetings annually for every resource student. In my role as caseworker I am responsible for planning, facilitating, and doing all the paper work for these meetings. In addition, I am responsible for dealing with a myriad of issues that come up during the year and many may necessitate additional meetings.

The typical annual IEP meeting deals with the student's progress and his or her transition plan for after high school. The IEP team consists of the student, the parents, teachers, guidance counselors, an administrator, vocational specialists, the resource specialist (me), and at times, the school psychologist. However the actual meeting attendees generally are the student, one parent, a counselor, a vocational specialist and me. On occasion, due to scheduling conflicts, the meeting may consist of only the kid, one parent and me. If necessary the meeting may be conducted by telephone. Every three years a *Triennial IEP* is held. (So far I have yet to hear anyone, administrators and teachers included, correctly pronounce the term *triennial*. They all say *triannual*.) The Tri is the critical meeting during which we determine the student's continued eligibility for special services. We assess eligibility through various tests that the school psychologist summarizes in the psych report, a document of at least a dozen pages. These meetings require all sorts of additional work and scheduling, and involve mountains of extra red tape.

While I am on this subject let me say a thing or two, all bad of course, about Priscilla the school psychologist, a middle-age blonde with a thick Texas drawl, who also coaches the girls' swim team. She is flat-out weird. When Priscilla presents the critical psych report at the meetings, she makes no effort to explain the complex report to the students and parents in language they might actually understand. Several times I have watched helplessly as Priscilla droned on and on, looking bored, her face tilted to the side and resting on one hand, her blond hair hanging to the table, reading word-for-word the key parts of the actual report which are quite technical and full of psycho-jargon. To date and without fail. after Priscilla exits a meeting I am facilitating, the parent asks me to explain what Priscilla has just said. Sara calls this part of our job *damage control.*

Now to those five IEP's:

Valerie, an eighteen year-old senior who is on track to graduate in June, sorta. Valerie is a freckle-faced bubbly pretty girl who has been taking all regular ed classes throughout her high school career. In special ed jargon she is known as a W/C (watch and consult). This term is used for students who have some relatively minor processing disorder that doesn't prevent them from succeeding in all regular classes. Teachers in these classes must provide the W/C students some individual accommodations (more detailed instructions, un-timed tests, etc.). Depending on the learning handicaps, resource kids can be enrolled in from zero to four resource classes. The resource classes offered are basically the core curriculum: English, several levels of math, chem survey, US government, economics and world studies. W/C students take all their classes, including electives, within the general ed population.

Valerie did quite well up to and through her junior year, but at present a severe case of senioritis is jeopardizing her graduation in June, and is also driving her mother crazy. I have had ongoing discussions with both Valerie and her mother throughout the school year and have a good rapport with both, although at times it has been a delicate balance. Prior to the meeting, I discovered Valerie had missed twenty-seven classes the first semester due to visits to the counselor's office, either for a scheduled weekly "girl group" or for various emotional "emergencies." Turns out she has been meeting with two different counselors and neither knew the other was also seeing her. Even more surprising, one counselor was totally unaware that Valerie was a resource student. Of course missing all that class time has been affecting Valerie's grades, and she is currently failing both English and US government.

Her parents were unaware of either the number of absences or the reasons for them, and to complicate things further, Valerie turned eighteen the day before the meeting. As you know, when a child turns eighteen he or she is magically transformed (by law, not the good fairy) into an adult with all the privileges (except drinking, as I am often reminded by my students) and responsibilities that come with this instantaneous metamorphosis. As eighteen year-olds, students may deny parents access to all their records, and they can actually (though most aren't hip enough to know this) excuse their own tardies and absences. During my pre-conference meeting with Valerie, one that took place on her birthday, we discussed her attendance and her excessive counselor visits. After wishing her a happy birthday, I asked point blank how she wanted me to handle these issues in front of her parents. We eventually worked out a strategy: If the subject came up Valerie would deal with it directly in her own words. It did come up, and everything turned out okay, but I made it clear to her parents that, in the eyes of the law, their little girl was now an adult. I had not been given any guidance about what to do or say in this commonly occurring situation, and when the meeting ended I felt uneasy.

Hoping for some answers and to ease my discomfort, I phoned Ethan and asked for his advice after the fact. Sgt. Putzmire acknowledged that it could be a problem at times. According to Putzmire, the rule of thumb in these situations is, unless the student is facing physical endangerment by the withholding of information, don't tell the parents anything the student doesn't want them to know. Then Ethan added that most of our students never realize the extent of their own authority when they become eighteen, and while we are legally required to inform them of their rights in writing, it is generally best not to emphasize this fact.

Natalie, a senior I have mentioned earlier in regards to her desire to leave SBHS and enter adult ed as soon as possible after she turns eighteen in March. Natalie's complaints, as you may recall, were about having no friends at school, her parents never being home, and most importantly, the fact her boyfriend lives in the East Bay. This IEP, Natalie's last before her departure, was to center on helping her with a smooth transition to adult ed. Like most meetings, Natalie's took place in my classroom. In attendance were Natalie, her speed-freak mom, her counselor, the vocational specialist and me. It didn't take long to discover that, yes, Natalie was leaving in March, but her plans had changed. She now planned to move in with her boyfriend, enroll in adult ed in Antioch (about 50 miles north of Hollister) and get a job as a nanny for her boyfriend's sister-in-law.

Oh, one more thing, Natalie is pregnant, and apparently very happily so. Her mother seemed genuinely excited about the pregnancy and went out of her way to thank the school for teaching Natalie about proper diet, nutrition and the do's and don't of having a healthy baby. Mom said something to the effect that her daughter knows more about good nutrition and child rearing than she did at Natalie's age. *Or at any age,* I thought snarkily to myself. Natalie is a real sweetheart, one of my best students, and I hope, despite the odds, that life works out for her.

Tara, a high performing junior, taking all regular ed classes, and like Valerie a W/C student. Tara wasn't in any of my classes, and I didn't actually meet her until a few days prior to the IEP. The meeting was a triennial, and the testing done a few weeks prior to the meeting had established that Tara was no longer eligible for special ed and all the accompanying services. That is a good thing of course; nevertheless some parents don't want to give up the perks their kids gain from being in the program. I wasn't sure what to expect at the meeting when we informed Tara and her mom of Tara's loss of eligibility for the first time. Turns out Mom and Tara were thrilled. Mom's only concern was about a smooth transition; I assured her I would do my best to shepherd her daughter into the mainstream.

Selma, a hard working, over-achieving developmentally delayed (nee: borderline retarded) senior. Selma has a 3.0 GPA and is on track to graduate in June except for one critical fact, she has not passed either exit exam. Selma is relatively close to passing the English exam, but I can see no way she will ever pass the math exam. Selma is a poster girl for the damage the exit exam can wreak on hardworking and dedicated students who simply are not smart enough to pass it. Her mother works nights as a hospital orderly and shows genuine concern for her daughter's future. Sadly complicating matters, Selma has a severely retarded older bother. I met her brother, Rico, when he attended his sister's IEP. Rico can't walk or talk, but he seems to smile and laugh a lot. Selma's hopes to eventually find work in the health field like her mom. I think she is capable of that. Because Selma has a hearing problem, her mother is currently checking to see if there are stethoscopes for the hearing impaired.

Selma is a joy to have in class, a refreshing antidote to all the negative, lazy and disruptive kids. Selma writes surprisingly well and one would never know that her IQ is as low as it is. Below is Selma's homework assignment from a few weeks back. It truly reflects the good, the bad and the ugly of her situation. (She was only one of three students who actually completed this homework assignment, a typical result for my classes.) In clear firm handwriting she wrote:

> If I were to vote, I would vote for Barak Obama or John McCain to join the presidency... Some of the reasons I would vote for Barak Obama, is that he wants to bring our troops back home and he knows that it will maybe take years for that to happen. Also Obama wants to protect our country as well, he shows that he really cares about the people in this country. And this the first time we might have a black president since Martin Luther King Jr. became president...

Garrett, a blond longhaired junior with an IQ of 130, is the intellectual flipside of Selma. What the hell is a boy with a superior IQ doing in special ed??? Here's the scoop as I know it: Although Garrett's IQ is higher than 97% of all his fellow students—as well as most of his teachers and every administrator I have ever worked with—test results demonstrate Garrett's relatively low performance in certain areas and are evidence of an underlying, neurological processing problem. In real world language, Garrett has legitimate problems organizing and performing administrative tasks. And one more thing, in his former caseworker Sara's exact words, "Garrett is a lazy fuck."

At present Garrett is enrolled in regular classes except for chem survey and has an overall 1.5 GPA. Apparently Garrett's *modus operandi* is to refuse to take any notes or do any homework. He relies solely on his inherent smarts to ace his tests, and he usually does. However Garrett's refusal to do class work drags his high tests scores down. Not surprisingly, Garrett suffers from a serious case of ennui at school and at home. This situation is a constant source of frustration for his alternate-life-style parents, as their son's behavior propels them down the road to wits' ends. Garrett's problem stems in part from a classic case of bored super-bright student in need of more challenge. But his primary problem is his total unwillingness to put out any real effort. This is seriously compounded by the fact that he has no idea what he wants to do when he grows up. Regardless of all this, and in spite of his continued technical eligibility for special services, Garrett's parents, with the support of the IEP team, decided to refuse special services and instead, to toss the boy into the pool with the general population next school year to see if he sinks or swims.

Saturday - March 8

I was going to start with a quick update on the usual extra-curricular bullshit, the war with the Ice Queen, IEP case work, budget cuts and pending teacher layoffs, but I was afraid I would get caught in my typical scenario of turning a quick update into a lengthy diatribe; so forget that stuff for a while and let's get back to the teaching.

Day by day, with an exception here and there, teaching gets easier and more fun. I can sense myself becoming better, more confident and more relaxed. I am reaching my stride and am traveling full circle back to the real me—the recognizable Eric who my friends and family know and love—the sweet compassionate Eric who often hides behind his sardonic veneer. My relationship with the majority of my students is strong. I appreciate them as individuals and most have some sense of who I am. I am more comfortable in my teaching skin these days, sometimes too comfortable. The kids I have been battling since day one, Toxic Tomas and Jorrid Jorge, remain serious problems and continue to adversely affect my teaching. Seems like the dance I have been doing with this duet is pretty much set in stone now, and I am close to giving up on the two of them.

Shit, who am I kidding? I have given up on them.

Wine for the soul

Laughter is wine for the soul—laugh soft, or loud and deep, tinged through with seriousness. Comedy and tragedy step through life together, arm in arm. The hilarious declaration made by man that life is worth living. Once we can laugh, we can live.

—Sean O'Casey

To the dismay of some, humor has always been a cornerstone of who I am (or who I think I am). I tend to use humor even if it has adverse results. I am a sucker for a joke, good or bad, even at my own expense. I have paid for this in the past and will no doubt pay more for it in the future. Even at my most hilarious, not everyone, even those close to me, thinks me funny. Sometimes I feel like I have some form of uncontrollable comic Tourette's syndrome. In the classroom I try to control myself somewhat, but occasionally I go too far out on a very shaky limb and am unable to scurry back to safety. Luckily, most of my dubious cracks zip straight over the students' heads and proceed unnoticed to their final resting place in bad-joke purgatory.

One thing I have observed about teenagers is that most have great difficulty understanding irony and self-deprecating humor. I think irony is beyond what their young and not yet fully developed minds are capable of grasping. In their need to project strength and maintain respect they mistake self-deprecation for weakness. The irony, in my mind, is that making fun of one's self is actually a sign of a healthy self-image, a fair indication that you are comfortable with who you are. I don't want to sound too scatological (heavy on the BS), but it seems to me that understanding and appreciating both irony and self-deprecating humor depend on certain life experiences that most of my students have not yet had. Humility and self-deprecating humor go hand in hand, and while teens possess insecurity in spades, few have developed a sense of humility. And the objective of satire, as we remember from the Cowboy James' favorite song saga, is often incomprehensible to the teen mind. For many their humor consists of inane putdowns—*that's because you're gay*—or finding something they think hilarious and then running it into the ground.

As an educator I try and turn every possible opportunity into a teachable moment, and. as you may have noticed, I tend to veer off topic whenever an opening presents itself. For example, last Friday was *Leap Day* and I had the kids do a *Quick Write* describing what they thought was unusual about the date, February 29. Even after I wrote the hint *leap* on the board most remained clueless, and even more shocking, less than a handful actually knew what a year signified astronomically speaking; many also believed that the sun revolved around the earth. Whoa! I stopped my planned lesson and changed courses midstream, and for the next twenty minutes I made a ardent attempt to explain to them, in simple language, a year, a month and a day.

During Fifth Block a smiling and cocky Michael insisted I was wrong, and moreover that he could prove that the sun went around the earth. He pointed out, with the simplest of logic, that you can see the sun come up every morning and see it go down every night; in Michael's mind this proves that the earth sits still while the sun spends its days circling around it. In an effort to introduce the heliocentric solar system to Michael and friends, I brought out my big guns. I went over to my desk, took out an apple and a grape from my lunch bag and did my best Mr. Wizard imitation, using the apple as the earth and the grape as the sun. One of my smarter students tried to bust me with, "Mr. Mandel the sun is much bigger than the earth, you should use the apple as the sun and grape as the earth."

"I decided to use the grape as the sun." I tell them, "because Michael seems to rely almost entirely on what he sees. I was trying to avoid Michael's obvious question to me about the massive relative size of the apple/sun, something like, *'Can't you see Mr. Mandel when you look up in the sky the sun is smaller than a dime?'*" I decide, in the interest of time and concern for my long-term sanity, to forgo explaining the difference between observational evidence and empirical proof.

THE ACCIDENTAL TEACHER

I have learned that to have any hope that anything I teach will actually stick, I must give the students knowledge in small portions; if I dump too much stuff on them they shut down. Oops, I just realized I did the same thing to you, the reader, spinning off on a tangent in search of enlightenment. I'd better find my way out of this digression fast.

Of course when you play with humor, sometimes you get burned. I have the scars to prove it.

[Months after school had ended I heard survey results that forced me to reassess the idea that my students' knowledge base was well below that of the average American. According to a poll conducted by the *California Academy of Sciences*, 50% of Americans don't know how long a year is, and 41% believe that men and dinosaurs walked the earth at the same time. Resource students have a built-in excuse for their inabilities; there is only one excuse for the rest of us—a systemic failure of our educational system.]

Mr. Mandel's Badass Shoes

One day a couple of weeks ago during First Block, as I was working my butt off leading a discussion on white-black-brown race relations as they pertained to *The Parrot in the Oven*, I noticed Tony, not Two-Fisted Tony, but Smiling-Good-Natured-Pain-in-the-Ass Tony, ignoring me and passing notes. I continued teaching and approached his desk, signaling Tony with my outstretched hand to give me the tiny, shriveled-up note. Tony complied. I took a quick peek at the poorly scribbled, quarter-sized memo and continued with my lesson.

The note reads: *mr mandels shoes are badass* (the badass shoes being the same brown, nerdy clogs I have worn all year). I chuckle to myself. I decide to ignore the harmless incident and go on with the lesson as if nothing has happened. Gotta love Tony. He works much harder at distracting me than he does on his class work and he has a D- to prove it. Another plus, Tony bears no grudges.

Last Thursday, with the incident all but forgotten, as I am trying to teach the same class, Smiling Tony, totally ignoring the lesson of course, picks a tiny, balled-up scrap of paper off the floor near my desk, and laughing, shows it to one of his partners in crime. Just like a note in a bottle washed up on a faraway shore, Tony's badass note found its way home; the same silly note I thought I had tossed in the trash a week earlier is now back in its place of origin, Tony's hand. Tony can't resist busting into my lesson and sharing his discovery with the class, resurrecting my badass shoes and laughing like it was the funniest thing in the world.

Sensing another one of those teachable moments, I harangue him with something like, "Tony it might have been funny the first time, but you always run your jokes into the ground. Look around the class. Notice the only guys laughing are you and your three stooges. You just can't repeat *badass* over and over and think that the more you say it the funnier it gets." Handing out sage advice like candy I explain, "It is funnier if you vary your jokes a bit from time to time, and not just blurt out *badass* over and over. "

Of course they got a real kick out of *me* repeating *badass* over and over. Eventually I did get back on track, finished my lesson and dismissed the class. I assumed, once again, the *badass incident* had been run into the ground and was buried for good.

And I was wrong once again!

Almost immediately after class ended I held a scheduled IEP meeting in one corner of my room. After the meeting ended and the participants were gone, I was sitting at my desk in my empty classroom eating yogurt and drinking root beer when I noticed five tiny shreds of paper hanging by scotch tape over the front edge of Tony's and the four neighboring desks. Curious, I stopped eating, got up, walked over and collected them one by one, starting with the by now hackneyed original, *mr mandels shoes are badass* and then in the following order: *mr mandels shirt is badass, mr mandels pants are badass, mr mandels watch is badass*...and finally with a flourish, from Josh's desk, *mr mandels smile is badass*.

I guess you do reap what you sow. I chuckled out loud to myself—it was pretty funny. I decided to share the story and the notes with Sara. I wasn't sure how she would react. Would she laugh or think I was a fool for letting the kids make an ass of me? Sara knows all the kids involved, and like most resource teachers has a good sense of humor, so I was almost certain she would appreciate the prank. She read each of the notes and cracked up. Sara thought it was wonderful, and to her it implied a positive bonding; however she then felt compelled to add the obvious caveat—not all teachers and administrators might view the incident in the same light. I told her I was well aware of that fact, adding that the kids are actually smart enough to know what they can safely get away with—behavioral relativism of a sort.

After patting myself on the back, another note passing story brings me, and my ego, abruptly back to earth. About a month ago I confiscated the following flirty, serial note between recent *badass incident* participant Zeke, a pierced-eye-browed, sometimes disrespectful, black t-shirted, black-jeaned, metal-headed slacker, and Amy, a pretty A student with a touch of attitude:

EVALUATION ROW

Zeke: *your name is Amanda...that sucks..jk(*just kidding)*...
I'm bored*
Amy: *NO! It's Amy (*she hates to be called Amanda and she let's you know it) *and I'm bored too.* ☹
Zeke: *It's tard!!!! JK!!...This class is boring..*
Amy: *Those guys (*the stooges) *where you sit won't shut the fuck up! lol...It's annoying.*
Zeke: *lol. Yea true and I'm getting in most of the trouble. I should have sat away from them.* (Zeke doesn't shut the fuck up either btw)
Amy: *Yea I know you got sent out and you didn't do anything. Lol. Sorry.*
Zeke: *Actually I did do the noise (*loud tongue clicking) *that time.* ☺ ☺
Amy: *Oh haha stupid.....how is Holly (*no idea who she is)?
Zeke: *lol, yea. She's doing good...she left Michael and is with Kyle S..*
Amy: *good! I'm happy she's doing better. Does she still get to keep her kids? And yea do they live with her? Or do they still see Michael sometimes?*
Zeke: *Yea Yep. She keeps them since Michael never sees them anymore....*

I didn't comment on the note at the time. Actually I didn't read it until after school and was a little encouraged by the fact that, while both Zeke and Amy complained that my class was boring, neither stated directly that *I* was boring.

When Amy showed up early for the next class I mentioned the note and as she blushed I said, "Well at least you didn't say *I* was boring."

She smiled and said nothing, but her friend Lisa, a cute, curt senior, enthusiastically chirped, "Well *I* think you are boring Mr. Mandel."

VIII

In Dubious Battle

Now the bricks lay on Grand Street
Where the neon madmen climb.
They all fall there so perfectly,
It all seems so well timed.
An' here I sit so patiently
Waiting to find out what price
You have to pay to get out of
Going through all these things twice.
—Bob Dylan

I have become painfully aware that my narrative has been hijacked by my struggle with Carol. In order to keep the focus on my students, I've have considered reducing Carol's role and elbowing her into the background. I know that my ongoing battle with her brings out the worst in me: the vitriol, the sarcasm and the hostility towards authority. But because the conflict has affected my whole teaching experience to the point of poisoning what has been for the most part a wonderful journey, to de-emphasize

THE ACCIDENTAL TEACHER

Ms. Havisham's role for literary reasons would twist my memoir into a work of fiction. I see no option but to march on with a smile on my face and a song in my heart, slogging my way through the turbulent noxious muck.

Take a load off Fannie,
Take a load for free.
Take a load off Fannie,
And [and] [and]... you put the load right on me...

Now I'll be the first to admit that I can be a pain in the ass, or even at times a smug asshole. (Yes, exactly like some of the students I complain about constantly.) Throughout my career I've been a model low-maintenance employee who in general was liked and respected both by my superiors and by those I supervised. All I ever expected from my bosses was respect, definable expectations and clear direction—the same considerations I provided all my employees. And if there was an issue with my job performance, all I ever wanted was to have it explained to me clearly and directly.

There are few things in life I hate more than playing the lemming—doing something I don't understand, for reasons I can't grasp, in a way that makes absolutely no sense to me —for the sole purpose of mollifying superiors, many who have been flat-out idiots. I hope you can understand how my frustrations are building day by day as I struggle with the incompetence of others and hobble along the final leg of my journey.

Sunday - March 16
I'm out of excuses and can't avoid writing about The Meeting any longer. I did meet with

Carol last week and it left me more frustrated than ever. She is a real piece of work, like a Dickensian cartoon character or an alien, animated and predictable with just enough volatility to keep me off balance.

About a week before the meeting with Carol, I met with Sara and Jen, the vice-principal in charge of new teachers (and also Randy's wife), to discuss options. It was a good meeting and basically we concluded I needed to find a way to adapt to Carol's "philosophy", however faulty and unreasonable it may be. Carol is in the upper echelon of management, and regardless of how little everyone thinks of her, like it or not she is my boss. Jen made it quite clear, even after implying I was getting screwed, that it was basically up to me to rectify the situation.

Jen did offer the suggestion that Sara be included in my next meeting with Carol. She was surprised that Carol had failed to ask my mentor teacher for any feedback, and she thought it sensible to have Sara there not only to support me, but also to hear directly from Carol what she expected from me. I had considered this option but hadn't mentioned it earlier it for fear of putting Sara in an uncomfortable position. While Carol garners little respect from her staff, many are afraid of her. Sara enthusiastically agreed to accompany me to my meeting with the Ice Queen. During her four years at San Benito, Sara had never spent any real time with Carol and she was curious to see for herself exactly what this woman was really like. (Interestingly, Carol effusively sings Sara's praises for being a wonderful teacher despite never having observed her in the classroom.)

The day of the meeting got off to a rocky start. On the way to school I got stuck in traffic due to an eight-car collision on Hwy 101 at Rocks Rd (I just had to use that road's name. This is an old suicide alley section of 101 between Salinas and Gilroy that still has lots of cross traffic.) I arrived about five minutes before the bell for first period, and as I was parking my car I noticed that my familiar red San Benito High School lanyard with my school keys on it was not around my neck, a first for me. (I never thought I would be one of those dorky teachers with a key necklace, but it is just so damn convenient.) Keyless, I dreaded calling the office and asking them to send someone to open my door. Thankfully however, as I was walking to my room I saw a groundskeeper. He had a master key and let me in my room. One potential disaster averted. I was relieved but still stressed when, as I was putting my lunch book bag away, I noticed that everything in my man-purse (a black canvas bag with *Art breaks all the rules* emblazoned above a colorful cartoon painting) was wet and sticky. "Shit." I muttered.

As I dumped the crap out of my bag, I discovered that the bottle of designer root beer I had put in my lunch bag was now only a third full. Some stuff was ruined, including my school planner, no real loss. Most things were drenched in root beer, but thank god, and I use that term lightly, my digital camera remained above the fray, apparently saved by the wool shirt I had stuffed in the bottom of the bag. The shirt, clearly oblivious to the consequences of its actions, had sacrificed its own well being for the survival of my camera. When the students began arriving I was still bouncing around the room, muttering to myself and trying to limit the damage. My wallet was wet and sticky. I am sure the kids got a real kick out of watching Mr. Mandel mumble a variety of expletives while using baby wipes to clean his credit cards, drivers license and other assorted crap. Eventually, I did get my act together, but on the whole, not an auspicious beginning.

The meeting with Carol was scheduled for 1:30. Sara and I met at lunch to map out a strategy. During the lunch meeting we decided Sara would facilitate and referee the meeting. I did insist on opening the meeting with some comments regarding my major complaint: how Carol could justify changing my earlier rating of *Needs Improvement* to *Does Not Meet Standards* after one twenty-minute observation. As the two of us walked together over to Carol's office, Sara offered these last words of advice to me, "Don't be confrontational."

I promised to do my best.

Karaoke in the Cuckoo's Nest

Funny thing, when we arrived Carol wasn't expecting us. She had mistakenly put the meeting on her calendar for the following Tuesday. But fortunately, or at least that is what I thought at the time, Ms. Havisham did have time to see us and she graciously invited us to follow her back to her office. Moments later I was disappearing down the rabbit hole with Sara following close behind. After adjusting to the unfamiliar surroundings, I cut right to the chase and politely asked Carol to explain her rationale for lowering my rating to *Does Not Meet Standards*. She took a few seconds to organize her thoughts and then began to ramble. Her reason for the downgrade was that I did not offer enough variety in my lesson plans. She based this conclusion solely on my posted agenda for the day of her visit and not on observing me teach. Carol had determined that I did not take her suggestions seriously, that I had ignored her earlier recommendations and had made no effort to modify and vary my teaching methods.

THE ACCIDENTAL TEACHER

When I asked why she hadn't talked to me about these concerns prior to writing the final report, Carol insisted that sometime in the past she must have mentioned to me that it is my responsibility to approach her with my concerns, either during the observation or after. Putting aside the fact that Queen Carol had told me no such thing, I informed her I had had no reason to approach her during class or afterwards because, as far as I was concerned, my lesson had gone well, and I did not know otherwise until she shared her thoughts with me in the written report.

In preparing to make my case I had brought with me to the meeting an outline and some related paperwork from the five-week lesson plan I had developed myself for *The Parrot and the Oven,* a sliver of which she had observed and used as the sole basis for her evaluation. I handed my support documents to Carol and asked that she read them later, and after reading them perhaps reconsider her ratings. Carol mumbled a few words that in no way convinced me she would ever take the time to read my materials. We went round-and-round until finally, Sara broke in. In her calm, firm, resource teacher manner she did her best to rephrase our opposing arguments—a classic diversionary strategy to find common ground and prevent things from degenerating further. Professor Havisham, with Sara taking notes and occasionally asking for clarification, proceeded to officiously pontificate her precious pedagogy. During the dissertation I sat there squirming, sometimes responding to her questions, sometimes biting my tongue in an effort to prevent career suicide.

I don't want to bore you with the details, nor force myself to go through it again, so let me try recounting the hour-long meeting in song.

The Diva opens the medley of greatest hits with *Teach.*

Teach. Teach, Teacher Man, a Beach Boy like ditty about her desire for me to use every last minute of the block to teach. She follows it up with a soulless cover of the classic *What a Wonderful World*'s opening line *Don't know much pedagogy,* in which she rejoices in her utter contempt for wasting precious classroom time on individual reading, library visits and dictionary use. She then seamlessly slips into her self-pitying country ballad *They Threw it All Away,* about the good times long ago when Ms. Havisham was principal, and about how much better things were in the days before the misguided powers dumped her (Carol's words, not mine). What a pity? All her wondrous efforts to reform education slipped away and, in the end, came to naught.

The Queen of Ice then effortlessly slides into *No Homework, No Cry,* a reggae number that extols her royal standards of hard work and higher-level thinking. The performance reaches a crescendo with her rendition of the country music classic *Do Write Man,* a song praising the Her Majesty's favorite teaching technique for resource kids, modeling over and over, ad nauseam, until all creatures large and small finally grasp whatever point you are trying to make. Mind you, I was very quiet and well behaved throughout the performance. (Where was Simon Cowell, or better yet, Chuck Barris, when I really needed him?) But when Carol hit those dissonant sour notes with *Model, Model, Model, Model,* I was ready to explode.

My mind was off and running, my thoughts like hot whips of pain raging over with a sarcastic, *Model!!! Model!!! Model!!! Teach me what you preach!!!! And why the hell don't you model for me and show me how it is done???"*

My face remained stoic; my mouth remained shut tight as I dug my right thumbnail deep into the fleshy area between my left thumb and index finger. I was close to drawing blood, but I just sat there like a good little soldier, glancing from time-to-time at Sara. My mentor seemed to be enjoying her first real encounter with the Ice Queen just a little too much for my comfort. Eventually Sara did step in and stop the bleeding, taking control by distracting both of us with her own summary of Carol's main points. By now it was clear that Carol was never going to change her mind. We were going around in circles, getting nowhere. Sara was trying her best to tie things up in the hope I might still be able to escape with some hope of salvation.

On the ropes

I could not resist a parting shot. After explaining that my signature does not signify agreement, only acknowledgement, Carol asked me to sign the evaluation. I told her I would have no problem signing it, but not then; instead, I would prefer to sign it in a few days so as to give Carol ample opportunity to read the papers I had given her at the beginning of the meeting.

Oops!! Big mistake.

Carol's deadly glare and her angry red face said it all. I had crossed the line and questioned her authority. In truth, all I was really trying to accomplish was to get Carol to read the damn lesson plan and then consider changing my evaluation. Sara's pained expression warned me to ease off and try to make amends before it was too late. Recognizing defeat, I reluctantly told Carol I would sign it, and then I asked politely that she explain, one last time, how my performance rating could change so significantly after one twenty minute classroom observation. I tried to frame the question in a way that made it appear I was at fault for not understanding her the first time.

So while I signed the document and scribbled some insipid comments in my own defense in the section entitled *Evaluees Comments*, Carol tried once more to clarify her reasoning. Hoping to simplify things for me, Carol used the following analogy.

"Imagine" she began, "that you taught a student, day-after-day, week-after-week, the proper way to write a decent paragraph. But despite all your efforts the student ignored your direction, refused to change and continued to write the same way he did before your instruction began. How would you feel?"

I was only too eager to respond with my own spin on her analogy, but timing is everything. I waited a few beats then, carefully measuring my words, answered, "How would I feel? Well it all depends, but one thing I know for certain. I would be fair to the student and read the paragraph in its entirety. I would not judge the entire composition on a single forlorn sentence."

Not sure if Carol even understood what I was trying to say, but it was time to leave. After the proper formalities, Sara and I got up and made our way out of the rabbit hole into the bright warm light of day. As we walked back to our rooms I asked Sara what she thought of her first real encounter with Carol. "Incredible. Pretty incredible." and then she asked how I was feeling.

"Fucking frustrated"

"I really can't blame you. And I have no idea why she couldn't have been a little flexible and told you she would take the time to read your materials and then possibly reconsider. But Eric, all that is beside the point. We really do have to come up with a plan to make Carol happy. You are both stubborn. And, like it or not, the woman has lots of experience and a few good ideas and you really need to be a little more deferential toward her in the future. But relax, I think you are doing a great job with your kids and I am sure they will ask you back for next year."

Sara's not the first woman to tell me to relax. And it didn't make me relax or feel any better. In truth, I felt like a battered boxer. There was, however, some small consolation in knowing someone with more teaching experience than I, after having visited *Havishamland* with me, validated my perception of the hole I found myself in.

At least *I* wasn't the crazy one.

Monday - March 24, Spring Break

I am a pretty tough guy when it comes to ignoring slings and arrows from someone whose opinions I don't respect. But even a tough guy like me, after several bruising beatings, begins to suffer some self-doubt. My rope-a-dope strategy doesn't seem to be working. Carol shows no signs of fatigue from the pummeling she is giving me. Maybe what I need is a new corner man? Sara at times seems to be way too eager to throw in the towel, to compromise, and besides it's probably not such a great idea to have a pacifist in my corner. Feeling a little punch-drunk after all the abuse.

Enough with the clever boxing analogies and back to my slipping self-confidence. I feel pretty certain that I am becoming a good teacher, but I am beginning to worry that some of my readers may have reached the point in my tales of woe where they are thinking, *"Maybe Eric's just fooling himself. Maybe Carol is right and he doesn't have a clue."*

Or some may now be thinking that I have inadvertently come to represent the oft-used literary technique of the unreliable narrator. A tactic employed by Poe in several stories including the *Black Cat,* and in more modern times by Scorsese in *Taxi Driver,* where the author creates a somewhat reliable first person narrator who, as the story unfolds, becomes more and more unreliable, eventually turning into, say, a paranoid, raging, psychopathic serial killer. I can assure those readers who may subscribe to this theory that, although I may share with him a sense and fear of being continually observed, I am no Travis Bickle.

Of course those who know me have faith in my objective self-awareness and assume, as I do, that I am doing as good a job as anyone in a similar situation could do. I got a nice ego-boost the day before spring break from the following observation notes from Randy. Randy knows better than anyone what I am facing, and unlike Ms. Havisham, he actually knows many of my students. While Randy's primary job is to offer positive strokes and gentle suggestions to anxious first year teachers, I sincerely believe he is in the position to have the most objective view of how I am faring.

Randy's observation:

3-19-08

Mr Mandell, (Randy spells my last name wrong, Carol my first)

I arrived at 2:17 you were playing a tape of the Great Gatsby. Great pause and questioning about the book. Eric good job of pushing them to a higher level....Good job of explaining what NYC is and what " marks signify on the quiz questions and good job when you explained what you meant by "aggressively" and Eric, great job of re-reading the questions and encouraging them to try. All the kids were trying to answer the questions. Good job of circulating about the room and making sure the kids were working. You offered just the right amount of help, without giving them the answers. You had your lesson agenda on the board and all materials ready. You had your state standards posted. You did a good job of getting the girl in the brown shirt (Jasmine) to try. You gave them clues in the questions, which was great.

Great job of keeping Jeremy on track when he insisted he needed to look in the mirror, by sticking to the point that it is more important to work on the quiz.

Eric of the 15 people I'm observing you have improved the most. You have become a teacher....

Ok now I am off to enjoy the rest of my break...

꿍ᐯᑎᘿ

The Peter Principle on Steroids: The Rise and Fall of a Bureaucrat

Now seems as good a time as any to tell the reader what I have learned about the background of Ms. Carol Havisham, the lady who once held the coveted throne of Principal and in whose hands my fate now rests. What I learned about Carol comes from personal research, first person accounts from reliable sources, and just a bit of out-and-out hearsay. I am quite certain that, while the details may be fuzzy, the tenor of the story is quite accurate.

Like many staff members at San Benito High School, Carol is a *Baler* for life. She graduated from the school in the late 1960's and then spent most, if not all, of her career working for the district. In addition, both her children are *Balers*: a college-age son (the interloper who called asking Mommy for money during one of our meetings), and a daughter who at present is a junior at San Benito. This royal family's DNA seems to breed and bleed red and white. (Some extraneous info I tripped over while *googling* Carol: she sold her house in Hollister in June 2006 for a little over one million dollars. It also appears from the home sale details that Carol is divorced.)

Carol began as a teacher, and despite obvious short-comings, worked her way up the educational hierarchy. She has held various administrative positions including Director of Counseling Service, High School Vice-Principal of Discipline, Director of Grants and Services, and Director of Special Services. In the summer of 2002, after twenty-seven years with the district, Carol reached her career pinnacle when, in spite of significant staff resistance, and following a contentious search, she was appointed principal of her beloved alma mater. According to an unimpeachable source, the decision to hire Carol as principal, despite her reputation as a poor manager and miserable people person, was settled decisively by that time-honored and generally catastrophic dictum: *It was her turn.*

Back in 2002, even before Carol took the helm, unrest and turmoil were brewing. In her past positions Carol had alienated much of the faculty and staff. So not surprisingly, within weeks of her appointment things began to fall apart; morale tumbled especially among Carol's office staff. They felt unappreciated, believed they were being treated poorly and that their legitimate concerns were being ignored. Things got so bad so fast that the school board took the highly unusual mid-year step of "reassigning" Carol to the position of Director of Special Services and appointing an interim principal to replace her. Within seven months of her coronation—her dream-job in tatters at her feet—the fallen monarch was forced to return, royal robe between her legs, to the backwaters and friendly confines of the Special Services Department.

After the announcement of her reassignment, Carol told the *Hollister Free Lance* on March 20, 2003, "I resigned from the principal's position to assume a position where I felt that I could continue to bring the best possible education and career opportunities to all students."

The *Peter Principle* as it relates to public education: *In the hierarchy of a school district every administrator tends to rise to his or her level of incompetence.* Carol's career is a prime example of the *Peter Principal* (pun intended) run amok. She must have reached her first level of incompetence a long time ago, but though grit, and who knows what else, she continued her rise, eventually becoming principal. And even after her fall, it is my humble opinion that the Ice Queen is still operating several rungs above her capabilities.

Don't you just love America? *Those that can't, teach, those that can't teach, manage those that can.*

And yes, it does comfort me some to know my principle tormentor has tormented hundreds of other poor insubordinates during her thirty-three years with the district. *Misery loves miserable company.* And if Ms. Havisham is a prime illustration of the *Peter Principal* run amok, I guess that makes me a poster boy for the damage done by the deployment of said principal.

Rainy Day Women

Saturday - April 26, one month later...
Good news and bad news to report.

IN DUBIOUS BATTLE

More bad news relating to my Kafkaesque battle with my arch-nemesis as it rages on towards its seemingly inevitable conclusion. But first the good news about what got me into this mess in the first place—the kids. They continue to amaze and to frustrate. Sometimes I think back to the old Art Linkletter TV show that aired in the late 1950's. Linkletter, the all-knowing host (later revealed to be a right-wing reactionary) interviewed young children, effortlessly eliciting amusing and accidentally profound responses. The show's catchphrase was *Kids say the darnedest things*. Updating the phrase for today's world: *Teenagers say some pretty funny shit*.

Classes are moving right along. My juniors have finished *The Great Gatsby* and I can say with confidence that after reading them the entire book aloud, showing two movie versions of the novel, and hammering home its major themes day-after-day, most have grasped Fitzgerald's main ideas and may even appreciate the book as literature. This week, in one final activity before burying Jay Gatsby forever, I had both classes write a two-page essay on one of five topics:

1. Many people say that "The Great Gatsby" is the best description ever written of the American lifestyle in the 1920's. Explain how this statement is true or false, using examples from the text to support your answer.

2. Jay Gatsby represents a person who is so caught up in the past that he cannot live for the present. Do you agree? Write an essay in which you support this statement with examples from the book or movie.

3. Money can't buy happiness. Do you agree? Write an essay in which you support this state-

ment with examples from the book or movie.

4. *"So we beat on, boasts against the current, borne back ceaselessly into the past."* What does this quote mean? Explain using examples from the book and from your own life.

5. There are several important symbols in Gatsby, including the eyes of Dr. Eckleberg and the green light. Pick one symbol and explore its significance in a well-developed essay. Use examples from the book to support your answer.

I realize that some of my topics were, to say the least, a stretch, and I was not astonished to discover that not a single student opted for either topic four or five. I was pleasantly surprised however, to discover that most were able to construct relatively coherent, corroborated, well-argued essays.

My seniors, after spending the last few weeks on prereading activities and historical background for the play *Zoot Suit* by internationally acclaimed playwright and local resident Luis Valdez, finally began reading/performing the play aloud last Monday and Tuesday. They seem to be enjoy reading parts and playing with the accents, and of course they really get a kick out of reciting the swear words in both English and Spanish. Many of my students who are fluent in Spanish enjoy the feeling of power they get in translating the Spanish for their non-Spanish speaking classmates.

An interesting discovery on my part, one I am sure is common knowledge among pedagogues and makes complete sense upon reflection—just because a kid is fluent in Spanish and can read English doesn't mean he can read Spanish. Some of my students who speak

Spanish fluently and are proficient readers in English, read Spanish poorly at best. This seems counter-intuitive. It seems logical that once someone has mastered the complexities of English pronunciation then reading in Spanish, a phonetic language, would be a snap.

Incorrect!! Evidently if English is the language that you learn to read first, in most cases you will still require additional instruction to learn to read Spanish, especially if you never look at written Spanish on your own, as is the case with most of my students.

Valdez employs, effectively for me and frustratingly for many of my students, both English and Spanish throughout his play. He shifts back and forth from one language to the other, neglecting to translate for the monolingual, and at times coining his own variety of *Spanglish*. I found Valdez's technique both appealing and contagious. For purely educational purposes I coined several words of my own, including my favorite and most useful, *quwhyatay*—the bastard offspring of an adulterous liaison between *be quiet* and *callate* (the Spanish word for shut up and pronounced ki-ah-tay).

Quwhy-ah-tay!!! Try it. It rolls off the tongue like warm honey and creates the perfect fusion—a healthy measure of civility with a dash of insolence.

Before the class actually began reading the play, I showed the first fifteen minutes of the movie *Zoot Suit* as a teaser, and to help students understand the concept of stylization in cinema and theatre. Showing segments of cinematic adaptations following the reading of the appropriate segments of a book or play increases the students' understanding and helps them to visualize the narrative. The downside of showing the movie is it invariably leads to an almost unanimous appeal to abandon the book altogether and just watch the film. My standard comeback, *"Trust me guys, I wish almost daily that this were a film appreciation class and not an English class."* does little to quell the clamor.

Lately I have been trying to vary my instruction, spending more time teaching vocabulary and the meaning and significance of adages and proverbs. Many of my students have great difficulty moving from the literal to the figurative. Working with adages, deciphering the obvious ones like *an apple a day,* and the more opaque ones like *still waters run deep,* has been a revelation.

At Carol's request, I am making a concerted effort to teach the art of writing compound and complex sentences. Surprisingly, many students actually know what simple and compound sentences are, but just when I think I am getting somewhere, I trip over another black hole of ignorance I could never have anticipated. One day last week for *Transition,* I asked them to define a play, a novel and a screenplay in their own words, and to give an example of each. Assuming—always a big mistake—everyone had some familiarity with Shakespeare, combined with the fact the class had already "performed" one act from the *Crucible* in December, I was taken aback when only a few had a clear idea of the distinctions between a play and a novel, let alone a screenplay. Incidents like this demonstrate how pointless and impossible it would be for me, or any teacher for that matter, to teach Carol's higher-level thinking ideals to resource students.

After explaining the characteristics and the meanings of these basic literary genres, I could not resist pontificating, mostly for my own amusement, on the unusual and arcane use of the term *wright* in play*wright*, in contrast to the common term *writer* in screen*writer.* When I conclude the tutorial by suggesting it might be fun for them to impress their parents by dropping this fact into an upcoming conversation, they look at me like I'm nuts.

Beavis and Butthead: Stan, one half of the senior, auto-dynamic duo I have lovingly dubbed Beavis (Oliver) and Butthead (Stan), always questions everything I do. Both of them seem fascinated by the sounds of certain words. Early in the year when I mentioned Bruce Springsteen in passing, the boys found the way I said it totally hilarious. Probably I said it too fast, or maybe it arced a memory synapse in Stan's and Oliver's brains recalling their *Sesame Street* days with Bruce Stringbean. Who knows. For weeks after, anytime I wanted to get their attention I just said *Bruce Springsteen* really fast. Recently Oliver has become fixated with the sound of the word *adage*. Sometimes he spews out *adage* three or four times in a row, laughing harder each time. (According to the neurologist Oliver Sacks, people with autism, Tourette's syndrome or OCD may become hooked on a sound or word and repeat it, or echo it, for days on end. And then suddenly it's gone and there's a new sound or word in its place. This phenomenon is similar to a *brainworm* or an *earworm*, two delightful and interchangeable terms used to describe the relatively common experience of a tune or jingle inexplicably becoming trapped in one's head.)

Whenever I begin a new lesson Stan inevitably blurts out some version of *This is stupid Mr. Mandel. Why do you always make us do this stupid stuff?* Usually I respond with some sarcastic and self-amusing quip. On rare occasions someone will get my joke and say something like *That was pretty funny Mr. Mandel.* A few weeks ago, after one of Stan's *This is stupids*, I came back with, "Stan I bet you were just the same and just as annoying in first grade. Your teacher writes the word *cat* on the board and says, *Class, cat is spelled C A T.* And cute little Stan counters, '*Mrs. Jones, cat, C A T, that is the stupidest thing I ever heard!*'"

I think that may have been one of the few jokes that the entire class appreciated, with the exception of Butthead of course.

I do realize that the kids are tiring of me pressuring them to learn things they don't think they will ever need to know, so I decided to give them a chance to get back at me. After introducing new vocabulary words they insisted they would never use or see, I had them break up into groups and work together to come up with popular teen slang words or phrases to teach *me*, the only caveat—*no dirty or sex-related words.* They groaned and moaned of course, and initially had difficulty coming up with anything. Eventually they hit upon a few, two of which I actually partially remember. I had them write their words on the board and use them in sentences, and then I attempted to come up with their meanings. The first was *gigindurdy* (sic). Without hesitation I deduced by its resonance it had something to do with dancing. Pretty damn close. According to my very unreliable sources it denotes *dancing while high on E* (the drug *Ecstasy*). Beavis and Butthead's group offered up the other slang word. The actual word has slipped my mind, but it was a lengthy meandering onomatopoeia that meant something like *humongous jiggling tits.* After they used it in a sentence about a girl running around the track, I guessed the meaning. I then went on to explain that the best slang terms convey their meanings in a covert creative shorthand, and that I saw no benefit in using a twenty-five-letter-long word to replace the simple, succinct and alliterative phrase, "bouncing boobs".

The trivial things my students notice and find

entertaining about their hapless teacher continually amaze me. Their images of Mr. Mandel are all over the place depending on time of day, his wardrobe, his hair and his attitude. Over the year students have told me I remind them of many people from House (brilliant, sarcastic, pill-popping TV doctor with horrible bedside manner and a limp) to Mr. Rogers (it must be the sweaters). I continue to hope against hope they will notice my enthusiasm, even just once, or allude to something I have taught them.

Well to be honest it has happened on rare occasions. One Friday about a month ago, to illustrate the effective use of opposing points of view when writing about uncomfortable situations one might find one's self in, I told them a story about when I was their age traveling in Europe with my friend Tom. I recounted the time Tom and I met some American sisters in Greece, paired up with them and hitchhiked through the Alps from Italy to Germany. We split up into couples in Venice, planning to meet back up in Munich the following day. To make a longwinded and complicated story brief, suffice it to say that within an hour of our departure I realized I did not want to be with the sister I was with. While she was very beautiful and spoke Italian fluently, she was also incredibly annoying in a variety of ways that I won't go into (paranoid being one). But we were stuck with each other for two days. By the time we reached Munich things were so bad between the two of us that I chose to sleep in a park rather than share a room with her for the night.

The kids relish hearing my stories primarily because they think they are getting me off task, and while I certainly realize this, I do my best to play the fool and trick them into learning something in the process. The Monday after I shared my story, Josh shared a story of his own about an incident from the weekend when he and some homeboys were trolling for girls in San Jose. They met some friends who knew some girls; the boys found said girls and picked them up planning to take them to a mall. As Josh told his story he mentioned that the girls seemed really hot when they picked them up, but as soon as the one sitting beside him opened her mouth and said something Josh thought, *"Damn, now I know exactly what Mr. Mandel was talking about."*

I smiled. One tiny step forward beats running in circles any day.

The students take great joy in the trials and tribulations of their teacher. Vital topics range from loud, loquacious laments regarding my lame set of wheels (a 14 year-old Volvo wagon), to the more critical issue of the state of my hair. My hair seems to be a constant source of entertainment, discussion and debate. *Did you comb your hair today Mr. Mandel? Do you have a mirror at home?* And my favorite, *Mr. Mandel does your wife see what you look like before you leave in the morning and still let you out the door?*

They were pretty excited early last week when my hair finally reached that point of unruliness requiring the use of gel, which transformed my look from casual-just-woke-up to slicked-back Pat Riley. I told them I was gellin' like,...oh, never mind. They were entranced for a few minutes until some new triviality distracted them. But the real thrill for them came about three weeks ago when one student noticed my shirt was in some type of fashion limbo. My guileless shirt was neither completely tucked in, nor completely pulled out. The whole class seems fascinated by this fashion *faux pas.* Taking advantage of the situation—in the interest of time I decided against debate—I immediately called for a vote on the question, *Shirt in? Shirt out?*

The *Shirt Outs* won in a landslide, so naturally I tucked my shirt in. Sometimes I really love my job.

⸏⸏

Thinking back over my short teaching career, in the beginning I hated teaching Third Block. For one thing it's after lunch. (Interesting POV aside: all teachers complain about how afternoon classes are much worse than the classes before lunch. A few months back I heard a student's perspective on the same issue. As we watched a film of SBHS student interviews during a staff in-service, a straight-A female student complained about how cranky teachers are after lunch and how this makes it difficult for students to learn.)

Third Block also has its share of interesting but taxing personalities: the two drama queens Jeremy and Gina, the whiny homophobic and often-obnoxious *Scene Boy* Zen/Irwin, the obstinate and arrogant Luke, the love birds Jasmine and David, Red-Headed Rick, arbitrator of justice, Cal the black poet, Tony the boxer, and William, the kid who showed up the final day of first semester and asked me to provide him with all his missing assignments so he could bring his grade up from below 50% to a pass. Over the months this class has matured and come together into a working unit; the kids have grown to appreciate one another, and most surprisingly, it has become my most enjoyable and engaging class. I can't believe I am saying this, but it is the class I most look forward to teaching. It is the one class in which I can try out more complex lessons. Still challenging, but well worth the effort.

Zen slips in and out of participating in class and doing

his work, and after failing first semester, he is maintaining a so-so C. He is definitely an odd duck with more phobias than any one duck is entitled to. Irwin loves doing grammar and exploring the roots of words. He carries around Freud and seems genuinely interested in psychology, although when I suggested he write a short book report on Freud for extra credit he turned in a perfectly plagiarized, three-page, psychobabble-laden, bootlegged report.

Zen seems to strive for amorality. His arrogance and prejudices are unrivaled; he proudly boasts that if you ain't a *Scene Boy* or a *Scene Girl* you ain't worth shit. This stuff can be disturbing, but also great fodder for my own entertainment.

Jeremy is, well, still Jeremy only more so; the new, improved, tattooed version with the same flamboyant daily trips to the mirror. His vanity is unsuppressed and unsurpassed. He is just way too busy primping to have a clue what is going on in class. Jeremy recently replaced his small lip ring with a clumsy looking larger one, and drones on day after day about sex. Jeremy could fail my class this semester.

William on the other hand, has made a remarkable turnaround. He does all his work on time and is currently earning a strong B. William was shocked into his turnaround when I failed him last semester, and while he is doing great at present, he can't seem to understand my refusal to change his first semester F to a D as a retroactive reward for his renewed effort this semester.

Speaking of my favorite class, get this: In one week last month, multi-talented but-unable-to-spell-her-middle-name Gina, earned first place for her original monologue at the *Ohlone Theatre Festival* at Gavalin Community College; Cal, in spite of a serious case of stage fright, made it to final round of the school-wide poetry slam, and lastly, Tony won the *California Golden Gloves Welterweight Championship*. That week I felt like a proud parent and went around bragging about my students' accomplishments to anyone who would listen. Winning the *State Golden Gloves Championship* means that Tony is the best amateur in his weight class in California. He has fought many bouts against men as old as thirty, is undefeated, and has yet to be knocked down. Tony moves on to the *Nationals* in late May and plans to turn pro when he becomes eighteen next fall during his senior year.

A few more odds and ends before I tie this thing up in a neat bow with another Beavis and Butthead tale. Josh was accepted into the Marines. He is excited, proud and all set to go to Camp Pendleton in early July. When Josh told me he was accepted he gave me that Marine-look straight in the eye, shook my hand firmly and earnestly thanked me for believing in him. I have mixed feeling about Josh becoming a Marine. He really wants it badly and I think he realizes what he is getting into. He lives with his grand-parents and has struggled to make it through high school. Josh is one of my brightest and most curious students, but he has some serious issues accepting authority. His hypersensitive *bullshitdar* can get him into trouble at times and could be a real problem in the Corps. Josh is looking for the family he has never had; he yearns to belong to a band of brothers.

Speaking of the military, Sara and I often discuss the pros and cons of military service in relation to our students. The military has a visible presence on campus, and unlike schools in Santa Cruz, San Benito goes out of its way to accommodate military recruiters. As a pacifist, Sara wants nothing to do with the recruiters and does her best to shield her vulnerable students from brainwashing.

Nothing demonstrates our different approaches better than our distinct attitudes towards the free lunches and free crap (mugs, calendars, pencils, etc) the recruiters give to the faculty on a regular basis. Sara refuses to go to the lunches or accept the blood booty on principle, while I go eat their food and take their doodads. I rationalize this smug self-serving approach by explaining that taking their stuff is a noble Gandhi-like sacrifice that reduces the money available to the military to buy guns and kill babies.

Back to Beavis and Butthead: Friday, April 18 about 11:15, Butthead Stan and Oliver Beavis arrive late as usual. They make their dramatic entrance, both waving yellow traffic citations and oblivious to the fact that I am addressing the class as they loudly bemoan their shared misfortune in getting pulled over and cited by the cops twice in the same morning. I ask them to sit down and be quiet for a few minutes, assuring them that when we are done with the current lesson they can share their sorrows with the class. Ten minutes later when the lesson is over I say to Stan, "Your turn. The class is on pins and needles."

Befuddled, Stan replies, "What are you talking about Mr. Mandel?"

Shit. At times like these, and there are many, I really wish corporal punishment were still legal in schools. Eventually the following details come out: On the way to school that morning Stan, driving his flame-decorated small Mazda pick-up truck with Oliver riding shotgun, gets pulled over by the police and is cited for tinted windows and having some object blocking his vision. Because of Stan's low frustration threshold, he was tense and befuddled as he told the story. Making things worse for poor Stan was that this was his second ticket for the same identical violation; a year earlier he had been busted and had had to replace the tinted windows. A few months later, since he was planning to sell the truck, he had put the tinted windows back in.

Oliver's ticket tale was more compelling. Oliver was even more frustrated than his partner, too frustrated even to tell the story. He handed me the ticket and said, "You read it."

At 10:30 the same cops pulled over Stan and Oliver, this time citing Oliver. The citation was for marijuana possession. When I read this I naively assumed the cops found some weed in the truck. Hoping to avoid hearing more than was good for me, I attempted to drop the issue. But Beavis and Butthead were having none of it, and they went on to proudly explain in detail to the enthralled class that when pulled over they were actually *smoking* weed. And they add, gratuitously in my opinion, that they often leave campus during breaks to get stoned.

Upon hearing this, the cloudy haze around *my* head lifted, the sun came out in all its glory, and suddenly things came into sharp focus. *Eureka*!! All their silly, inane behavior over these months was due not to ADD. No, they were stoned almost every day in my class! How could I have missed the obvious: the blank looks, the silly sneers and the constant talk of food. Naturally everything seemed funny to them. No wonder they enjoyed my class so much.

I put on my best *you-guys-are-in-real-trouble* act and sternly lectured them to never smoke weed during school hours again. I warned them if I ever discover them stoned I would be obligated to turn them in and they would not graduate in June. Stan seemed genuinely surprised with my reaction and said something like, "Why do you care Mr. Mandel? You live in Santa Cruz."

THE ACCIDENTAL TEACHER

Interesting observation, I thought. I asked them both to stay after class and then I tried to get back on track and finish my lesson for the day. After class the two of them approached my desk acting like they had no idea why I wanted to talk to them. I explained to them the stupidity of their behavior, how they were putting their approaching graduation at risk, and the problem they had created for me. I told them that many teachers would send them to the office, which would lead to their certain suspension. They looked at me, utterly unimpressed, and then Stan asked, "Can we go now?"

Partners in Crime

I have been meaning to discuss my aides for months. I think I have mentioned all of them at one time or another in passing, but I am afraid I have failed to give these five women their due. As you recall, when Carol hired me she promised, because of my inexperience, to provide me with a strong aide. As with most of her promises, it wasn't honored. Most resource teachers work with just one or two aides that makes for a more consistent educational and work environment. I started the year with four aides: Vera for First Block, Rayna for Third, Linda for Fourth and Kitty for Fifth; second semester Eva replaced Rayna. I have no serious complaints about any of them.

Their personalities range from formal and business-like to fun-loving and easy-going. Vera can trace her lineage all the way back to California Spanish land grant days. Linda has a daughter in one of my classes. Kitty is fun, and Eva is tough and all business with the kids when they act up. I believe four of the five graduated from SBHS. All are experienced. Some are bright, others not

IN DUBIOUS BATTLE

so much. They all do their work willingly. Work consists primarily of circulating around the room and helping students one on one, running errands, assisting with pupil management and inputting grades. Aside from the problem of inconsistency with so many aides, my major complaint is their high rate of absenteeism. At certain times during the year I have been teaching without an aide for half my classes for weeks on end. One aide spent more time on the phone dealing with family problems than she did working with me.

I often wonder what these women say to one another about me; after all, they have the best vantage point to observe and judge my performance. Kitty, my aide for the Beavis and Butthead gang, is probably the one I feel closest to. She and I have similar personalities and try to have a good time no matter how badly things are going. Kitty views the bad boys as an entertaining distraction and an amusing break from the rest of her day working as an aide for a difficult, "mainstreamed", autistic, devout Mormon. The kid is very bright and has many issues related to his autism that drive Kitty nuts: a short fuse and a religious fanaticism for example. For Kitty, Beavis and Butthead, et al must seem like a trip to *Disneyland*. I realized for the first time the other day, no matter how often I have insisted they call me by my first name, I don't think any of them has ever called me Eric.

My back is on fire. It's time to take a break, to lie in the sun and do the Sunday crossword. I will wait till tomorrow to report on my final and less than epic battle with the wicked witch.

IX

Beer and Loathing in Steinbeck Country

They're selling postcards of the hanging
They're painting the passports brown
The beauty parlor is filled with sailors
The circus is in town

—Bob Dylan

Sunday - April 27

When last we met, the Ice Queen and me, with Sara acting as moderator, Carol mentioned she was planning an additional drop-in observation sometime during the first week after spring break. In Carol's mind she is doing me a big favor by giving me one more chance to demonstrate my ability to incorporate her wisdom and insight into my fledgling lesson plans. Of course to me Carol's begrudging benevolence is just another truckload of horseshit providing me nothing more than one final opportunity to crash and burn. In early April Pete Pecksniff, the asshole in charge of human resources, promised to let me know by the first of May whether I would have a job next year, so I think Carol, being the person who will make the decision, might be feeling pressure to make it soon.

I spent spring break relaxing and catching up on some things I had ignored or delayed doing since this all began in early August. I visited my regular doctor for a general check-up, went to my pain doctor and got an epidural steroid injection in hopes of reducing the chronic pain in my lower back, had my first eye exam in five years, got a haircut, ordered my first real pair of glasses (picking out frames is a story for another day), and closed a long dormant checking account. It is curious how completing a few relatively simple tasks gives me such a satisfying sense of accomplishment.

On Thursday of spring break I drove up to San Francisco, picked up my friend Donny, and headed up to his summer cabin in the Sierra to spend some well-earned do-nothing time before returning to work on Monday. On the drive up Donny and I estimated it would take an hour or so to open and clean up the cabin after its winter hibernation; however we were greeted with a little surprise as we entered the kitchen. The cabin's co-owner had, in a well-meaning effort to save the world's dwindling supply of fossil fuels and reduce the cabin's carbon footprint, decided in late fall to unplug the well-stocked refrigerator and prop the doors open in the belief that the cabin's consistent winter temperature of thirty-five degrees or below would preserve the food until spring.

The plan might have worked, but the cabin's winter residents had other ideas. In the absence of human interference, the mice had moved into a new, cozy, safe and well-stocked home. What a great way to start a relaxing weekend. It must have taken us five hours to clean out all the mouse turds and nesting material, to throw out the contaminated food, to clean and sanitize the entire refrigerator, and that included removing the freezer's sub-floor. Despite the surprise welcome, Donny and I enjoyed our stay: drinking beer, preparing and eating good meals, listening to music real-real loud with no one there to tell us to turn it down, bullshitting about our good ol' days, and partaking in some herbal nostalgia.

A Guide to Pedestrian Pedagogical Survival

A few nights ago while we were at dinner with a group of friends, one of them who has taught for over thirty years asked me to describe my teaching style. My initial instinct was to give him some smartass reply like *I don't got no stinking style*, but instead I said, "You know, I don't have a clue."

He responded, "You have a style. You just have never tried to articulate it before. And knowing you like I do, I'm betting within five minutes you'll come up with some brilliant full-blown half-bullshit theory."

He was wrong. It took me significantly longer than five minutes and the bullshit content of the ensuing hypothesis was considerably greater than fifty percent.

Originally when I took this job I just assumed, foolishly as it turned out, that I would have substantial help in developing an effective method for teaching English to teenagers. However it didn't work out that way; necessity forced me into the comfort zone of my life experience and I was free to make up my own system. Looking back to my first weeks of teaching, my only goal was survival, but of course there must have been some method, conscious or otherwise, to my madness. When I started to deconstruct my teaching method I realized that my approach to teaching was essentially an adaptation of my management and parenting styles. This was inevitable—I had nothing else to fall back on.

From my work experience I adapted my people skills relying on the following tried and tested theories: Don't sweat the small shit, many problems will solve themselves, and just because someone is above you in the hierarchy doesn't mean they are smart. I know this going to sound lame, but I really believe that the most critical thing in teaching, as in life, is to follow the *Golden Rule*. (And in my case, never to forget my own behavior in high school.)

And from my parenting, well for me, teaching is basically just parenting on a grand scale. Everyone who has raised children knows that despite all the outside influences, it is basically a process of trial and error—trying anything, and then either returning to whatever worked the last time or trying something else. And while it is possible to educate (or over-educate) one's self on the most modern "effective" techniques of child rearing, most of us—like our parents and grandparents before us—fall back on our instincts.

When it comes to raising children and teaching students there are several universal truisms, among them: Everyone has advice to offer whether you want to hear it or not. No two children are alike, and its corollary—every individual child has a host of personas. Just because a technique works the first time is no guarantee it will work again. Don't think too hard. I could go on but I think you get the point.

Regardless of our best intentions and efforts we end up making and repeating thousands of mistakes. I'm the first to admit that as a father and a teacher I have fucked-up many times in the past and will fuck-up more in the future. But to date, as far as I can tell I have never seriously damaged my own kids or my students and I am confident that I have done far more good than harm.

Another good analogy for my teaching experience comes straight from the kitchen: Imagine you are a gourmet cook who specializes in small intimate meals. Suddenly you find yourself forced—minus your *sous chef*, your dishwasher and proper equipment—to feed one hundred hormone-infested teenage diners whose tastes range from the awful to the repulsive. They prefer *Twinkies* to fine pastry and *Happy Meals* to a two-star *Michelin* dining experience. They wouldn't know a good meal if you put it on their desks.

So what do you do?

Get cooking…

$\sim \sim$

During the deconstruction exercise I also discovered that the *diversion theory* of education I so glibly promoted during the job interview actually works and has intuitively become the backbone of my teaching. I'm not so stupid as to think I was the first person to think of this technique. All good teachers are inherently entertainers. I did my best to make my class fun, and lots of my students, and there were many among them who hated school in general, loved coming to my class. I know being entertained is really not the purpose of school, but it is a great way to keep the students awake and hold their attention so they are ready to learn. At this point I am a better entertainer than a teacher. But if only they'd give me a few more years…

THE ACCIDENTAL TEACHER

One pill makes you larger and one pill makes you small...

Returning to work after the break refreshed and re-charged, I was relieved as the first week came and went without a single Carol sighting. As the days went by I decided that I would rather not see the bleak-faced Ms. Havisham, clad in one of her bizarre long-past teen-style ensembles (i.e. poodle skirt), set foot in my classroom again; I would prefer instead to have her decide my fate based on the evidence already in her possession.

No such luck.

On Tuesday, April 8 at 9:30, the Grim Reaper appears at my door, slips into the classroom and sits at the aides' desk located about thirty feet away from and kitty-corner to my desk. *Great.* I think. *Here we go again.* Since her last observation, in an effort to demonstrate a willingness to take her advice and against my better judgment, I had dropped SSR completely and had increased the number and variety of instructional activities in my lesson plans. Ominously, for the second time this year, on the day Carol chooses to observe me I am all set, have a solid lesson planned, prepared and posted, and it all goes out the window when a half dozen of my better students notify me as class begins that they will be leaving in fifteen minutes for another campus tour of Gavilan Community College.

Unbelievable!

I did what any reasonable educator would do in similar circumstances. I jettisoned my planned lesson and pulled together something supplemental that would be educationally worthwhile but not jeopardize curriculum continuity for the missing students. In one sense I was relieved because, just before Carol's surprise entry, I had decided at the last minute *not* to show the movie *Best in Show* as an example of satire and parody. You can imagine how well that would have gone over with Carol. Instead I decided to go with a portion of a lesson that I had been mulling over for some time using a segment from NPR's series on famous American fictional characters. The NPR segment I chose was *Eric Cartman: America's Favorite Little $@#&*%*. The plan was in its earliest stages and I thought it might be a fun and an interesting way to assess the lesson for future use. Trial and error plays a large part in my lesson plan development. Sometimes ideas I think are brilliant just never pan out, forcing me to abort lessons mid-flight and try something else. And sometimes lessons that start out shaky, after some jumps and starts, evolve into real winners.

I'll let Carol's own words describe what she saw, and I'll use both my official and unofficial responses to explain my observations of her observations. As soon as class ended, with Carol's counter-intuitive advice in mind—that it is my responsibility to explain to her any potential problems before I am aware there are any potential problems—I sent off the following clarifying email to Carol:

4/8/08

Carol,

I want to explain the situation in my first period today. I had planned to do some more traditional activities (vocab and historical background for Zoot Suit) and complete senior letters with my class; however since six of my most motivated students left at 9:15 to go on a field trip to Gavilan, I decided to shift gears and do something to engage the remaining students. I was hoping to channel some of their excess "creative" energy into a lesson on character development. Although this wasn't my original lesson plan for the day, I believe that I did address the following standards: Literary Response 3.0., Writing Applications 2.0, and Listening and Speaking Applications 1.0.

If you have any questions please give me a call.

As expected, I got no response. The next time I heard from her was when she sent me the following note with her observation attached:

Erik,

I recorded what I observed on April 8th in your English 12. Rather than me put evaluative comments I thought you might benefit from a reflective activity.

Please rate your lesson under each standard and write evaluative comments as well as several recommendations under each standard and put a copy in my box by April 18th. We can then meet the following week.

Thank you.

Carol's April 8th attached recorded notes:

As I entered at 9:30, Mr. Mandel got up from his desk to address the class, Students were working on an assignment which consisted of drawing an original cartoon character and write a descriptive paragraph. Mr. Mandel and the aide circulated around the room checking student work. At 9:40, Mr. Mandel asked students to supply names of their make believe characters. Students volunteered names such as Dirty

BEER AND LOATHING IN STEINBECK COUNTRY

Bubble, Kratos, Spider Dude, Tattoo Face….

I left at 9:54 as Mr, Mandel began next unit……

Mr. Mandel appears to have established open rapport with his students. They respond to his questions and directives. However, Mr. Mandel needs to more effectively utilize class time whether or not all students are present (He indicated that half the class was on a field trip to Gavilan College and he had revised his lesson plan accordingly…

The lesson observed "Drawing cartoons and writing a one paragraph descriptive essay" is far below state standards for high school seniors. Level of this particular activity is listed under Grade Three on page 18 of <u>English Language Arts Content Standards for California Public Schools Kindergarten Through Grade Twelve.</u>

Did she just say my lesson was third grade level??

And after seven months Carol is giving me my first opportunity to do a reflective activity and evaluate myself. Wow, lucky me!!!

Here is what I would have loved to send to Carol:

Carol,

You gotta be kidding? Do you really think me capable of such a high level reflective activity as evaluating myself? I guess I should be flattered that an expert in the field of education such as you has recognized some intellectual growth in me. You are a real piece of work. When you hired me and I shared my anxieties about not having the background and tools to teach high school English, you assured me over and over again in that annoying squeaky voice of yours that you would make certain I would have everything I needed to be a successful first year teacher. You promised me that by the time I completed the New Teacher's Academy I would have at least two weeks of lesson plans ready for the start of school. You promised a curriculum map and class outline for both English 11 and English 12, and you assured me I would be teamed up with an experienced instructional aide to make my transition less difficult.

Well the academy came and went, school started and guess what? You failed to deliver on any of your promises. No curriculum map, no lesson plans, no nothing. To be fair, on the experienced aide promise you outdid yourself. Instead of the one aide who would have provided both the experience and the continuity you promised me, I got four! (I am the only teacher I have met who has more than two.) They are all capable, but the lack of continuity and consistency that results from their sheer numbers creates a major headache for me. And then there are their numerous absences: some weeks I feel lucky to have an aide half the time.

Once I was onboard you disappeared, never asking me how I was doing or what you could do to help. Never. Not once. And the one piddly-ass phone call I did get from you—well, it was you calling to check up on one of your fellow administrators.

I do want to thank you however for candidly and unprofessionally sharing your negative opinion of other school administrators. It was eye opening to see how little you respect your peers. Thanks also for sharing your past failure as principal.

In summary, you did everything in your power, without lifting a finger, to make sure I would not succeed. The irony is that while I am failure in your eyes, everyone else who has observed me, including me, realizes the remarkable growth and progress I have made in an incredibly difficult situation without any substantive administrative help.

Another startling fact is that not once the entire year did you give me a verbal compliment or a pat on the back. I have experienced some miserable managers in my thirty plus years in education, and you may not believe this, but you are the worst. Despite your self-proclaimed belief that you are student-oriented, you are a detriment to the students and the staff at San Benito HS.

Thanks for nothing.

Eric (with a 'c')

ps: In the future you may want to learn the proper spelling of your employees' names.

Boy that felt good.

Here is what I actually sent, including the self-evaluation Carol requested:

April 20, 2008

Carol,

Thanks for the opportunity to do a reflective critique of my lesson you observed two weeks ago. As a new teacher with no real classroom experience I have spent most of the year pondering, formulating, attempting (sometimes successfully and sometimes not so successfully), reflecting on and revising lesson plans. I have made substantial progress, but I still have a ways to go before I reach the level of competence all teachers strive for.

THE ACCIDENTAL TEACHER

On the day you observed me I had originally planned a pre-reading jigsaw activity for *Zoot Suit* on the Zoot Suit Riots in Los Angeles in the early 1940's. But when I realized that morning I was losing a good chunk of students to a field trip to Gavilan, I shifted gears and switched to a lesson I had been planning to use in the near future; one that I had not completely fleshed-out. I thought my original plan for the day too critical to the understanding of the play to present with so many students missing, and I hoped to use the time with the smaller group to present and fine-tune the upcoming lesson on character development and how writers sometime use their characters to promote political agendas. Needless to say, I wasn't completely satisfied with the outcome and hope to present the improved version in the future.

Lesson Plan

Goal: Demonstrate through various means how writers develop characters

+ To connect the common themes and motives of two works by Mexican-American writers: one, *Parrot in the Oven,* we had completed earlier this semester and the other, *Zoot Suit* we will begin as soon as STAR testing is complete. In addition I hope to show to the students how a writer's political ideology may be reflected in their work.

+ To engage all students by utilizing their interest in popular culture, to hook some students who seem to have a real interest in drawing, and to demonstrate the common techniques used in character and plot development in all forms of creative enterprise from great works of literature to TV cartoons.

Transition: Who is your favorite animated character and why?

+ Go over agenda and relation to *Parrot* and *Zoot Suit*

Anticipatory Set: Brief intro on what to listen for and then play radio story *Eric Cartman: America's Favorite Little $@#&~*%* from NPR's ongoing series on indelible American fictional characters, *In Character: Tricksters, Vamps, Heroes and Scamps.*

+ Short teacher led discussion on story and how *South Park* creators invented and refined Cartman.

+ Review literary devices used for character development that we had learned with *Parrot* to uncover how author created protagonist (action, dialogue, interior monologue, etc).

Activity: Have students create animated character via a drawing and a one-paragraph description. Students share creations. Discuss student-generated characters and relevance to readings. (future revision: have students create character that reflects their personal agendas and discuss what they can use to show their thoughts/beliefs through their creations)

+ Connect to possible future activities developing plots, and perhaps have students characters interact to demonstrate how characterization, plot and ideology intersect.

CFI: (future revision) Have students rate each other on a class-created rubric

Standards addressed: Reading 2.1, 2.4, 2.5
Literary Response 3.9
Speaking 1.1, 2.1

My Self-Evaluation:

STANDARD I – Engaging and Supporting All Students in Learning

- Connecting students' prior knowledge, life experience, and interests with learning goals.
- Using a variety of instructional strategies and resources to respond to students' diverse needs.
- Facilitating learning experiences that promote autonomy, interaction, and choice.
- Engaging students in problem solving, critical thinking, and other activities that make subject matter meaningful.
- Promoting self-directed, reflective learning for all students.

I think this is one of my strong areas. In general I have worked hard at finding engaging, relevant material for all my students, and this semester I have emphasized the Latino experience. All my students seem more engaged when I find activities they can relate to and connect to their own lives.

This lesson engaged most students, and pop culture seems to be of interest to them all. I also did make sure that they all understood the assignment and I spent substantial one-on-one time with those students who were having difficulty. My quick dropping of the senior letter activity was more a result of not having all students present, than it was on the few who had actually taken the assignment home on own volition and then failed to bring the letters back to class.

RATING: Meets Standards

RECOMMENDATIONS: Improve my techniques for more reflective, self directed activites.

STANDARD II – Creating and Maintaining Effective Environments for Student Learning

- Creating a physical environment that engages all students.
- Establishing a climate that promotes fairness and respect.
- Promoting social development and group responsibility.
- Establishing and maintaining standards for student behavior.
- Planning and implementing classroom procedures and routines that support student learning.
- Using instructional time effectively.

I think connecting with students is another strong area of mine. I have worked very hard at establishing trust and encouraging open discussion and the free exchange of ideas. And while I think my classroom management skills are satisfactory, next year I plan to be more consistent and follow through more on consequences. I have come to realize that there is a fine line between establishing trust and respect and allowing students to get away with too much.

RATING: Meets Standards

RECOMMENDATIONS:

1. create an environment with higher standards
2. make sure AFS notifies me a few days prior to field trips.   DONE
3. be more prepared for unforeseen events. have emergency lesson plans with basic, consistent activities that are not critical to all students understanding of central theme of novel or other work in progress.
4. be more consistent and demand more from students

STANDARD III – Ensuring Progress of Pupils Toward the State Adopted Academic Content Standards as Measured by State Adopted Criterion Referenced Assessments through the Understanding and Organization of Subject Matter for Student Learning.

-Demonstrating knowledge of subject matter content, **State Content Standards,** and student development.

-Organizing curriculum to support student understanding of subject matter. -Interrelating ideas and information within and across subject matter areas.

-Developing student understanding through instructional strategies that are appropriate to the subject matter.

-Using materials, resources, and technologies to make subject matter accessible to students.

-Achieving identified state adopted academic content standards by **all** students taught.

By far my weakest area and I do realize I need to challenge my students more. As you know, I am still familiarizing myself with the content standards and have a ways to go before I am able to remember and incorporate them into my lessons. Another big problem for me is figuring out effective methods to deal with the wide range of student abilities in my classroom. There are some kids reading or writing at or above grade level, and others at 3rd grade level, and some seriously developmentally delayed students are challenged by most higher level skills. I have yet to discover the best method to push the higher level kids without losing the lower performing ones.

RATING: Needs Improvement

RECOMMENDATIONS:

1. learn and utilize State Standards
2. devise methods to reach wide range of students
3. become more proficient in Schafer Method and enhance my skills at teaching all forms of writing.
4. more modeling

STANDARD IV – Planning Instruction and Designing Learning Experiences for All Students

- Drawing on and valuing students' backgrounds, interests, and developmental learning needs.
- Establishing and articulating goals for student learning.
- Developing and sequencing instructional activities and materials for student learning.
- Modifying instructional plans to adjust for student needs.

Another area I need work in. The Agenda for the day you observed was incomplete due to the fact that I had changed the lesson plan as class began; however since our survey conference I have been posting detailed agendas with corresponding standards. I realize that my sequencing of activities and efficient use of instructional time needs improvement. This will come with experience and hard work.

RATING: Needs Improvement

RECOMMENDATIONS:

1. observe experienced teachers to learn tried and tested methods
2. work with my mentor to improve my weak areas
3. continue collaborating with the English Dept in developing an effective English curriculum map
4. when English map complete, work with Sara and other resource teachers to develop effective map for our program

Hope this is what you had in mind.

I realize we have butted heads a few times this year, but I hope you believe as I do that we both have only the students' best interests at heart. I can assure you my apparent resistance to your advice is neither a sign of disrespect nor an attack on you. I can be stubborn at times, and while we don't always see eye-to-eye, I am working hard, with Sara's invaluable help, to incorporate your suggestions into my teaching.

I know I have a long way to go to become a highly qualified educator. This year has been an incredible learning and teaching experience for me; much harder than I ever imagined, and much more rewarding. I sincerely believe I am doing a good job, and if provided the opportunity to return next year, I look forward to incorporating the tools I have acquired this year to improve my pedagogy.

Eric Mandel

Yeah, pretty pathetic groveling and ass-kissing (and yes, I tossed in *pedagogy* for my own amusement). Really not my style, and even after the above sycophancy I was pretty certain my days were numbered, so I decided to try one last tactic, a tactic I had been avoiding for fear that it might threaten Carol's testicular fortitude and that it could result in her taking it out on me. I decided to enlist Randy, the New Teacher Support Specialist, to my cause. Randy's been one of my biggest supporters and is universally respected on campus. I explained my situation to Randy and asked him to write me a letter of support, which he did willingly.

THE ACCIDENTAL TEACHER

Randy's letter:

Dear Carol,

As you may know since Jen (Randy's wife and VP), can no longer be both the new teacher support person and an evaluator, this year Debbie Fisher and I have been hired by the school to observe and assist new teachers. One of the new teachers I have worked with this year is Eric Mandel. Yesterday Eric and I had a lengthy discussion in which he shared some of his concerns about his evaluation.

I feel that of the 15 teachers I have been working with this year, Eric is by far the most improved. He has shown tremendous growth and continues to improve at a rapid rate. I continue to observe his classes on a regular basis and I have seen the change in his teaching and in his relationship to students. There is no question that at the beginning of the year that Eric was at the bottom of a very steep learning curve. He has responded to the challenge in an impressive manner. He has sought out help from his mentor Sara Stasi, me, and others at the school.

Eric did not come to us with the educational background and experience of other first year teachers. He had done no student teaching, so in truth his experience at the beginning of year *was* his student teaching. In spite of all these deficiencies, Eric is learning, adapting and seems to me to be on a path to becoming an excellent teacher. He has learned the IEP process, learned to differentiate instructional delivery to his students, and in my opinion has done a fantastic job in connecting with a very difficult group of students at a very high level.

I have observed his 3rd block 12 to 15 times this year. During this time they have read Of Mice and Men and The Great Gatsby among other works. Eric has done a wonderful job of bringing these stories to life for these kids, using many different modes of instruction. I was present for the summation Of Mice and Men and for a test on Great Gatsby. Students were answering higher order questions, formulating strong opinions, and more importantly, backing them up with reasons.

Like many new teachers, Eric has struggled at times with classroom management and curriculum content issues. But unlike many new teachers, he did not give up and shy away. Instead he stepped up and worked hard to improve his teaching strategies to better serve his students. Eric is always open to new ideas and suggestions from you, Ethan, Jen or anyone else. I look forward to helping Eric implement any suggestions you might have. In addition I would be willing to work with you in helping Eric implement your suggestions.

It is my sincere belief that Eric is on track to becoming an excellent educator. I encourage you to observe his 3rd block. It is a very difficult group of kids, but it is the group that I have witnessed make the most growth.

Thank you for your time and attention.

Respectfully submitted,

Randy

Randy hand-delivered his letter to Carol on Thursday morning, April 24th. Little did we know at the time—it was already too late.

THE ACCIDENTAL TEACHER

∽の∾

While I am proctoring the STAR test (something I plan to rant about at another time) the morning of April 24th, I get a phone call from Peggy at HR; she asks me to come up to talk to Pete as soon as I can. I explain to Peggy that I am right in the middle of STAR testing. Peggy schedules me for 2:15 that afternoon during my prep period.

My fate was sealed. Now I just had to make it through the STAR test and my two classes before being officially told to fuck off. In retrospect, I had been pretty certain at the end of the previous week that I was already toast when Carol ended an email granting me a deadline extension for my self-evaluation with, *That's okay.* **Have a good weekend.** *Carol.* I realized at once that this, her first superfluous pleasantry to me the entire year, was not a good omen. Guilt must have gotten the best of her.

After testing is over for the day, I drop in on Sara to tell her about my appointment. Sara does her best to put a positive spin on it, but she knows I'm not buying. So at a little after two I make my away across campus to Pecksniff's office. It's a strange feeling to be approaching my own demise under my own volition—a dead man walking. When I arrive Pete is out of his office. I sit in the small waiting area, the same alcove where eight months earlier I had nervously awaited my job interview. After several excruciating minutes Pete appears and casually waves me into his office. I follow him and sit as far away from his desk as possible. Pecksniff doesn't even bother to sit down. Standing over me he opens with the insipid rhetorical question, "I guess STAR testing is over for the year?"

I look up at him and reply curtly, "Can you please just get this over with?"

He complies immediately, "Last night in a closed

session the board elected not to ask you back for next year." And then he hands me the following letter from the superintendent:

Dear Mr. Mandel:

On April 24, 2008, in accordance with subdivision (b) of Section 44929.21 of the California Education Code, the Board of Trustees of the San Benito High School District decided not to reelect you to your position for the 2008-09 school year.

The Board thanks you for your service to the San Benito High School District and wishes you well in your future endeavors.

I really, really want to tell the schmuck about the time Havisham phoned me to spy on his ass, but for now I decide to take the high road and I say something like, "This is bullshit and I am really upset and frustrated. I am a good teacher and I would be even better next year. It's obvious you guys never had any intention of asking me back."

Pete remains silent, then I ask him a question I know he will never answer, "Any chance you can give me the reason for the decision?"

Pecksniff stands above me and remains mute. After a few seconds of silence I get up and walk out of his office passing once-friendly smiling faces that are not smiling now; instead, they are staring straight down at their desks doing their best to pretend I am invisible.

The deathwatch has begun.

Feeling a combination of numbness, frustration, anger and, strangely, an acute sense of liberation, I walk back to my empty classroom. As I do, I notice for the first time what a warm and beautiful day it is. With May approaching, Hollister will be starting to heat up and I'll be pulling out the fans soon.

X

Running on Empty

Saturday - May 10

When I get back to my empty classroom I sit down at my desk and stare at my computer monitor trying to decide who to tell and how to react. I send the following email to Sara, Doug the Librarian and Randy, my friendly observer:

Sent: Thu 4/24/2008 2:38 PM

To: Randy, Doug, Sara

Subject: Too little, too late...

Pete just called me up to his office and curtly told me I was not coming back next year. Needless to say I am upset as I believe I have done everything possible to try and adjust my teaching to Carol's unclear and un-reasonable standards. Not sure what I can or want to do about the unfair treatment I have received from Carol.

Anyway thanks for all your support. You have all helped me become a better teacher, and in spite of what Carol's thinks, I know I have done as good a job as I could do under the circumstances.

I then walk over to tell Liz who teaches resource social studies, one of my few confidantes and the person whose refrigerator and microwave I have used daily throughout the year. Liz's first reaction, "You're fucking kidding... right?" When the truth sinks in Liz repeats, "I'm sorry." about a half a dozen times.

I then go to Bryan's room and tell him the news. Bryan is a first year resource science teacher and former San Benito High star quarterback. (In fact for all you football fans: In his senior year Bryan was the starting quarterback and his understudy was Cade McKnown. McKnown later went on to star at UCLA and start a couple of seasons for the *Chicago Bears*. The highlight of McKnown's career, in my eyes, was the moment during a big game in college when he steps out of the huddle, pukes on the gridiron, calmly steps under center, takes the snap and plays on.) Bryan offers his condolences and sends me off with the universal male-to-male panacea for everything, "Let's go have a few beers before you go."

When I return to my room Sara is waiting for me. As I enter she tells me, with tears in her eyes, how sorry she is and how unfairly she thinks I have been treated, repeating at least five times, "I can't believe it."

At that moment I feel sorrier for her than I do for myself. We commiserate a while, and after Sara leaves I read email replies from Randy and Doug. Doug writes that the school is notorious for mistreating new teachers and that I shouldn't take it too personally because Carol is an idiot. The always-earnest Randy in the following email, offers his sympathies. Always the student advocate, he goes on to warn me not to let my students down, or worse—attempt to use them to fight my battle.

RUNNING ON EMPTY

Dear Eric: I would recommend speaking with the Union to see if it's something that a grievance could be filed on or if they don't have to give you a reason. I also will stand by my word and would be happy to write you a letter of recommendation if you would like. It's also important to keep in mind that there are 6 weeks left, and it will be easier for you if you keep your intensity level up. If you go into "safe mode" the kids will sense it. I also don't think it's anybody else's business especially the kids. If you want to contest it go through the CTA, but it never works out trying to get the kids involved. Thanks for trusting me enough to tell me, and I will keep it in confidence. I will still continue to come to your class and will resume observations next week. Whatever I can do to help, please let me know, Randy.

My reply:

Randy, I hope you know me well enough to realize I would never short-change my students and just phone in the last 6 weeks. My frustration is not directed at them. They are the reason I stuck it out the entire year with no support from my administrator. I also would never try and get the kids involved, though I do plan to tell them, not sure when or what. Some have been asking me about next year since the pink slips went out.

I will continue to put out my best effort. It won't be easy but I owe it to my students.

THE ACCIDENTAL TEACHER

A Bukowski fantasy

The frustration and helplessness I feel after being informed that I am not wanted, combined with Randy's lack of faith in my commitment to my students, are downright liberating. I'm tempted to cut the tenuous lines that tether me to convention and return to the imprudent inclination I voiced at my job interview—to use Bukowski in the classroom:

On the last day of school, in lieu of finals, I offer an alternate lesson plan on writing composition. I drop all the *Shaffer* bullshit and turn to the *Bukowski Method* on becoming a great writer. I share with my class these opening lines from Bukowski's poem *how to be a great writer.*

> *you've got to fuck a great many*
> *beautiful women*
> *and write a few decent love poems.*
>
> *and don't worry about age*
> *and/or freshly-arrived talents.*
>
> *just drink more beer*
> *more and more beer...*

The kids would certainly appreciate this sagacious advice, and I can easily imagine the spirited discussion that would follow. A spectacular teaching moment; a day to remember; a lesson my students will reminisce about for their entire lives.

I wish I had the balls to pull off this fantasy. The funny thing is—if I did, there is a good chance no adult outside of my classroom would ever know.

RUNNING ON EMPTY

❧

I did in fact talk to the union. Initially they told me that as a first year teacher with an emergency credential there was really nothing they could do to help me; however, after hearing my story they suggested I attempt a *Hail Mary*. Currently we are working with two sympathetic board members, one of whom is my student Cal's father, asking that they revisit my case. It is a real long shot and I am going to continue teaching with the expectation that I won't be back. It is nice in a way—I can now do exactly what I think best for my students without fear of reprisals. First thing I did was to reinstitute SSR and the bi-weekly trips to the library. Things are more relaxed in the classroom these days, and I think the kids even notice the looser (or perhaps to be more precise should that read *loser*?) atmosphere.

So far, so good.

Excerpt from email to school board member (Cal's dad) dated May 6, 2008.

Dear Mr. Gardner,

I was notified two weeks ago by the HR director, that the board had voted not to offer me a contract for next year. I realize that the board only acts on rec-ommendations from the administration, and I feel the need to explain and express my frustration with the decision and with the unfair treatment and the lack of support I have received from the district. I do not take this step lightly; I understand the situation and realize there is little if any chance of a reversal of the deci-sion. Before becoming a teacher last July I had spent over twenty-five years in public education as a classi-fied director. This experience gave me knowledge and insight into how school boards operate. In spite of the overwhelming odds against me, I am taking this step to relieve some of my pent-up frustration and hopefully to illuminate some problems in the district so they might be corrected for future new hires. I have no desire to rip a particular administrator or portray myself as a victim of a conspiracy; however I feel strongly about the unfair nature of my dismissal...

[Deleted section is a long-winded *rewhine* of the situation I have been dealing with all year.]

...I could go on and on, but I will spare you more sob stories and end with this: Although I now believe that I was hired primarily as a disposable placeholder until a more qualified candidate showed up, I loved the kids and I loved the teaching. It was much harder than I ever expected, and also much more rewarding. Modesty aside, I did a great job with the kids. I pushed them and I challenged them. They were engaged, they were curious, and most importantly they learned. I honestly believe my absence will be a loss to them and to the school. As unlikely as the prospect is, I would like nothing more than to teach again at San Benito High School next year.

I prefer you not share this letter with others. If you have any questions please call or email me. Thanks for letting me vent.

A few days after my notification I found out that I was one of six first-year teachers to be released. I was pleased to discover that another member of the dirty half-dozen was the original burr in my butt, Sally Smuts. Ah, a shred of silver lining. Speaking of nemeses (Aside: I just discovered a debate raging on the internet about the plural of nemesis.), two days after proclaiming me a dead man walking, Carol had her assistant Nydia call to set up a meeting for Tuesday to discuss my end-of-the-year *Summary Evaluation*. Of course my initial reaction was, *Fuck off! Such gall! Why would she want to meet with me after she had me fired?*

But my curiosity got the best me. I surmised that Diva Havisham could not resist an encore performance, and I perversely relished the prospect of one final trip down the rabbit hole. *Havishamland* is always sure to entertain. I waited until Monday to confirm my appointment.

I showed up on time and Carol, dressed in one of those Donald Duck sailor outfits with the navy blue, knee-length shorts and a navy blue, floppy white-collared blouse, led me back to her office. Once settled, she handed me my final evaluation and asked me to read it. I put it down on the table without looking at it and said, "This is pretty silly don't you think Carol? You just fired me and I won't be using any of this."

Carol looked stunned by my response and I thought for a moment that I had done the impossible—seriously underestimated her cluelessness. She attempted to convince me to read the entire evaluation and insisted that if I did I might be pleasantly surprised. And she added that her advice could come in handy if I were to seek a teaching job closer to home next year.

Ah, I thought to myself, *so she's actually doing me a big favor firing me! She's doing it to protect me from my dangerous ninety-mile daily commutes!*

What a doll!

I told her I was not really interested in my final evaluation, and that in fact I was finding the whole conversation surreal and pointless. Carol validated this point by suggesting that a positive letter of recommendation from her might be helpful for me in gaining a future teaching position.

"Carol, don't you see the paradox? You're willing to write a letter recommending me for a teaching position two days after letting me go because you think I am unfit to teach here?"

I don't recall her exact response but she made some lame attempt to convince me that I have the makings of a good teacher. We tap danced round-and-round with this, and then I asked pointblank, "So why did you decide to get rid of me?"

I was sure Carol had been instructed by Pecksniff not to give a reason so I did not expect an answer. (When the law does not require the employer to give a reason most employers do not, because if they were to give a reason, the employee and the union might have grounds to appeal the action.) Carol hemmed and Carol hawed, and Carol went on and on about how she couldn't answer my question. Then she reminded me that she had warned me months ago about the possibility of my being replaced by a more qualified candidate, one with a special ed credential and appropriate subject and grade-level experience. This not so subtle wink and nod all but confirmed for me that Carol had recently offered my job to someone she thought better qualified.

Several minutes of uncomfortable silence followed

until I began to mindlessly restate my case: my hard work, the strong rapport I had developed with the students, the lack of support, the simple fact that she had not once asked how I was doing or if there was anything she could do to help, etc, ad nauseam. My protestations, bordering on the pathetic, fell on deaf ears. Carol got all huffy and shrieked, "That's not true!! It's not my job to support you, that's what we have mentors for, but if it makes you feel better to blame me, go ahead."

Eventually I signed the damn evaluation without reading it, set it on the table, and without another word, staggered out of *Havishamland* for the last time.

A week later, after the March results of the CAHSEE's (exit exams) were released, I could not resist one more jab at Carol:

Carol,

I realize this is too late to change anything, but I wanted to point out that 17 out of my 19 seniors who had not passed the English section of the CAHSEE as of the beginning of this school year have now passed the test. I am neither vain enough nor naïve enough to take all the credit for their success, there are other factors (readers, prep, etc) for this, however I do think I played a major role in strengthening their language skills and building up their confidence thus making their success possible. Done tooting my own horn.

Eric

PS: Excerpt from summary evaluation: **…However, Mr. Mandel fell short in regards to providing the necessary modeling, instruction and rigor that would have adequately prepared his students for CAHSEE passage…**

The final passing rate on the English exit exam for my senior resource students was an amazing 96%!! Well above the district goal of 70%.

Not surprisingly, I never got a reply from Carol.

✣

A couple of weeks after our final meeting I recovered enough to go back and actually read Carol's end-of-year evaluation. Below are Carol's written *Summary Comments*:

> As previously stated, Mr. Mandel has had a steep learning curve this year. New to the teaching profession, he came to the district with no classroom experience. Despite his lack of experience, Mr. Mandel has demonstrated classroom management skills. He has developed positive, professional relationships with his students and maintains ongoing rapport with them. He has strengthened his skills in the area of case management, so that presently he writes IEP goals and completes all IEP forms with few errors. He has followed IEP time lines and has kept his caseload compliant with state regulations. As of the end of April, Mr. Mandel continues to struggle in the areas of planning and delivering an appropriately challenging, standards based lesson. His lesson delivery lacks the sufficient modeling required by students for mastery of new skills and concepts. When planning, Mr. Mandel continues to create too few activities for a 100-minute block and has not yet mastered the incorporation of state standards into his lesson development. Mr. Mandel needs to continue to explore and utilize additional teaching strategies; incorporate the state standards into his lessons and increase his planning and preparation for his

classes to continue his growth and development as a special education classroom instructor. He is to be recognized for the work and progress made during his first year as a classroom instructor.

And one final comment that stuck in my craw: Mr. Mandel has received extensive coaching in the areas of classroom management and instruction.

Children Left Behind

As the school year comes to a close it's time to discuss the students who did not make it. Some dropped out, some transferred to adult ed, and some were sent to San Andreas, the regional school that falls somewhere between public education and state prison. Five come to mind, most of whom I have already written about.

The first one to leave was Jesus. As you may remember, Jesus got expelled after getting busted for blazing (teen slang for smoking weed) in broad daylight behind the metal shop. Then came Melody, that unforgettable Melody, my most talented and most troubled student; her tune lingers on long after her final exit. I have not heard a word about her since her last disappearance.

The departure of Melody was followed closely by the departure of Ernesto, *sweet Ernesto*. This former senior was powerless to resist the temptation of nooners with his twenty year-old *Juliet*, and eventually was expelled for truancy. Then Natalie, one of my favorites, with the whacked-out f-bombing mom, became pregnant and left school in late March on her eighteenth birthday. Carlos, a pleasant, smart, sensitive, habitual truant with bleached hair, a bright smile and a shitload of potential, so feared confrontation he just stopped coming to school altogether. Eventually, when Carlos turned eighteen, he was taken off the books for good. The last I heard, Carlos was living with his 20 year-old girlfriend and working at *McDonald's.*

And, last but not least, there was Vanessa, that cute, bright, flirty, troubled, potty-mouthed junior. I have mentioned her a time or two—her drunkenness, her perpetual disorderly conduct and her unlikely career goal of becoming a pharmacist—but to this point I do not believe that I have given this Diva of Discord her due. Vanessa, with seeming effortlessness, arrived fashionably tardy on a daily basis. Her dramatic and disruptive grand entrances never failed to grab the spotlight as she single-handedly turned harmony into discord. A real virtuoso, Vanessa was suspended several times during the year until she was finally kicked out for good in April for jumping and beating the crap out of a fellow student. Here are two essays Vanessa wrote for me during her final suspension. She is a great speller, but like many of my students never bothers to break her essays into paragraphs.

Topic One: Explain why you were suspended and what you learned from the experience.

I got suspended three weeks ago for fighting a girl named Ami Jones. I believe that was her name. Well anyways one day after school my friend decided she wanted to fight her. So when we walked to Taco Bell Ami was in front of us. My friend confronted her but she didn't do nothing. So knowing I didn't like her, Ami decides to say something I didn't like so I grab her by her hair and we started fighting. So when we, meaning me and my friends, went to school the next day they called us into the office. Made us sit there for like half the day. Then we got locked up in juvi for 3 days and 2 nights. To tell you the truth it was not fun. I hated it in there. What I hated most was not being able to talk to my boyfriend. But when we got out and went to school they told me I was out. Pretty gay I thought. They only kicked me out. But I don't know. I learned that nothing is fair in this world. Also nothing comes easy. I know what I did was wrong. Not the right thing to do. There's other ways to handle problems. But know I know there are good things to take risks for. But that wasn't one of them. Let's just say it won't be happening again. You can count on that.

Topic Two: What are you planning to do for your senior year?

Well first I was hoping to graduate from San Benito. But now that everything happened I kinda just gave up on that. Because I mean I know I'm not the best student. Yeah I might talk alot (damn). But I'm a hard worker. I'll get my stuff done. Just tell me what I got to do and explain it to me and I will do it with no problem. But now its just like I want home school. I know I can get my stuff done with no questions asked. Probably even be better on my part. What I mean by that is I get tired of people. They bug me so I'll say something. I won't stay quiet. I don't think that's gonna happen. So my Senior year I probably will be out of school by then. Or at least done with high school. That's all I really want. Go to Gav (local community college). Get my basic. Maybe take a training. Just start getting my act together. Get started with my life. But who knows we'll all see by tomorrow's meeting on which path I plan on taking.

Sometimes when I'm having problems with bright, disturbed and disruptive students like Vanessa and Melody, I wonder if the school, in an admirable but misguided effort to protect the general ed population from chronic disorder, uses resource classes as dumping grounds for these troubled kids.

A Teacher Left Behind

The lack of support I experienced is not universal for new teachers on campus. Most first and second year teachers are part of the *Beginning Teacher Support and Assessment program* (BTSA). BTSA is described on its website as *a state-funded induction program, co-sponsored by the California Department of Education (CDE) and the Commission on Teacher Credentialing (CCTC) designed to support the professional development of newly-credentialed, beginning teachers and fulfill the requirements for the California Clear Multiple and Single Subjects Credentials.*

Evidently as a non-credentialed first-year teacher I was ineligible to attend the monthly two and a half hour induction meetings or other BTSA workshops. It is ludicrous beyond irony that the state does not offer, or even mandate, assistance to teachers in my situation. It is possible that the state is blameless in this matter. While researching BTSA I came across another state teaching program the *California Internship Teacher Preparation Programs* (CITPP). Described as an internship program that *provides opportunities for intern teachers to engage in systematic study and supervised practice of teaching while they serve as instructors-of-record with compensation. Intern programs may be offered for Multiple*

Subject credential candidates, Single Subject credential candidates, or Education Specialist credential candidates. It seems from the description that CITPP would have provided me an invaluable opportunity—if only someone had bothered to mention it to me.

When You Wish Upon A STAR...

Now on to STAR testing. Until recently I knew nothing at all about the STAR. Like many important matters this year no one had taken the time to explain to me about STAR testing and its significance, and everything I learned about it I learned through research, observation and osmosis.

STAR stands for *Standardized Testing and Reporting.* STAR testing is required for all students in California public schools in grades 2-11. The test takes place over four or five days and is used to rate students' proficiencies in various subjects. The proficiency ratings are *Advanced, Proficient, Basic, Below Basic, and Far Below Basic.* Students are tested only in math, science and English. Students are not tested in civics, government, or American history. STAR results are the sole criteria the state/fed (NCLB) uses to rate a school's success, and as a result many schools emphasize the tested subjects at the expense of the other academic areas. It should come as no surprise therefore that a recent poll found that 66% of American adults couldn't name the three branches of government. And while STAR test results are critical to a *school's* overall performance rating, to most students the testing means little or nothing. Unlike the CAHSEE, they do not need to pass the STAR to graduate.

Schools do everything they can to hype the test and

improve results for their own survival. San Benito High School had a STAR Pep Rally during which various school clubs, including the cheerleaders, did a sales job (or more accurately, a con job) on a pretty cynical student body. At the rally the Drama Club performed silly skits misinforming the students that if they did not do well on the test the school would lose its athletic and extracurricular programs. This is pretty much bullshit. Just before the rally was to end, Krystal, the school principal, *Baler* alum and hyper-proactive proponent of school spirit, took the stage. In hopes of working the crowd into a frenzy, she announced that she had made the following bet with the principal of the school's biggest athletic rival, the dreaded *Mustangs* of Gilroy High: the administrators at whichever school did worse on the STAR would have to wear the other school's football jerseys for a week.

Big mistake.

Drawing crazy patterns on your sheets...

During the first morning of STAR testing the faculty received the following email from Krystal:

To: Certificated
From: Krystal, Principal
Subject: One more issue **URGENT**

I just received a parent phone call about STAR testing and she is very concerned, as she is hearing that students are bragging about making nice designs on their exams answer sheets with random bubble fillings so we do poorly on STAR.

Please check every answer document when you

collect your materials at the end of the testing time
and look for designs, etc...

I am requesting that you speak to the student first
(if this is the case) and email me the names of the
students because I will be calling their parent(s) (and
talking to the student) about the issue. You know your
students well, and will be able to identify whether they
did their best on the exam.

The rumor is that our students are texting each
other to do poorly on STAR so we can go into program
improvement and they want me to wear the Gilroy jersey. I am VERY disappointed to say the least!!

I hope our students rise to the occasion and show
their Baler Pride!!

Thanks,

As you know by now, I am no fan of standardized
testing. To many teachers, and some administrators, data-
driven education is a failure and does students a serious
disservice. One thing I have learned during my year in
education is that while my students thirst for knowledge
they are actually drowning in useless information. We stuff
them with often out-dated information that may come in
handy on standardized tests—information they will never
need once their high school years are behind them—while
what they need is knowledge that can actually help them
in the real world, and the critical-thinking skills that will
give them the ability to figure things out on their own.

I proctored for four students with IEP's that required
they have a "reader" for the STAR, and I was obligated
to listen along with the students to the official CD whose
narrator "read" every question. Although the test was all

multiple-choice with no writing, it was brutal. The English test consisted primarily of passages one to three-pages long, followed by five or six questions related to each passage.

Students without readers are able to read the questions first and then scan the text for correct answers. But the students I was proctoring were forced to listen to the narrator read every single word, including the meaningless copyright information, and had no way to review the narration once they read the questions. I did encourage them to read the questions before I played the passages, but it was really a pointless exercise. The *Futile Four* seemed to be in a constant state of bewilderment. I am fairly certain that when their results are released they will find themselves in the *Far Below Basic* category.

The test for English 11 was really hard. There were a few questions that *I* would have had trouble answering correctly. There were questions about passive and active voice, and I remember one about personification. I found the following example from the 2007 STAR:

The Wood-Pile by Robert Frost

Out walking in the frozen swamp one grey day
I paused and said, "I will turn back from here.
No, I will go on farther—and we shall see."
The hard snow held me, save where now and then
One foot went down. The view was all in lines   5
Straight up and down of tall slim trees
Too much alike to mark or name a place by
So as to say for certain I was here
Or somewhere else: I was just far from home.
A small bird flew before me. He was careful   10
To put a tree between us when he lighted,
And say no word to tell me who he was

RUNNING ON EMPTY

Who was so foolish as to think what he thought.
He thought that I was after him for a feather—
The white one in his tail; like one who takes   15
Everything said as personal to himself.
One flight out sideways would have undeceived him.
And then there was a pile of wood for which
I forgot him and let his little fear
Carry him off the way I might have gone,   20
Without so much as wishing him good-night.
He went behind it to make his last stand.
It was a cord of maple, cut and split
And piled—and measured, four by four by eight.
And not another like it could I see.   25
No runner tracks in this year's snow looped near it.
And it was older sure than this year's cutting,
Or even last year's or the year's before.
The wood was grey and the bark warping off it
And the pile somewhat sunken. Clematis 1   30
Had wound strings round and round it like a bundle.
What held it though on one side was a tree
Still growing, and on one a stake and prop,
These latter about to fall. I thought that only
Someone who lived in turning to fresh tasks   35
Could so forget his handiwork on which
He spent himself, the labour of his axe,
And leave it there far from a useful fireplace
To warm the frozen swamp as best it could
With the slow smokeless burning of decay.   40

25. In line 35, when the poet mentions "Someone who lived in turning to fresh tasks", he is referring to a person who
A likes things to be organized.
B rarely completes his projects.

C dislikes hard work.

D feels at home in the outdoors.

26. One feature of this poem that classifies it as modern American poetry, rather than poetry of the Colonial period, is that

A it is not strongly moralistic or religious.

B it has only one main character.

C it provides a description of nature.

D it lends itself to various interpretations.

27. What is ironic about the winter setting of the poem?

A Animals cannot make use of the wood because they are hibernating.

B The wood could be keeping someone warm, but instead it is rotting in the swamp.

C The speaker would not have noticed the wood-pile if the trees had not been bare.

D The person who cut the wood wanted to come back to it, but the snow hid his tracks.

28. Robert Frost wrote and published from 1894 until his death in1963. What literary trend of Frost's era can be found in this poem?

A focus on everyday things

B intricate rhyme schemes

C instances of dialogue

D dramatic ending

And finally from the Science STAR an example not related to any passage:

56. Which instrument would be used by a scientist to measure time?

A goniometer

B hydrometer

C chronometer

D anemometer

Hey STAR Masters, how 'bout a clock?

I firmly believe the emphasis on standardized testing is detrimental to our nation's clumsy quest to overhaul our failing educational system. Something needs to be done soon. I don't want to come off as an apologist for teachers as I think many of them don't belong in the classroom, but change needs to be made from the top down and no sector should be spared. Some form of merit pay is undoubtedly part of the solution, but not if merit is based primarily on standardized test scores and administrative evaluations of teachers. After my experience as administrative evaluation road-kill, it should come as no surprise that I think there needs to be another method of evaluating teacher effectiveness. And while all the evaluation standards must be tied to student performance, one criteria (or for you grammarians, one criterion) should measure a teacher's rapport with his or her students.

Reflections on the possibility that I lost my job to an appropriately trained and "highly qualified" neophyte: Today, *No Child Left Behind* is the driving force in the area of performance assessment. With the passage of NCLB early in Bush's first term, the federal government mandated many new goals and regulations but provided little or no funding to help schools achieve them. One particular edict in NCLB that played a negative role in my development and success as an educator is the requirement that after a transitional phase, schools shall hire only "highly qualified" teachers. At first glance this seems a worthy goal, but of course as we (my students included) know *The devil is in the details.*

THE ACCIDENTAL TEACHER

To paraphrase a former president, it depends on what *highly qualified* is. As some may remember, in a time before NCLB there was a serious movement to waive certain teacher requirements in an effort to get effective but not necessarily "trained" teachers into classrooms, But in NCLB, *highly qualified* is based totally on front-end quantitative qualifications: the paper qualifications a teacher brings to the job: credentials, degrees, special certificates, etc. (Just realized that this is the identical debate I had with Sally Smuts during the new teacher in-service.) The rating of *highly qualified teacher* is determined solely by points on a bureaucratic checklist. Effectiveness is not a factor.

Bottom line for my situation: my effectiveness as a teacher was basically irrelevant in determining my fate; schools are at times forced to replace an effective and potentially exceptional but theoretically unqualified educator (like me?) with a potentially less effective but "highly qualified" one.

A rumor is currently circulating at school that a credentialed, experienced resource teacher, one who happens to be related to a well-respected science teacher, is all set to replace me next year. In retrospect this rumor makes a lot of sense. Looking back over my earlier talks with Carol regarding my status for next year, it seems likely that she had a specific replacement for me in mind for quite a while, and I wouldn't be surprised if she had promised my position to someone very early in the school year.

It's likely that I never had a chance and that I was in fact, little more than a disposable placeholder.

Sucks.

RUNNING ON EMPTY

They sat together in the park...

On a somewhat more positive note Zeke, one of my brow-pierced, black t-shirted, black-jeaned metal boys, turned in the following somewhat disturbing story. I was surprised when I read it as prior to this story Zeke had never shown any evidence of having a flair for creative writing. When I first read *Twisted Fate* I was suspicious, plagiarism at worst, derivative at best. I *googled* some passages and found nothing, and after a gentle interrogation I've come to believe that Zeke probably did write it. What most impressed me, aside from the inventive spelling, was the shifting of POV at the beginning and the end.

Twisted Fate

You awoke in shock, to find yourself in closed spaces. You struggle to get free but, it's no use. It's dark in every turn you make, slimy, thick but piercable layers, wrapped around you with no way out....

It was a bright and beautiful day, a Tuesday perhaps. Becky had just locked her front door, and turned to her car. She was aged around 23-26, hair color of Burnette, roughly as tall as 5'9". Wearing a White large shirt, a short blue jeaned skirt, with white shoes. She was also pregnate, as far along at 8 1/2 months with a baby boy. Becky had just sat in her car and started for the ignition. She had a sharp pain in her stomache and shreiked. Clenching at herself, she started breathing heavy. Not a moment later had she been relieved of this pain, she sighed greatfully, then started turning the key. The engine started puttering, and turned over. She put it in reverse, pulled out, threw it in drive, and took off.

Becky pulled to a stop light, and noticed she was low

on gas. She thought to herself, how she would make it to the Doctors in time. As the light turned Green, she made her way to the nearest gas station. Becky pulled into "Jared's Gas at Lowest" but unfortunatley, every pump was taken, and with few cars trailing behind each "Crap, Becky yelled, and turned away to search for another. Driving around, coming to a second Red light, Becky looked in her rear-view mirror and saw a Black Corvette zooming passed each car cutting them off. The vehicle pulled along side her, and waiting for the light to turn Green, reved the engine a few times. The black tinted windows rolled down, and a man with Black shades turned to her, smiled sharply, and look forward. At the sight of Green the mysterious man sped off forward, and Becky stared at his License Plate wich read: LC666CF

The thought of that made her stomache churn. She pressed on the gas, and turned into the next gas station. The sign read: Burney's Dine and Gas. It didn't seem much of a Dining place, for nobody bothered to go inside much, just wen for the gas was all. Becky had pulled into Pump 3, got out, and walked over to the pump machine, and slid a Credit Card though the card reader. After the beep, she took opened her gas cover, took off the lid, and put the pump inside the gas tank. Squeezing it once, it locked for the remainder of the time being. Leaning against her car, the License Plate burned an image into her mind, and she could not stop thinking about it. Not a moment to soon had she collapsed to the ground on one knee, and clenched her stomache again. A puddle beneathe her face, showed not only her face, but a man behind her. The same man from the Black Corvette, but her face, was different now, it looked to be dripping of Black oil. She freaked out and jumped back, feeling her face, looking around, but no oil found, nor the mysterious man. What she did find, was shocking, blood laid on the ground underneath her skirt.

The pump had clicked and the handle released. Becky stood up as quickly as possible, took out the pump, dropped it, and closed both the nozzle cap and gas cover. She raced inside her car and took off. In panic,

Becky sped to the Hospital. Arriving there she parked in the Handicap space, turned off her car, got out and rushed inside. She came up to the Receptionist and told her about her appointment. In reply the Receptionist said: "You're late... the Doctor will see you now." Yes, thank you..." Becky told her. She made way through the halls, and into the Doctors room. Ahh, at last, Becky, how are you today? spoke the Doctor. Becky said: "Doctor Friedmen, the pains gotten much worse an-" "Contractions" interupted Dr. Friendmen. "No, much worse, they were painful, I bled just before I got here at the gas station." Dr. Friedmen moved closer to her and felt her forehead, she felt fine. He spoke to her and said "You might be having a miscarrage. We'll need to perform an ultrisound right away."

Being in the Ultrisound room was quite uncomfortable for Becky. But no matter, she stuck to it to find out if she was truly having a miscarrage. She was sitting on a small, yet rather comfortable chair, with the Monitor to her left, and the Dr. to her right. Dr. Friedmen had a small sensor connecter to the Monitor in his hand. The Monitor showed everything that Dr. Friedmen went over with the sensor. "Hmmm, nothing seems to be out of the ordinary, and there doesn't seem to be anything wrong with the baby.."

At an instant Becky asked the Doctor in fear, "What it is, what's wrong??" "There seems to be something attached, or around the baby..." Replied Dr. Friedmen. "What do you mean.." Becky spoke in crazed emotions. "Never you mind my dear, I'll take a copy photo and figure this mess out. What I want you to do is take your mind off things, go shopping for this baby. It was a boy, no?" "..Yes.., he is."Said Becky. "Ok then, off you go, and take it easy." Becky told the Doctor, "Ok, thank you Dr. Friedmen, I'll see you soon."Dr. Friedmen smiled and walked her to the door.

Becky was driving through the town, thinking about the facial expression on the doctors face, and kept wondering what he meant by "Something wrapped around the baby." She drove to the Store, like the Doctor had told her to, and she parked close by in a shaded area. When she got out, she noticed the same Black Corvette from earlier. She clentched at her stomache for a brief moment of pain. With a discrete look, she moved into the Store, took a shopping cart and made her way to the baby section. She spotted out the cutest baby outfit on the hangar racks, and picked it up to look at it. from the corner of her eye, she saw a black suspicious object moving. She couldn't help herself but look at revealed it to be the mysterious man. He too was in the baby section, and he made his way past her. For a sec Becky could swear time was slowing down. As he passed her, he pulled down his shades and stared at her.

His eyes were as Black as Night. As he pulled his shades back up he walked away, and Becky had the same pain from before, but it hurt alot **(DAMN!)** more this time. She fell onto her back, and she couldn't think straight. Screaming in agony, people stopping what they were doing to watch. A few people had rushed to help her but had no idea what was going on. Becky kicked, and freted. Screaming and yelling. Blood started gushing out of her, and soon, her stomache had torn open, with a small hand holding out, black with oil running down. Everything leaped back in fear. Becky was still screaming for a short a while, but resumed to be dead after.

You jump out of Becky's stomache, and land onto the floor, free at last from the fleshy prison, standing there, staring at everyone, frightened, and running everywhere, leaving trails of Black oil.. People are shrieking, running around, pushing and shoving. You come across a mirror, and see yourself as a monster, with dark Black oil dripping from yourself. Behind you is a tail, with a point at the end, swaying back and forth, from side to side.

You look down at you hands as they seem to be like claws, only the nails are as sharp as razors. You can't help but have the urge to kill people, everyone.. All of them... As a women screams at the very sight of you, you leap onto her, bite her neck, taking a chunk out of her, and digging your nails into her lungs, killing her within seconds. One after another, you kill people, watching there blood drip to the ground, and them fall after.

A hand was layed on your left shoulder, and you look up to see the mysterious man standing next to you. He speaks, "Come, it's your time in this world..."He moves his hand before you both, and a shroud of darkness covers all, pulling you both into what feels like a portal, but you are still in the Store, but it's not the same.. everything is destroyed.. The mysterious man is gone. You are left alone, and you walk to the door, as it's broken down, with glass shattered all over. Stepping outside, everything lies in ruins. Vehicles rusted down, buildings collapsed, roads torn up, and Bridges broken down. People are either dead, or walking in single file lines with creatures flying above them with what appears to look like a weapon of some sort. Creatures running around, taunting the humans. You smile at the sight of it all. Walking out to see more, the creatures kneel to the very sight of you. The thought crosses you mind, that you rule this world...

To Inherit the Wind

Many pages back, when the school year was young, my hopes were high and the possibilities were unlimited, I promised to provide the course summaries of what I attempted to teach my students. What follows are for English 11 and 12, beginning with the descriptions in the school catalogs and followed by my course summaries for the appropriate grade levels.

English 11 So Called Intelligent Design (aka: Description from Course Catalog): English 11 is designed to improve students' reading and writing skills and to create readers and writers through an in-depth study of the different genres of American Literature and the historical, cultural, and philosophical influences which (sic) shaped it. The course flows chronologically from the Native Americans through the Puritans, the Age of Reason, Romantic, and Realist periods, to the 20th century. Core work read includes such novels as *The Catcher in the Rye, Of Mice and Men, The Great Gatsby,* and *Bless Me, Ultima.*

Students will continue their study of *Schaffer Writing Model* components and strategies beginning with the concept of weaving and concluding with sentence blending. These strategies are designed to retain the advanced skills of literary and linguistic analysis while increasing freedom of style and student voice. Students write a combination of critical and creative pieces based on the literature and using the writing process. Students also write an "I Search" paper and research, write, and deliver an informative speech. Independent reading is also a major focus of this course. Instruction, activities and assessment focus on the concepts and skills outlined in the *California State Content Standards* for language arts.

English 11 Evolution (aka: summary of my actual course of study): English 11 was intended to improve students' reading and writing skills and to create readers and writers through an in-depth study of the different genres of American literature and the historical, cultural, and philosophical influences that shaped it. The instructor did his best to adhere to the substance of the designers' intent in the absence of a curriculum map. The teacher developed the course into a contemporary version of the original design through an evolving, organic process of natural selection and improvisational collaboration with the students. The course primarily dealt with the 20th and 21st centuries and touched only lightly on the Puritans. There was no real sense of chronology other than that provided by reading the novels, short stories, and plays from front to back, or more literally, from beginning to end. Students began the year listening daily to poems from NPR's *The Writer's Almanac.* When that didn't go over well, the class merged into the slow lane on the *American Dream Highway* beginning with *Of Mice and Men,* detouring back a couple of centuries to Jonathan Edward's fire and brimstone sermon *Sinners in the Hands of God,* and then on to Arthur Miller's *Crucible.* They continued on their dream-shattering journey with an in-depth reading and analysis of *The Great Gatsby,* and finished off the literary adventure with a song and dance entitled *Zoot Suit.*

The instructor determined it was more important to fill critical gaps in the students' background knowledge as soon as they became evident during instruction than to waste precious time on studying linguistic analysis. As a result there were many circuitous detours involving relevant and sometimes not-so-relevant topics from astronomy to zoology. Students wrote regularly, actually using the *Schaffer Writing Model* on occasion. The instructor emphasized narrative writing and used the discovery of one's voice as a strategy to stimulate student interest in the writing process. Students delivered a couple of presentations that fell far short of an actual informative speech. Vocabulary was based on the literature at hand. The teacher employed adages and proverbs to help students understand such literary terms as metaphor, symbolism and theme. Independent reading in the form of daily *Silent Sustained Reading* was a high priority until it was reduced and then later completely eliminated by administrative edict. The teacher designed instructional activities and assessments to emphasize the importance of critical thinking and the acquisition of knowledge necessary to live a well-informed life. Some of these concepts and skills may actually appear in the *California State Content Standards* for language arts.

English 12 So-called Intelligent Design (aka: Description from Course Catalog): Students in English 12 read novels, short stories, poetry, essays, and plays including: *Kitchen God's Wife, Antigone, Macbeth,* and *Things*

Fall Apart. Through reading genres of both classic and contemporary periods, students gain an appreciation of the universal values shared by writers from different cultures. Students will continue their study of *Schaffer Writing Model* components and strategies beginning with the concept of weaving and concluding with sentence blending. These strategies are designed to retain the advanced skills of literary and linguistic analysis while increasing freedom of style and student voice. Writing is critical, analytical, and reflective in nature and based upon class reading and outside research. There is an emphasis on collaborative work and presentations relating to topics relevant to the literature.

English 12 Evolution (aka: summary of my actual course of study): Students in English 12 read four short stories, some poetry, a couple of essays, one novel and one play. The short stories included: *The Black Cat* by Edgar Allen Poe, *The Other Wife* by Collette, *Marriage is a Private Affair* by Chinua Achebe, and *What You Pawn I Will Redeem* by Alexie Sherman. The one novel was *Parrot in the Oven* by Victor Martinez, and the one play was *Zoot Suit* by Luis Valdez. They also watched the Polanski film version of *MacBeth.*

The class explored various literary forms and genres with a major emphasis on the contemporary primarily because the students had a difficult time appreciating themes and genres that did not in some way connect to their own lives. The class sampled some of the other recommended readings, but found them either too difficult or of no interest whatsoever. The instructor used modern culture, including music (hip-hop, rap, rock and metal), fashion, movies and television, to encourage critical and reflective thinking and to foster an appreciation of diversity. Students worked on their writing, primarily creative writing, using narrative to develop voice, perspective through POV, plot weaving and character development. Teaching of vocabulary, adages, poetry and SSR details were identical to English 11 above. Outside research was assigned early on and was an immediate failure; many students suffer from ADD and for them to succeed it is important they have someone overseeing their work to keep them on track. The instructor emphasized collaborative work. The oft-neglected literary form, humor, was the heart of most successful student presentations.

A major component of both the English 11 and English 12 curriculum is the mandated Workability Program to assist all high school resource students with their transition from high school to college, vocational ed or the work world. This program offers career planning services including job placement, resume building, college field trips, help with grant and scholarship applications, job shadowing and more. Since English is the only class all students are required to take every semester, many of these services are delivered through the resource English classes. I invited several guest speakers to talk to the class about career opportunities with the US Forest Service, State Parks and the automotive repair industry. I estimate that thirty-minutes of class time per month was dedicated to the *Workability Program.*

I realized for the first time after reading the official description above that there are **NO** California state standards and benchmarks for seniors. Duh!!! Student progress is not assessed during their final year in high school, therefore there are no benchmarks for them to reach, ergo no need for standards.

Now they tell me!!!! Someone should let Carol know.

You don't have to be a professor of pedagogy to notice both the lack of curricular gravitas and the lowered student expectations for English 12 as compared to English 11. Reasons for the discrepancies are probably a combination of the following: the indolence and lack of effort by English 12 teachers to develop a serious curriculum, the loss of interest by the district once students become seniors and are no longer subjected to STAR testing—and so no longer effect the school's oh so important academic performance rating—and finally, a proactive effort by the administration to divert the lethal confluence of widespread faculty malaise and serious student unrest during the annual outbreak of virulent strains of senioritis.

After several seconds of intense self-reflection, I submit that any reasonably cognitive being would conclude that my real-world, rag-tag, hobbled-together curriculum is equal, if not superior, to the virtual curriculum designed by the pedagogical professionals who remain separated from classroom life by the thick fog of rarified air that surrounds their ivory towers.

XI

Muttering Small Talk at the Wall

Friday - June 6

Well loyal readers who have stuck with me to this point, if you were hoping for a Hollywood ending, a cavalry of students armed with picket signs and petitions riding to the rescue, you can forget it. Feel free, with my blessing, to stop reading now and allow your imagination to end the story in its own way. I won't mind in the least, and I will even offer a few alternate endings for you to consider:

1. The powers that be come to their senses, admit their mistake, rescind Mr. Mandel's termination and make a public apology.

2. Mr. Mandel morphs into the most unreliable of narrators, slips into a deep psychosis, and on the last day of school goes postal.

3. The entire student body, led by William, Gina and Cal, participates in a massive school boycott followed a day later by a faculty and staff walkout.

The unrelenting attacks gradually cause the hapless Ms. Havisham to fall apart one piece at a time, rambling nonsensically and issuing ineffectual edicts, until finally, while the students and staff celebrate Mr. Mandel's reinstatement at a large victory rally, she has a total meltdown and is carted away in a straight jacket. As Carol is wheeled off she looks directly into TV news cameras and offers her final farewell, "All right, Mr. Pecksniff, I'm ready for my close-up."

In the end there was no Frank Capra ending, no rousing speeches, no stirring music, no fireworks, and no affirmation of the *American Dream*. Like most things in life this story ends with a fade out, if not a whimper. One minute I am a teacher, the next minute I am in my car returning home to my former life as if the last ten months had all been a dream. I imagine the sensation is analogous to how one might feel returning home from a yearlong stint as a Peace Corps volunteer in some faraway place; within days all that will remain will be memories and a handful of souvenirs from my tour of duty.

Perhaps a more apt metaphor for my teaching experience and its transitory nature is me, like the *Discovery Channel's Survivor Man*, parachuting alone into a vast wilderness carrying only a flint, a broken bicycle pump and a Swiss army knife, relying on my own wits, my grit and my single-minded will to survive, eating unspeakable items and doing whatever is necessary to get along with the natives and stay alive in a hostile environment. In the end, the fact I made it through the entire school year without being airlifted to safety is one measure of a successful journey.

MUTTERING SMALL TALK AT THE WALL

As I sit at the dining room table in a friend's elegant eighth-floor condo on the Embarcadero in San Francisco, surrounded by notes and mesmerized by the panoramic view of the bay, a large weathered tanker surrounded by sailboats is moving under the Bay Bridge. In the wake of my journey I am trying to regain my focus and report on its final segment. This will be my final entry, and while I have a great deal to write about, I am not really sure how to find the words, so I will just let my mind wander and my fingers try to keep pace.

On June 4, 2008 the school year ground to an end. My major league career now over, I've taken my final hacks and I've made my last pitch. And although I have been callously cut from next season's *Baler's* roster, all in all for me it was a career year. Before I unveil the last of my student stories, one more digression I am helpless to resist: I think today's teenagers get a bad rap. Most teens are funny and friendly. Many crave attention, some just want to be noticed, and most do their best to make themselves invisible. There are some real jerks and losers in the mix, but the majority of the kids I have worked with are neither. They simply view high school as an annoying, unavoidable hurdle they must endure before moving on to a future most are unprepared to face and many are secretly, or not so secretly, scared shitless to confront.

My generation, the vanguard of the *Baby Boomers*, had the Viet Nam War as its defining issue to shape and unite most of "us" against most of "them." The war inspired us to protest, to engage, to drop out or to run away. We felt empowered and audaciously believed we would change the world. Our future was unlimited. Today's kids also have a war, but it is not their war. The war in Iraq hardly affects them. Most teenagers, like most Americans, are totally un-touched by it. Their future is unimaginable. Most don't care about changing, or even learning about the world, and because American teens have been constantly bombarded their entire waking lives with nothing but bullshit and fantasy, they unconsciously shut out everything that does not directly impact their day-to-day existence. When confronted with outside pressures they do what modern teenagers have always done—turn inward for comfort to their circles of friends, their music, their fashions and more. They seek and find kids who think (think may be too strong a word) and feel as they do. Education and books do not stand a chance against the web of distraction they face daily, the 500 TV channels, *MySpace*, movies, *iPods*, hip-hop, *Grand Theft Auto*, cell phones and texting. In this day and age the real miracle is that any kid willingly picks up and reads a book.

The vast majority of teens find groups to join, but there are some loners. Among my students were metal-heads, cowboys, pig farmers, car freaks, jocks, *emos*, potheads, gun-freaks, gang-bangers, geeks, god-freaks, and a very small group of intellectually curious kids (nerds?) that actually wanted to learn. And there are extremes, such as my solitary spiked-hair Scene Boy Irwin/Zenebula. While Zen technically belongs to a group, on this campus *Scene Kids* are such a small fringe population that being one by itself is an act of rebellion. Surprise! I am going to digress in the middle of this digression.

I never, and not from lack of trying, did find out exactly what the *scene* in *Scene Kids* is; as I have mentioned before, I did learn that Zen is the most smugly judgmental and vainly bigoted teenager I have ever encountered. Many times Irwin preached one irrefutable belief—the only people worth knowing are *Scene Kids*. Irwin would rather hang out with a pathological-raping-murdering *Scene*

Boy than waste his precious time associating with friendly run-of-the-mill kids.

Okay it's time to sum up this Andy Rooney moment: At San Benito High School there are good kids, not so good kids, bad kids and total asshole kids, but the bottom line is that the kids I have dealt with this year really aren't that different from the generations that preceded them.

Final tales from the crib...

Jeremy! Jeremy! Jeremy!

As difficult, self-absorbed and oblivious as he is, I have come to appreciate and actually enjoy Jeremy in small doses. In many ways Jeremy has become a parody of himself. He talks of himself in the third person, believing that doing so somehow gives him added gravitas. I was never sure if his over-developed feminine side and lack of interest in anything non-Jeremy was a result of cognitive disorders or just a result of his family dynamics––the strong mother, silent father, and thrown in for good measure, the vibrant hair-stylist older sister. His unique appearance and personality seem to constantly get him in trouble with his fellow students.

In many ways Jeremy invites hostility, and has on occasion received serious threats of violence against his person. In fact, during the last two weeks of the year his mother, fearing for Jeremy's safety, kept him home right up until the final day of classes. According to Jeremy, some kids were threatening to hurt him. The police were called in which of course only made things worse. Jeremy did return to school just in time to perform miserably on his English final, eventually ending up with a sympathy D.

Right to the end, Jeremy's slothfulness never wavered,

and his final performance amazed even cynical me one last time: he attempted to answer only four of nineteen vocabulary questions even though the vocabulary section was multiple choice, even though I had given the students the actual words in advance, and even though I allowed the students to use all their notes during the test.

Even more incredible, I learned from other students that Jeremy tends to be quiet and somewhat shy in most of his other classes. That certainly says something about my teaching, not sure what thing, but something.

Jeremy encore: One recent Friday as the class was leaving, I asked Jeremy if he had any plans for the weekend, "A new tattoo or piercing perhaps?"

He excitedly replied he had plans to see a movie with friends on Saturday.

"Which movie Jeremy?"

"Jeremy's gonna go see *Sex and the City*, Mr. Mandel."

And for about the millionth time this year, I bite my tongue, grin broadly and chuckle to myself.

Tony Morales, the *California State Golden Gloves Welterweight Champ*, went to Grand Rapids in early May to compete for the *National Golden Gloves Championship*. Tony won his first two bouts and then lost his third fight in a disputed split-decision to the eventual winner, a twenty-five year-old boxer from Syracuse, NY. Tony told the class about his trip to Michigan and all about his defeat. From what he said it sounded to me like he was robbed, but he took it quite philosophically. Tony remains resolute in his belief that he will one day be the middleweight champion of the world. I wouldn't bet against him. A few days later when I finally revealed to my students my own crushing defeat by TKO at the hands Hammer'n Havisham, I used both Tony's loss and mine as an opportunity to offer a life lesson in perseverance and making the best of a bad situation.

MUTTERING SMALL TALK AT THE WALL

And then there is Brad, a white boy who favors plaid Bermuda shorts that sag down to his ankles giving him the appearance of a gangster golfer. Brad is a good-looking, do-nothing, good-for-nothing junior with zero interest in class work. He is a member of an elite group of three students who actually failed my classes the final semester. Despite his obvious shortcomings, or maybe because of them, Brad is a babe magnet. At the beginning of class a few weeks ago Vera, my aide, confiscated from Brad a *graffitiesque* full-page cartoon of a handgun on a background of the number 187, the California criminal numeric code for murder. Evidently, and news to me at the time, 187 is a common gang-banger symbol and proclamation of impending bloodshed. At first I thought *no big deal*, but Vera went on and on about the inappropriateness of Brad's artwork. Stepping up to my role as authority figure, I called Brad up to my desk and demanded an explanation. Of course he had a good one: His counselor, in an effort to suppress Brad's creative urge to paint graffiti on school buildings, had encouraged him instead to draw graffiti in his notebook. "Good one, Brad." And I followed it up with, "Why don't you go sit down at your desk while I call your counselor."

He looked pretty glum as he shuffled his baggy-saggy-ass back to his desk. Surprise—his counselor had no idea what I was talking about and asked me to send Brad to her office immediately. Vera escorted Brad and his execution of execution to the counselor's office. Later Vera returned without Brad and informed me that on the way to the office Brad had threatened her with *"Snitches get stitches."* At the time Vera appeared unruffled, but when she mentioned that Brad lives on her street and that there was a recent unsolved murder a few doors down from her house, I began to understand her initial reaction to the drawing. When I suggested she write up her own incident report and possibly file a police report, Vera told me that aides aren't permitted to fill out complaints on students.

Wait. This makes no sense to me. Every school employee has the right to file a complaint. I catch a whiff of *Eau de Carol* and ask Vera where she got her information, and when she explained it all started to make sense. According to Vera, during a meeting with aides earlier in the year, Carol complained about the volume of what she called "unjustified" complaints. Carol's solution was to issue a fiat: from that point on only certificated staff could file complaints against students. Carol has an uncanny ability to make things as difficult as possible for the people she is supposed to be making life easier for.

I shared with Vera my feelings about Carol's stupid, self-serving solution and assured her she had every right to file a complaint. To further encourage her I called the principal and she verified what I had told Vera. She filed the complaint and talked to the police and Brad was suspended from school.

Mr. Mandel, Why can't we just watch the movie?

As both the school year and my teaching career wound down, I slowed my pace, lowered my expectations for the final time, and tried to give the kids a taste of some important works of literature we would not have time to read. In an effort to save time, and to everyone's delight, I replaced reading the actual works of literature with watching the movies. I had my seniors sit through Polanski's bloody *Macbeth,* and my juniors, Frank McCourt's memoir *Angela's Ashes.* Both movies were rated R, which theoretically required that before I showed them in class I either obtained permission from the administration or sent permission slips home and waited—who knows how long—for their unlikely return. I did what any lame duck faced with a similar choice would do, neither.

The seniors enjoyed *Macbeth* more than I thought they would. I tried to prime them with all the standard Shakespeare bullshit: how incredible Shakespeare was with his psychological insight and all, but I think the boys mainly appreciated the blood, the guts, the heightened sense of honor and the naked girls. *Angela's Ashes* was a great success with my juniors. Before I found myself in a crippling bureaucratic quagmire, I had hoped to introduce *Angela's Ashes*, the book, to supplement the English 11 literary theme of the *American Dream*. To fill a gaping hole in the curriculum, I had planned, without asking Carol, to introduce it after *Of Mice and Men* and *The Great Gatsby*. I thought it important, after studying two cynical critiques of the *Dream*, to tackle a work that in some ways confirms it. *Angela's Ashes* is also the funniest and most heart-wrenching memoir ever written about childhood. I also hoped the story might reveal to my students that as bad as some of their lives are, most people in the world are far worse off.

During a recent, horribly hot afternoon with both my not-supplied-by-the-school fans impotently spinning at high speed, the temperature in my classroom reached ninety-five. I decided to show *Casablanca* under the pretense, if anyone were to ask, that the classic movie's relevance to the curriculum was its setting during the exact same timeframe as *Zoot Suit;* providing the students the opportunity to compare barrio life in wartime Los Angeles to bar/cafe life in wartime Casablanca, as well as the opportunity to contrast the life-altering choices and failed romances of the respective protagonists. It is remarkable what bullshit the mind can come up with when necessary and yes, *necessity is* certainly *the mother of invention*. I tried to set up the movie as best I could, considering the circumstances, but due to the unbearable heat I was getting nowhere fast. I dropped that effort and instead encouraged them to just enjoy the movie, adding that I would award points based on how long they were able to stay awake. By the end of class at least two-thirds of the kids, some drooling and some snoring, were fast asleep.

Letting the cat out of the bag

I put off telling the kids of my dismissal for as long as possible, but on May 19th I decided to just get it over with. For weeks I had been mulling over when, how and what to tell them, and I finally decided to spill the beans to only one class. It made no sense to officially notify my seniors because it would not affect most of them, and besides I knew these kids well enough to realize that once I told one class, within a day everyone everywhere would know. I decided to tell Third Block, the Gina/Jeremy drama group.

I wait until the last fifteen minutes of class and then matter-of-factly announce I won't be coming back next year. For one of the few times in the entire year it gets real quiet. The quiet lasts about ten seconds until smart-ass Luke breaks the silence with a way too hearty, "Yay!"

Coming to my immediate defense Cal barks. "Why don't you shut the fuck up, Luke!!"

The others seem stunned. When they finally do get around to asking why they canned me, I make it clear it was not my choice to leave and that I had been looking forward to being around for their graduation next year. I then ask if they remember the unsmiling woman with the clipboard who observed me during the year. Most do. I tell them that she was my boss and that she didn't think I was doing a good enough job teaching, that in her opinion I did not push my students hard enough. They offer some choice epithetical epitaphs and ask if I want their help to help save my job. "Nah, but thanks. I don't want to work for someone who doesn't want me around."

I then attempt to use my dismissal, as I had a few days earlier with Tony's disputed loss in the ring, as a teaching moment. I explain that most of them at some time during their lives will find themselves working for a stupid boss or a person they don't like. I remind them they have all survived bad teachers in the past and to take each setback as a challenge. I do my best to twist my sad saga into a positive event; I almost begin to believe my own spin! After a few minutes of *you were great's* and *we are gonna miss you's*, Jasmine asks me if I would come to their graduation next year.

"Jasmine I am pretty sure you won't even remember my name when school starts in August. I can already imagine you asking David, *Hey, what was the name of that English teacher we had last year?*"

As the news sinks in, some of the kids realize they might be able to leverage my bad luck to their own advantage. Tony comes up with, "Hey Mr. Mandel, now you don't have to give us a final. Why don't you just give us all A's?"

"Sounds good to me Tony. I think I will give everyone an A except smartass Luke. Luke gets an F."

Luke protests immediately with a loud "What the f??"

And when I remind him that he was the only one to greet my announcement with joy, he attempts—unconvincingly——to persuade me that he had only been joking.

As predicted, within a day all my classes know my fate. Many students seem genuinely upset. Some do their best to make me feel good. Chris in Fourth Block, during the middle of a lesson, raises his hand and when I call on him says, "Don't worry Mr. Mandel. I think you're cool."

Beavis and Butthead announce in two-part harmony that my class was the only class they enjoyed. Beavis then says to Butthead, "How cool would it be if Mr. Mandel taught one of our classes at Cabrillo (local JC) next year?" I cringe at the thought.

RJ, of *fenetik* spelling fame, sums it up nicely with, "I learned a lot from you Mr. Mandel. And you did the best anyone could have done with this group of clowns."

∽੭ଈ∾

Soon after receiving my notice of release I decided to burn some of my ten sick days before year's end—*use 'em or lose 'em.* Prior to being fired I had been a loyal soldier, coming to work in pain everyday, rain or shine, stressed-out or not. A lot of good that did me! I needed to get away for a few days. Being the consummate educator, I spent way too much time preparing lesson plans for my sub. By the time I finished, they were my most detailed and well thought out lesson plans of the year. With all my lame ducks in a row, I headed for Calistoga for an extended Memorial Day weekend.

During my two-day absence rumors were rife—*Mr. Mandel has ditched school in anger and is gone for good.* So when I reappeared on Thursday, the kids and aides were very pleased to see me. They shared some stories about the sub: She asked the class to copy the five adages I had left for them, and then she refused to explain their meanings. (I had assumed the sub would know the meanings and therefore had not bothered to write them down.) She had told them that there were no wrong answers and so they would all get full credit for the assignment. They weren't buying her explanation; how, they asked me, would they learn the true meanings? Well at least I have taught them to have a healthy dose of skepticism.

The substitute teacher, Ms. Rivas, left these revealing comments on the *Comment Form for Substitute Teacher* under *class conduct:*

> **Block 1**-"Talkative, but ok." **Block 3**-"Talkative, had trouble staying on task during study time. Good during movie.**" Block** 4-"They were very good. On-track." And last but not least **Block 5**-"General conduct ok, but Tomas and Jorge were drawing on each other and talking instead of watching the movie. I asked them repeatedly to put their pens and pencils away unless they were taking notes on movie. After they finally put them away, they talked for a couple of minutes and then just got up and walked out, defying my requests to remain in the classroom exclaiming 'this class is gay!' The aide wrote out misconducts for them and called their counselors. I am going to take misconduct forms to the office."….

I couldn't have described the disdainful duo's behavior better myself.

Over the next few weeks kids came to me from time to time telling me how much they enjoyed my class. One day last week, William, not the old William I had failed last semester despite his lamentations, but the new-improved-good-student William, came into my room while I was eating lunch and said, "I still can't believe it. It sucks."

"What sucks?" I asked.

"That they fired you Mr. Mandel."

"Oh that." I said matter-of-factly, while secretly feeling pretty good inside.

Sweet William then offered his help and even volunteered to go on strike. I told him thanks, but no thanks. Later that same day Cal gave me the best compliment of all when he blurted out during class, "Two years ago when I had Ms. Bobbey I thought she was the best teacher and I wanted to have her every year. Then last year I had Ms. Stasi, and I thought she was the best teacher ever, and then I had you Mr. Mandel and you were just as good and I really wanted to have you for my senior year."

I'll take that.

Before I forget, one good piece of news. Sara was voted the San Benito High School *Teacher of the Year*, quite an accomplishment for a fourth-year teacher among a faculty of over 150. I may have been the last person to hear about her award. To avoid further embarrassment (perceived embarrassment to be honest), I skipped out on the end-of-the-year awards BBQ luncheon last week. I opted instead to quietly grab some chicken, beans, salad and a can of Pepsi and then, balancing my lunch on my arm, return to my room to eat in silence. Well not actually silence, more like solitude—I had music blasting. I chose to eat lunch as I had almost everyday of the year, alone.

About an hour later, the luncheon over, Sara, who had recently broken her foot in a car accident, zipped into my room and right up to my desk on her bright red gimp-scooter, gushing, smiling ear-to-ear, without a hint of conceit or look-at-me-ness, and proudly showed me her *Teacher of the Year* plaque. I stood up and gave her a big hug. For some reason, after the hug (perhaps to CFU) Sara told me she is the type of person who loves getting awards and that she was walking on air. I smiled and reassured her, "Sara, I knew that."

Before I move on to the sad saga of my increasing isolation from my colleagues, I want to talk about a small sub-group of my students, euphemistically called the *developmentally delayed* (DD), or sometimes more accurately the *developmentally disabled*; a group once labeled *mentally retarded*. Sometime well into the school year, I became aware that I had three students classified as high functioning DD in my classes. All three were earnest and hard working, and as a whole performed better than most of their classmates.

While I am discussing categories and acronyms, I need to mention the acronym ED. ED kids are seriously *emotionally disturbed*. Most live in group-homes, are volatile, apt to go off at any time, and require one-on-one aides. Melody, as you might have guessed, was one such student. Halfway though the year I discovered I had two other ED students. ED students generally do not have congenital leaning disabilities and many, if kept on task, perform well in school. One major complaint I have (one of many) is that no one red-flagged these kids for me in advance. This is a serious oversight and I feel fortunate I was able to learn enough on my own to avert real disaster.

Returning to my original stream of thought on my developmentally disabled students: all three have beautiful handwriting and write in clear simple sentences (one of these students, Selma, writes quite well), and all three are better than average spellers. However, I found that they have great difficulty moving from the literal to the figurative. Kari is a sweet, very hard-working senior who was never able to make the leap. (Kari was one of only two seniors not to pass the English exit exam. Jorge was the other.)

As I mentioned in an earlier entry, over the last few months I had been using adages and proverbs daily to help my students navigate from the concrete to the metaphoric. Generally speaking it was a success. Here are a few examples from Kari's final exam to demonstrate the limitations she faces despite all her effort and hard work. On the final there was a list of twenty adages we had recently reviewed. I asked the students to pick ten and explain their meanings. As I have also mentioned previously, the final was an open book test and the students were allowed to use their notes. In other words I had spoon-fed them most of the answers. (Unfortunately, during these feedings most kept their mouths closed and jaws tightly clenched.) Here are four of Kari's attempts:

He who hesitates is lost. *This means if somebody is lost, you might not find them.*
Two heads are better than one. *If you have two heads it means you can't think.*
The apple doesn't fall far from the tree. *Since the apple doesn't fall far, somebody can pick it up.*
Beggars can't be choosers. *If you beg for something it doesn't matter you still won't get it.*

This brings me to spelling. Many of my students have disorders that make correct spelling all but impossible. Gina, for example, is smart but cannot remember how to spell her middle name. In fact Gina can be brilliantly articulate at times, evidenced by her winning first place at a countywide arts festival for an original monolog she wrote and performed in dialect. Here are her answers to some short answer questions on the final.

Use two adjectives to describe the following characters from *The Great Gatsby*:

Daisy:	*spolled, cniving*
Tom:	*agresev, rude*
Myrtle:	*nosie, winer*
Gatsby:	*msteyers, oquwerd*
Mr. Wilson:	*nieve, dume*

Although she stretched my deciphering skills to their limits, Gina's choice of adjectives was the most precise and accurate of all her classmates.

Speaking of finals, for the last time I promise, in the vocabulary section I asked them to match *thesaurus* with its meaning. *Thesaurus* was a last minute entry I decided on after discovering to my surprise that a majority of my students had no idea what a thesaurus is. At the time of the discovery I walked over to the bookshelf at the far back corner of the room, picked up one of a dozen thesauri (or thesauruses, if you prefer), strolled back to the front of class holding the bright orange book up and said, in English, "This is a thesaurus." I then went on to describe in some detail that it is a reference book to help writers or readers find synonyms. (Yes, I did define *synonym*.)

To cut the tension (not really sure how many of them actually felt any tension) I added a dose of humor to the final exam. (As with just about everything else I tried during the year, it amused me more than it amused them.) I included one erroneous and extraneous meaning along with the correct meanings in the list of definitions. There were 19 words and 20 definitions.

Word: thesaurus

two of the choices: A. reference tool to find synonyms
B. a small three-legged dinosaur

I assumed that while some kids would take the bait, most would either chuckle to themselves or blurt out something like *Ha ha Mr. Mandel, pretty funny?* While there were some shout-outs and some chuckles, I estimate that more than 30% believed a thesaurus to be a small three-legged dinosaur.

❦

One morning last week I had a final chat with my one-time rival and fellow death-marcher Sally Smuts. As I was walking back to my classroom I noticed Sally approaching. She came up to me and asked pleasantly if I had found a job for next year. At first I was taken aback by the fact that Sally knew I had been released, but I recovered quickly and we went on to have a friendly conversation about our situations.

Not surprisingly, Sally has decided on a different tactic than I have in response to her release. While I am working behind the scenes with the union in a futile effort to save my job, Sally has pulled out the big guns and put together a packet of letters of support from students, parents and teachers and presented them, along with a speech, to the board in closed session. According to Sally, the board members listened politely and then sent her on her merry way. She is under the impression that the board had voted to let a certain number of teachers go without being told by HR which individual teachers they were releasing.

I try to be upbeat, but I mention I think the odds of a reprieve are very long, and if the board were to rescind its earlier action, board members would essentially be voicing a vote of no confidence in the administration. We then commiserate about how badly we were treated. Like me, Sally thinks she was let go primarily because of an unfair evaluator. She still believes, despite all evidence to the contrary—a student petition seeking her removal, numerous complaints from faculty about her behavior—that she is a wonderful, dedicated and well-liked teacher. In fact she may well be right about the dedicated part—Sally has already interviewed for a job in Salinas and she has every intention of remaining in Hollister so she can continue to be the voice of the *Lady Balers* at all home basketball games.

Without tipping my hand, and hopefully without sound too patronizing, I share the following extemporaneous insight: In my view there are only two possible reasons for being fired, either they don't like the way you teach, or they don't like you. Sally however has suspicions that in her case there is a third possibility: A few months back Sally became sick in her classroom and was carted away in an ambulance as asshole Pecksniff watched. Sally sincerely believes that the cost of the medical emergency, and the fear of future costs to the district, played a major role in her release. Aside from the fact that considering medical conditions and costs as factors in an employment decision is both unethical and illegal (neither of which would stop or even slow down Pecksniff if he wanted to get rid of an employee), I try to explain that I think it highly unlikely that the medical incident alone could affect her tenure, but I tell her it's quite possible that the incident was the final nail in her coffin.

Two mismatched souls—united only by a common fate, in search of answers they will never find—talk a little longer, wish each other luck, and then, off one soul strolls into her metaphoric sunset.

That's no way to say goodbye...

And now for a description of that fleeting instant when I saw the Queen of CHAOS for the last time. It was really a non-event, but still, in its own way, symbolic of the arc of a once promising relationship. Lately I have been wracking my diminishing brainpower to find the right words to describe Carol more accurately. She is like a character straight out of Dickens, one of those hapless, doltish, but not entirely unpleasant persons born into power but utterly unequipped to wield it competently. But not even Dickens could have created Carol Havisham without the aid of modern day psychogenic medication. For those more versed in Dr. Seuss than Mr. Dickens, let me try this comparison: Carol Havisham resembles the Cat in the Hat, minus the hat, the smile and the personality.

Even with the *Dickenseussian* mixing of metaphors, I wasn't happy with the resulting fusion love-child of Dickens and Seuss. I had almost given up finding the perfect metaphor for Carol when I inadvertently discovered what many teachers have been calling her behind her back for many years—The Turkey Lady.

Fucking pitch-perfect!! Turkey Lady: the long skinny neck topped by a badly bobbed haircut, the annoying voice with a whiny, grating, fowlish quality to its timbre–

–a voice the Turkey Lady seems unable to modulate.

A couple of weeks ago I needed to drop off some papers for Ethan at the special services offices on the other side of campus. Ethan had called me earlier that morning, anxious because the parents of Valerie, one of my caseload seniors, were demanding an immediate meeting in order to blame the school for the fact that their lazy-ass daughter was failing two classes and wasn't going to graduate. (I had expected that her pushy mother would do everything in her power to force the school to graduate her daughter.) Ethan asked me to get him copies of all my correspondences with Valerie's mom as soon as possible. Like a loyal subject I did as I was told. (I did manage, through sleight of hand and venial deceit, to avoid attending the actual meeting a few days later. Sgt. Putzmire punished me by refusing to reply to my email asking him about the meeting's outcome.)

As I approached the double-glass doors to the special services offices, Putzmire papers in hand, I caught sight of the shadowy figure of Carol Havisham alone in the large reception area. To my subjective eye the Turkey Lady appeared to be grazing in some high grass, but I will give her the benefit of the doubt and assume that she was looking for something on a minion's desk. As I pushed the door open she caught a glimpse of me, quickly turned around and silently scurried off to the safety of her office, like a wild turkey taking cover in the brush.

And like that, she was gone.

In my room

Following the announcement of my departure I felt increasingly isolated. Students had no problem commiserating and talking directly to me about my situation, but adults were another story. Initially my closest colleagues reacted sympathetically, but as the days went by and the end neared, most avoided the subject and treated me like I had cancer or worse, some contagious flesh-eating disease. I wasn't really expecting a faculty uprising, and I do realize how busy teachers are at the end of the school year, but I assumed that a few would approach me and offer their condolences. To be fair, Sara touched base frequently, and one teacher I had known casually approached me to tell me how impressed she was with my performance despite all the obstacles. Oh, and there was Daniel, the amiable custodian and fellow chronically-aching-lower-lumbar sufferer who cleaned my room; towards the end Daniel spent more and more time commiserating with me and less and less time doing his job.

The following is a delightful digression regarding a fellow school employee. (This is the sort of stuff I missed out on by holing up in my bunker and licking my wounds.) I inadvertently discovered this account a few weeks after school ended while researching background material for the journal. One can only guess how many other interesting stories I missed out on during my year at San Benito High School.

Who says *ignorance is bliss*?

Details from local paper:

> Nancy Polizzi a cafeteria worker at San Benito High School was placed on an unspecified "leave" shortly after her March 27 testimony in the Santa Clara County murder trial of 26-year-old Fresno resident Francisco Vega, District Superintendent Rose said at the time.

Frankie Vega, along with 23-year-old Hollister resident Joshua Joseph, were convicted of first-degree murder and sentenced to life in prison without the possibility of parole for waiting outside David Owens' San Jose home then entering the house and shooting him several times with a .22 caliber handgun.

During her sworn testimony, and in a subsequent interview with the Free Lance, Polizzi said she gave the two convicted killers money to buy the handgun used to kill Owens as well as money to start a "marijuana operation." She also said she was involved in a sexual relationship with both Owens and Joseph - who is her stepson - and that Joseph warned her that "David is dead" before the murder.

Polizzi has not been charged in the case, and Santa Clara County Deputy District Attorney Daniel Carr said he will consider that her possible involvement after he finishes a current murder trial expected to last through this week.

Below the article were the following comments from readers (*noms de plume* in bold):

Tuned in in Mtn View: Nancy should not only be fired from San Benito High School she should be arrested and charged with first degree murder for her part in the killing of David Owens. She was the mastermind behind the murder. She had sex with David Owens and he dumped her. She felt disrespected and paid Joshua and Frankie Vega to kill David Owens for her. She provided the motive, the transportation, the gun, the latex gloves, a map to David's home, cleaned

the car afterwards and paid Joshua $1,000 in addition
to clothes, a motorcycle and a car. She deserves the
death panalty. We should have a big party in Hollister
when she is arrested -- interested?
Jimbo: Did you ever think she may have been flori-
dated by the communists. We all need to join the fight
against this floridation stuff. Join me in the fight. Vote
Jimbo June 3rd
Convict Nancy Polizzi: Jimbo you are an idiot, I hope
Nancy gets you next!

My comments: This is incredible stuff. I guess when
you work in a place with so many employees you are bound
to have your share of felons, reprobates and generic weir-
dos. But jeeze, I mean like man, no way I could make shit
like this up. And I think one can safely assume that Nasty
Nancy continues to collect her full pay while she remains
on administrative leave.

∞

In spite of everything, I continued to perform all
my duties, including my caseload work, in a professional
manner. Right up to the end Ethan never mentioned my
dismissal. He expected me to meet all deadlines, whistling
as I worked as if nothing had happened. Ethan made it
apparent in other ways that he was not unhappy to see me
go; he no longer replied to my emails and he kept piling
on the work. I think he was worried I might intentionally
screw things up before my departure. I am certain my release was a sovereign decision involving both Her Majesty
Carol Havisham and her princely handmaiden, Mr. Ethan
Putzmire.

XII

The Grand Allusion

Ripple in still water,
when there is no pebble tossed,
nor wind to blow.

—Robert Hunter

Disclaimer: My wife has admitted to being wrong only once during our marriage (regarding the proper handling of raw poultry), and when she read the following paragraphs in which I attempt to connect my journey as a teacher to the journey Fitzgerald created for Jay Gatsby. she said bluntly "You need to cut this out." She complained that they were self-aggrandizing and egotistical. As you may have noticed, I have more than a few sophomoric tendencies, among them a penchant for literary allusion—or perhaps, grave *dallusional* tendencies? I just can't let it go, so I have decided to leave it up to the reader to decide if my wife was right. And yes, I do realize most readers will see right through my not-so clever ploy to have it both ways: to preserve my literary allusions while remaining a self-reflective and sympathetic figure.

THE ACCIDENTAL TEACHER

I spent most of the last weeks holed up in my bunker, avoiding end-of-year meetings and parties and finally, in the end, ducking out of school for good two days early. This self-imposed exile eliminated most situations in which I would cross paths with my colleagues. I don't want this to degenerate into a pity party, and I know that my own behavior played a big role in my isolation, but I can't resist the poetic temptation to compare my isolation to that of Jay Gatsby, coming full circle from my job interview ten months back when I unwittingly introduced Gatsby into my journey, to today, with my dream, like Gatsby's, wrested from my grasp. Gatsby my partner in crime, my wingman, my Sancho Panza; the two of us together on our quixotic adventure, battling our respective windmills and windbags. We have much in common. Both Jay and I tried to re-invent ourselves, he his past, me my present. We both were on dream quests––Daisy for Gatsby, teaching for me. Overmatched from the beginning––Gatsby by class and old money, me by a soulless data-driven educational system––our dreams came crashing down, terminated at the hands of misguided loners. And then––most dramatic and over-the-top––in the end, no longer of use to anyone, we were both totally alone––Gatsby dead, me on professional life-support abandoned by my colleagues. Okay, I still have my family, my friends and my dogs, not to mention three more paychecks, $2000 a month in unemployment benefits and a decent pension, but you can't blame a guy for trying. And besides, Gatsby was merely a man of fiction; save your sorrows for a man of flesh and blood, a complicated man, a man of real emotions, a man of shameless hyperbole.

Fitzgerald ends his novel with:

THE GRAND ALLUSION

And as I sat there, brooding on the old unknown world, I thought of Gatsby's wonder when he first picked out the green light at the end of Daisy's dock. He had come a long way to this blue lawn and his dream must have seemed so close that he could hardly fail to grasp it. He did not know that it was already behind him, somewhere back in the vast obscurity beyond the city, where the dark fields of the republic rolled on under the night.

Gatsby believed in the green light, the orgastic future that year by year recedes before us. It eluded us then, but that's no matter—tomorrow we will run faster, stretch out our arms farther....And one fine morning——

So we beat on, boats against the current, borne back ceaselessly into the past.

Brilliant, fitting and profound, I could, pompously and mercifully, end my opus right here, but as always I have more to say and I want to end this on a positive note with something about the stars of the show, not the supporting cast.

The final word

I do realize a few pages ago I promised that I was writing about finals for the last time. But it looks as though I have once again, worked myself into a corner. I have more to say about my kids *and* my finals and I can't write about the last days without talking about both. So that leaves me a few options:

Option One—take the easy route, play dumb, ignore what I wrote earlier and finish this entry.
Option Two—go back and edit out the "last time promise" and finish this entry, no one the wiser.

Option Three—tap dance on my keyboard for a few sentences and then get back to the business at hand.

No surprise, I'm going with number Three.

The last week of school was *Finals Week*. The schedule was truncated, two blocks instead of three per day with school ending early. On Monday my Beavis and Butthead blockheads took the last English final of their lives. I had done my best to prepare them, but because they were my biggest fuck-ups and my least motivated class, I had little hope that few, if any, would perform well enough to raise their grades. Actually I was worried most might drop down a grade. And for some dropping down a grade would be as good as a death sentence: it would prevent them from graduating.

I did my best to make the final as easy as possible. I eliminated the sections on grammar and concentrated instead on recent class novels and plays, vocabulary and adages. I reduced the writing section from two essays to one, and decided to provide them the actual essay topics a day in advance so that they would have the opportunity to write the essay at home. In addition I provided a study guide, reviewed some actual questions, provided them a new folder for final notes, and spent time in class helping them get all of it organized. As my kids have learned this year, *You can lead a horse to water, but you can't make him drink*. And it came as no surprise that few paid serious attention to what I was saying, fewer studied, and fewer still (less than a handful) worked on their essays at home.

On Monday in Fifth Block I had no sooner handed out the tests and sat down at my desk (to try and finish up the mountains of paperwork so I could get out of Hollister for good on Wednesday after my last final was done and my grades were recorded) when I heard Michael whine from the back of the room, "Mr. Mandel this final is too hard. I don't know any of the answers."

So much for getting anything done while this beleaguered and befuddled bunch of knuckleheads took the test. I did my best to encourage Michael and the others, "Come on Michael, you have your notes. We have reviewed most of the questions, I gave you the essay topics in advance and you have all the books with all the answers right on your desk. What else do you want me to do? Take the test for you?"

You can guess his reply, and he then added something like, "You promised you would make it easy because they fired you and you were pissed off."

Not.

I gave the class some routine advice about first answering the questions they knew, and then going back and looking up the ones they weren't sure of. It was quiet for a while as most of the kids plodded through the test. But Michael, who has that unnamed and incredibly annoying humor disorder that causes him to repeat something he thinks is funny over and over again even when it is apparent to everyone but him that it isn't even remotely amusing, could not let it go. He would work quietly for short stretches and then blurt out comments such as: "This is too hard. What score do I need to get to get a D? If you fail me I won't graduate." repeating them over and over as if they were mantras.

Michael was on the verge of working himself into a state of paralysis so I had Kitty, the classroom aide, sit with him, calm him down and try and help him get through the test. Eventually Kitty's presence had the desired effect, but not before Michael attempted to punish me for my meanness with some choice pleas to the almighty: "I hate you Mr. Mandel. You are mean and old. Your wife hates you. Your kids hate you. Your dogs hate you. I hope when you go home tonight your wife divorces you and takes all the dogs with her."

I had to laugh, and then replied, "Michael you sure knew how to scare a guy."

The Fifth Block final, because of the distractions and poor time management on my part, took longer than I had anticipated and some students worked right up to the bell. I gave free reign to those who did finish early (within certain boundaries of course) to write farewell messages and drawings on the whiteboard. As the class ended I gave a half-hearted, truncated farewell speech thanking them for all the fun and games, and as they left my room I shook their hands firmly, looked 'em in the eye and said "Good luck."

Stan popped his head back in my room with these last words, "Bye Mr. Mandel. See ya at a kegga in Santa Cruz."

And before I knew it they were gone. Suddenly alone, I convinced myself I would do better with my remaining classes.

Wednesday, my last day, I got off to a late start to school because I had to return home to get my wallet, and then I got stuck in road construction for thirty minutes. I was tardy for the first time all year. I had called ahead to make sure the room was unlocked and to tell the aide what to do until I got there. When I arrived about ten minutes after class started I was surprised to find Mr. Pirl, of *Pepto Bismol* fame, "teaching" my class. Apparently it was Bruce's prep period and the office had sent him over to cover my class until I arrived. (I had hoped to avoid notifying Pecksniff and his crew, but it seems someone had told them of my late arrival.) Mr. Pirl was not a happy camper. He had already handed out the finals, and as I entered the classroom the kids were attempting, without success, to convince him that the test was open-book. I quickly thanked him, made some small talk about how strange it must feel to return to his old room, and then shook his hand and sent him on his way. I calmed the kids down and got them on track.

After he was gone I noticed that he had erased all the student drawings and comments on my whiteboard. I realized Bruce was unaware of the unorthodox relationship I had nurtured with my students, and probably had erased the comments in an effort to protect my feelings, so I hid my displeasure from the class.

Below is a recreation of a section of the whiteboard before he erased it. A parting shot to aptly bookend the opening classroom scene of Mr. Pirl's bottle of *Pepto Bismol*. (As bad as things got I actually never required *Pepto Bismol*.) The quote, as you might guess, is from Michael, who in spite of his anxieties did fine on his final and earned a solid C.

Mr Mandels wife

is going to say

he is dumb and old

and tell him to leave

THE ACCIDENTAL TEACHER

The remaining finals and farewells did go better. I left more time at the end of class for bullshitting and goodbyes and delivered a little goodbye/good luck speech. I also took photos and short videos of the kids and had the aides, or had one of the few kids who refused to be photographed (like Zen or Jeremy) take some class photos of me and the gang. There were some heartfelt remarks and *thank you's*. It was more emotional than I thought it would be. I had spent a great deal of time with these guys, and the more we had gotten to know each other, the better things had become. I do think I reached most of them in some way. I figure if just once in the future, just once in their lives, when they hear an adage we discussed, or the name of a literary character we read about, and they think *Hey I knew that*—or better yet, if I have awakened in any one of them a curiosity or an interest in anything—except perhaps serial killing—I have done my job.

After the finals, I worked straight through to grade the tests, enter the scores, compute the final grades and send them off to the registrar so I could get out of Dodge before sundown. Computer software makes computing grades a snap. You set up your rubric, enter the grades by assignment, click the mouse and the final grade instantly appears rounded off to the nearest hundredth. I can only imagine what a pain computing grades was before computers. Computer software isn't fail safe, and I have learned to be careful with the rubric; it is possible to really skew and screw grades up by subtle unintentional manipulations, such as having too few assignments in one category, or by calculating F grades too low by using the actual percentage score on the assignment of 25% or zero as the grade for example, instead of translating the score into the F grade range of 59%.

THE GRAND ALLUSION

Comparing my first semester grades to my second semester grades I discovered one of two things; either some of my kids got smarter and some got dumber, or my grading became more accurate over time. Without going into too much detail, the first semester I gave out six Fs and five A's, and second semester I only failed three students and gave out only two A's. Even with the reduction in Fails, the overall GPA dropped from 2.35 to 2.2. Interestingly, the cumulative differences between the classes narrowed by year's end. In the end, my seniors in First Block had the highest, a 2.56 GPA, while the seniors in Fifth Block had the lowest, a 1.58 GPA.

The last few days I worked late into the evenings to get my grades in, my room cleaned out, all books and equipment returned, caseload files organized and returned to Sgt. Putzmire, and everything else that was required of me. I finished by Wednesday evening so I could take the last two workdays off—in my mind, a well-deserved, two-day early retirement. In the end, after weeks of inner struggle resisting my initial desire to seek public revenge on those who I believed had treated my unfairly, I decided to take the high road and leave as gracefully and as quietly as possible.

In the early evening of June 4, 2008 I turned in my keys, and as I walked across the lawn I allowed my mind to meander to a final literary allusion (yes, an allusion of meander). I imagine myself as Jay Gatsby, my metaphorical sidekick who seems to have shadowed me since day one. Heading out of San Benito High School for the last time I can almost make out in the distance Nick Carraway's last words to Gatsby: *They're a rotten crowd. You're worth the whole damn bunch put together.*

In a sane, rational world this is the way it would have ended, but not so fast.

THE ACCIDENTAL TEACHER

Echoing El Pachuco from *Zoot Suit*

There

are

other

ways

to

end

this

story

ese

watcha chale.

THE GRAND ALLUSION

Gonzo Gulag

The next morning at about nine, as I lay in bed listening to NPR with my two Jack terriers' warm bodies nestled up against my legs, enjoying the first morning of the rest of my life, the phone rings and effectively shatters the moment. We have a talking, albeit phonetically challenged, telephone that *she-manishly* sounds out who is calling. "San bnito hig shol" it stammers and stutters. I don't answer, letting the call roll over to the downstairs answering machine. When I hear an all too familiar male voice leaving a message on the machine downstairs I mumble out loud, "Shit, I can't believe this is happening."

I do my best to stay put, but too angry to relax, I climb out of bed, trying my best to *let sleeping dogs lie*, stretch my back, take the requisite morning piss and then hobble downstairs. Before I disclose the message I want to mention that until this moment I had not received a single phone call at home from anyone at work since Carol called me in August to offer me the job.

The message verbatim:

> Hi Eric, this is Pete Pecksniff at human resources, Eric ah, it has come to my attention that you have turned in your keys and called in ill. Hm, eh, I want a doctor's note for today and tomorrow if you are ill. That was number one. Hm, number two, you do need to check-out. We have a formal checkout procedure system here, so you need to go through it and pending that we will be holding your check. So please do it correctly Eric, I would appreciate that. Give me a call if you have any questions. Thanks.

THE ACCIDENTAL TEACHER

As you can imagine, my blood was simmering at *Hi* and reached a rolling boil by the time I got to *number two*. And to think that earlier in the week I had suppressed my ardent self-righteous indignation and decided to leave quietly without causing so much as a ripple!

Doctor's notes are rarely required unless a teacher has a history of abusing sick leave. You would think Pete would let this go. He was never going to see me again and it would have been so easy to do nothing. I knew he was a loathsome prick, but I never guessed that he enjoyed being one to such an extent that he would willingly make more work for himself and his staff just for the satisfaction of sticking it to me one last time. While his archenemy Carol is a well-meaning, hapless character, Pecksmith is far more devious and sadistic.

I went upstairs, took a deep breath and composed the following email and copied the union president:

Subject: Checkout
Date: Thu, 5 Jun 2008
From: "Eric Mandel"
To: "Peter Pecksniff"

I have been having serious back pain for the last few months. In spite of the pain and the shabby way I have been treated, I have been doing my job and serving my students in a professional, dedicated and loyal manner. I am quite aware of the checkout procedure, so when my back pain flared up earlier in the week I began it. I have been checked out by Spec Ed for my case files, final exams and for my room. In addition I have recorded and turned in a hard copy of my grades, I have returned all books and equipment, I have returned my copy card, and most importantly, I have turned in my keys. Sara will

THE GRAND ALLUSION

turn in my checkout sheets on Friday.

Considering everything that has happened over the last year I have no regrets about taking the job; I enjoyed the teaching, the kids and learning from my colleagues. In my humble opinion and the opinion of others, you are losing a good and potentially excellent educator.

You might want to re-think the way you do business. No one wants to be treated like a disposable commodity.

Pecksniff's reply:

Eric,
We will need a Dr note.
We will also need you to check out.
If everything is OK on the Checkout then you are good.
However, until the checkout is verified we are required to hold your check.
I hope your back is better soon.
Let me know when you can come in.
Thanks,
Pete

Email to the union accompanying a copy of above email from Pecksniff:

This is not the way I wanted to leave, but Pecksniff forced my hand by calling me this morning at home and chastising me for not coming in to work today (I have no classes, no sub needed). He left me a short lecture on the proper checkout procedure and how I should do things the right way, and then demanded I get a doctor's note to excuse my two-day absence.

Can he do that? I thought a note was required after three consecutive days. I won't have a problem getting a note, I may even send Pecksniff an x-ray of the two screws in my lower back, right next to the knife he stuck there at the end of April.

Let me know.

And sorry to be such a pain in the ass,

Eric

Peter Pecksniff will have to wait until hell freezes over before I report back in or send a doctor's note. I am curious to see if he pushes the issue and forces me to file a grievance. I guess I will have to update my readers when I report on my next impersonating gig, *Call Me Doctor: My Year as a Proctologist*. Unlike teaching, I will be entering a field in which I have extensive experience.

THE GRAND ALLUSION

Nothing is real and nothing to get hung about....

July 12 - Saturday

Mary thinks that the bitter tone of my ending overrides my inspirational story. I'm not quite ready to admit she is right, but I have had a few weeks to reflect on the final weeks and the finality of the good-byes and it hit me; I will never see the kids again. As you may have noticed, unlike my mentor Sara I do not wear my emotions openly for all to see. Like most men I hide them, ignore them, deny them, restrain them, or flat out just don't have them. I will spare my readers another one of my gender benders and just say that if I have learned anything over my thirty years of marriage, twenty-eight years as my daughter's father and twenty-five years as a boss, it is that men and women are more unalike than I ever could have imagined decades back when I was a naïve, bleeding heart advocate of gender homogeny.

Speaking from my feminine side, it troubles me that I probably will never know what became of my students—who succeeded and went on to live a good life, who came up short, who exceeded expectations, who ended up in prison, who went on to live their dreams. Perhaps one day I will bump into one of them or maybe read something about one of them, something great like Tony Morales becoming *World Middleweight Champion*, or Gina getting a part on a popular sitcom, or maybe something not so great that I don't even want to contemplate.

So now I am going to end this thing once and for all with one last story intermixed, of course, with a digression or two.

Despite my best efforts in my struggle against administrative injustice, I did have to return one last time, long before hell froze over, to San Benito High School. My battle with Pecksniff ended with a compromise arranged by the union: I would not have to provide a doctor's note, but I would have to return to school to complete paperwork and have an exit interview.

On Thursday, July 3, after putting off the inevitable for as long as possible, I left home around noon, made my way out of Santa Cruz down Highway 1, past the strawberry fields of the Pajaro Valley, skirting behind Elkhorn Slough past farms and ranches, and on through the lovely mission town of San Juan Bautista (setting for some crucial scenes in Hitchcock's *Vertigo*). Then I turned left onto the back road that snakes through rolling hills for several miles before it reaches the vast river flatlands, and on past the *Sugar Plum Farm*. And then finally, over the new seldom-used bridge that spans the dry San Benito River into the southwest corner of Hollister and directly on to the campus of the school.

It was a nice, warm afternoon, traffic was light and my plan was to get in and out of the school as quickly as possible. I had my camera with me and I hoped to take some pictures of the school and the surrounding area: a surreal broken-down quarry on the banks of the San Benito River, a dilapidated farmhouse with huge black Angus bulls napping in the front yard and loitering on what remains of the farmhouse's porch, and maybe even a few photos of the exposed fault lines running through some Hollister homes bordering the campus.

Being summer I assumed the school would be devoid of students, but as I approached I noticed some kids and then remembered that summer school was in session. Focused on getting the unpleasant task over quickly, I found a parking place under the majestic sycamores on

Monterey Street in front of the main building. I got out of the car and stepped to the curb, and before my feet hit the sidewalk I was shaken from my meditative state by a boyish voice shouting, "Mr. Mandel? What are you doing here?"

I turn around to see a smiling William, his black oily Tom Petty haircut shimmering and bouncing as he breaks off from a group of his friends and heads towards me. We shake hands and I tell him I have come back to pick up my final paycheck. We make some small talk and William reminds me, good-naturedly, that he is stuck wasting his summer in school because of me. I remind William, equally good-naturedly, that I had little to do with it, that he had failed my class all by himself. He's not convinced. I ask William who his summer school English teacher is and if he is enjoying the class at all. William tells me a name I don't recognize and goes on to say the class is not a resource class but a regular English class, it is just okay, kind of boring, and he is getting a C+. I let him know I'm impressed.

I get a nice feeling from our conversation. Here is a kid I battled with early on and who at times drove me crazy, a kid who had flunked spectacularly the first semester and then did a complete turn-around the second semester and became a good student. And now this kid seems to be genuinely pleased to see me, beaming at his good fortune in running into Mr. Mandel, the teacher who failed him.

We shoot the breeze for a more few minutes, shake hands for the last time, wish each other luck and then, after a goofy half-pirouette, William swaggers off back to his friends.

THE END!!!

Acknowledgments

Thanks to everyone at San Benito High School, the heroes and the villains for without them there would be no story to tell. Thanks to my family and friends for putting up with my frustrations and my mood swings as I forced my stories upon them, all too often ignoring the fact that they had their own lives to live.

And a very special thanks to Nancy French for spending weeks on end trying to refine my crude prose and make it presentable to the outside world. She was a worthy adversary in our battles over semi-colons, commas and other—in my mind—insignificant minutiae. She raged on, ignoring my pleas to not sweat the small shit and to only worry about misspellings and incorrect word usage. The resulting book is better for her efforts and so am I.